Charlie Elder is a journalist. For the last twenty years he has worked for papers ranging from the *Times of Tonga* in the South Pacific to the *Telegraph* and the *Evening Standard*. He is currently chief sub-editor on the *Herald* in Plymouth. He lives with his wife and two daughters on the edge of Dartmoor.

D0872838

www.rbooks.co.uk

CHARLIE ELDER

WHILE FLOCKS LAST

*An armchair birdwatcher
goes in search of our
most endangered species*

TRANSWORLD PUBLISHERS
61–63 Uxbridge Road, London W5 5SA
A Random House Group Company
www.rbooks.co.uk

WHILE FLOCKS LAST
A CORGI BOOK: 9780552157544

First published in Great Britain
in 2009 by Bantam Press
an imprint of Transworld Publishers
Corgi edition published 2009

Addresses for Random House Group Ltd companies outside the UK
can be found at: www.randomhouse.co.uk
The Random House Group Reg. No. 954009

The Random House Group Limited supports The Forest Stewardship
Council (FSC), the leading international forest-certification organization.
All our titles that are printed on Greenpeace-approved FSC-certified paper
carry the FSC logo. Our paper procurement policy can be found
at www.rbooks.co.uk/environment

Typeset in 12/14½pt Bembo by
Kestrel Data, Exeter, Devon.
Printed in the UK by
CPI Cox & Wyman, Reading, RG1 8EX.

2 4 6 8 10 9 7 5 3

Mixed Sources
Product group from well-managed
forests and other controlled sources
www.fsc.org Cert no. TF-COC-2139
© 1996 Forest Stewardship Council
FSC

To
N + E + B

PREFACE

I AM ABOUT AS FAR NORTH IN BRITAIN AS YOU CAN GET and it is freezing. Gale-force winds are pummelling me and I'm kneeling in damp heather trying to hold my binoculars steady. I have trudged across sodden moorland to an upland loch which looks more like a large muddy puddle than a lake. The surface has been whipped up into waves. At the far edge tapering stems of sedge are bent over like tiny fishing rods while close by the foaming water is gnashing at the shoreline. There is nothing to shelter behind: not a tree or bush in sight, only a few wet sheep, but they are heading over the hillside towards the sea. Even the midges are keeping out of the wind, clinging to rocks for fear of being swept away to Greenland. This is no place to be out in the open, and were it not for the fact I have a reserve warden alongside me I could be arrested and jailed for being here – though it seemed like the kind of bleak location to which prisoners might be banished in any case.

I have driven for a couple of days and taken a flight and two ferries to reach this remote protected spot, and while I am no hardy wilderness type who bathes in mountain streams and thrives on discomfort, I can hardly feel the cold because less than 20 feet in front of me bobbing about on the water picking insects from the surface are a pair of one of our rarest and most endangered breeding birds, a species I have never seen before and will probably never see again. More than that, after a year struggling to get to grips with bird identification, I actually knew what they were.

So what had possessed me to travel so far to see a dainty reddish-brown variety of wader? They didn't owe me money. What made them so special?

The answer was a damp piece of dog-eared paper stuffed in my rucksack pocket: a list of names – not of my own making, but compiled on behalf of everyone with an interest in the fortunes of our most threatened birds. It had brought me to this desolate moor, just as it had led me to coasts and cities, marshes and mountains across Britain on an ornithological treasure trail with binoculars around my neck and a bird guidebook in hand. Seeing these unique birds was another milestone in a quest to which I had devoted the previous twelve months and I was elated and relieved. I was also exhausted, but after thousands of miles on the road my journey was finally nearing an end.

At least I thought it was.

CHAPTER ONE

I DON'T USUALLY GET LAUGHED AT DURING MEETINGS.
Well, not that often. So it came as something of a
surprise.

'If you could have more of anything, what would it
be?' the management consultant asked us.

We had spent the best part of two hours discussing the importance of setting goals to achieve success,
and I was tired and hungry and perplexed by the
enormity of the question. I surveyed the empty plates
on the tea trolley beside me and considered saying:
'Biscuits.'

The consultant paused, peering out of the window
across the business park where our Devon newspaper
offices were based, then turned to a flipchart beside him

and raised a red marker pen over the blank top sheet of paper awaiting suggestions.

'Control,' someone piped up, and he copied it down.

'Respect,' another added.

'Time,' came the third response.

It was obvious the dozen or so fellow staff had got into the spirit of the leadership skills seminar. But my mind went blank as my turn approached. I wanted to say something perceptive and meaningful, only I let myself down. 'Money,' I said.

And at that moment a laugh rang out. An urgent, mocking laugh.

I looked around me. It hadn't come from anyone in the room. Nor was it my imagination playing tricks on me. Yet even though I was sure everyone had heard it, there was not a single flicker of acknowledgement in the faces of either my editorial colleagues beside me or the consultant, who was busy trying to get his marker pen to work properly.

After a second or two the peals of laughter came once more, ringing from the trees outside and piercing the heavy air of the boardroom where we sat.

I recognized the source of the sound with a smile. It was one I had not heard in a while, and I was itching to share both the satisfaction of knowing and the joy of hearing. But you can't very well interrupt a management course to announce: 'Did you hear that? That's a green woodpecker!' before rushing across the room, throwing open the window and beckoning everyone to join you in the hope of catching a glimpse of the bird. Not, that is, if you have any ambitions of promotion.

I excused myself, pretending I needed to make an important call, and headed downstairs and out into the summer sunshine, striding across the car park to a neighbouring woodland from where I guessed the sound had come. In the six years since joining the newspaper I had never ventured this way before. When the woodpecker's cry came again, '*Heeu! Heeu! Heeu!*', I followed the sound down a muddy path, feeling a little overdressed in a shirt and tie. It called again and I crossed a clearing and then a stream, drawing closer. The elusive bird didn't lead me through the forest to a magical kingdom – then again, in a roundabout kind of way, perhaps it did – instead I found myself behind a nursing home close to the A386 squinting in the bright sunshine at a pointy silhouette clinging to the side of an oak tree. I shielded my gaze with a raised hand, and as I did so the bird took to the air, swooping low across a clearing revealing its apple-green back, red cap and yellow rump, then landed on a branch, gave me a hard stare and disappeared between the trees. It isn't an uncommon bird at all, and it wasn't the best sighting, but as my encounters with nature over the previous two decades had largely been limited to whatever hit my windscreen on the drive to and from work, it certainly felt special.

Birds had been missing from my life for far too long. And that, I resolved with the kind of determination that would have made the management consultant proud, was going to change. Uplifting moments like this, standing with mud on my shoes scanning the canopy for flashes of colour and movement and natural wonder, were the answer to his question.

Having said that, a little more money wouldn't hurt either.

In my early teens I was fascinated by natural history. I spent nights catching and identifying moths in the garden of the north London home where I grew up; I kept a weird assortment of pets; I dissected owls' regurgitated pellets and identified the bones of their victims, and I helped set up a nature club at school. But as the years passed my priorities changed – and the harsh realization dawned that girls aren't generally impressed by collections of bird pellets. I turned my back on my childhood enthusiasm. At university I swapped a degree in ecology for the chance to take things easy in the English department. The trendy crowd I befriended thought an ornithologist was someone who fixed teeth. My RSPB membership lapsed, and I hid my old birdwatching magazines under my university bed inside a copy of *Playboy*. I buried my interest.

And that is the way it stayed for the best part of twenty years. While I remained keen to identify whatever birds flew past me, I didn't want to be identified with them. Birdwatching has something of an image problem, and the longer I lived in cities the more uncomfortable I became with assuming the label. As for the modicum of knowledge I had picked up along the way, it was relegated to the function of useful pub quiz trivia.

It took a move from London to the West Country to change all of that. The people I met in Devon had hobbies – they sailed at the weekend, or went surfing, or fishing, or horse riding, or hiking, and they weren't ashamed of what they enjoyed. One could freely admit to being a member of an amateur dramatics group or line-dancing club without being laughed out of the room. A shame really. But it did give me the confidence to embrace my own secret enthusiasm and to finally come out of the closet and declare: 'Hi, my name is Charlie and I'm . . . er . . . interested in birds.'

However, I had a lot of catching up to do. Up until that point I had seen embarrassingly few British species, and barring a family of bitterns setting up home by our village pond or ospreys dropping by for bread crusts on the lawn I realized I was never going to see them unless I made the effort. If they weren't going to come to me, I would have to visit them. And as I thumbed through a handbook that I received on rejoining the RSPB one thing stood out: an alarming number of pages had red strips across the top, denoting the fact that the species beneath were of conservation concern. In the period I had turned a blind eye to birds, many had suffered catastrophic declines. I felt guilty for not having cared more, and ashamed at never having made the time to see them. My new mental list of 'birds I would like to see' was replaced with 'birds I feel I must see' – in some cases before it was too late. So one Sunday over lunch I announced to my wife and two young daughters: 'I'm going birdwatching.'

Showing the kind of respect for their father that one would expect from a nine- and an eleven-year-old, my daughters seized on the chance to offer kind words of encouragement.

'Boring!' my youngest grinned.

Her elder sister added eloquently with a sneer: 'Birds are, like, so whatever.'

My wife came to my defence: 'Girls, don't be rude. If Dad wants to waste his time wandering around with his nerdy binoculars looking at brown sparrows, so be it.'

'Er . . . thanks,' I said.

They had suffered enough, to be honest. Ever since moving to the country our walks had become increasingly punctuated with pauses while I chased after this or that bird, and they had learnt to adopt the brace position in the car whenever I slammed on the brakes to identify something flying overhead.

'How long will you be gone?' my wife asked.

'A year,' I answered calmly.

'A year?!' They laughed. But it petered out when they saw I was serious.

'Well, I'll be back during the week for work, though I might try to get time off in the spring, and I'll leave some weekends free, so it won't be too bad . . .' I began, then explained my plan. I wanted to see all of Britain's 'Red List' birds – those species considered to be in most trouble. I had been a frustrated armchair birdwatcher for too long and finally needed to get out and encounter birds I had seen so many times in books. There were, at the time, forty species on the list, and I decided I would give myself exactly a year to see them. Any longer and I calculated my marriage would also end up on the 'threatened' register.

'But why can't you search for exciting animals like

tigers and polar bears?' my youngest daughter asked. 'Then we could come.'

'Because these are our own special species. They matter too. And they're not as boring as you think,' I replied, getting the RSPB book down from the shelf.

'We know, Dad,' her elder sister sighed, seeing a sermon coming.

I flicked through the book, stopping at the first Red List species I came across. It was a type of warbler. Small, plain and brown. Not the ideal choice to make my point, so I quickly chose another page, opening it at the hen harrier, the picture showing an impressive silvery-grey male with dark wing tips that looked as if they had been dipped in black ink. I had always wanted to see one – more than I wanted to see a tiger. And I turned to the mysterious dusk-flying nightjar with its gaping whiskered mouth; the glossy black grouse whose pumped-up macho males strut and pose to impress the females, and the small, shy lesser spotted woodpecker whose secretive behaviour has earned it the nickname 'never spotted woodpecker'. It was my daughters' generation that stood to lose such birds – although they looked far from bothered.

I noticed my wife weighing things up as she helped herself to more salad, and I added quickly: 'Don't worry, I'll make sure I fit all the travelling around family arrangements, and do it all on the cheap . . .'

'I thought we'd scheduled in your mid-life crisis for next year,' she replied coolly.

I realized that if I was going to go traipsing off around the country at every opportunity to see these special birds, I needed, in fairness, to make a family offering of some kind.

Five minutes later I had agreed to both a puppy and a holiday.

Bother.

Still, I was bursting with such enthusiasm for the challenge that awaited me that I hardly cared. And having bought their blessing I became fired up with a missionary zeal concerning the importance of what I was doing. I eulogized about the wonders of nature, and despaired at how we had polluted and ploughed up and paved over huge swathes of our countryside. I pondered how our relationship with birds had changed over time so that we had moved from eating wild birds or keeping them in cages to be admired, to a situation where we fed wild birds and ate battery caged ones. I pontificated about how we had a duty as guardians of the planet to safeguard species, and how by supporting conservation organizations, going out and seeing birds at risk and spreading the word about their uncertain futures I could play some part in safeguarding our natural heritage.

'If just one bird can be saved as a result,' I proclaimed, with all the hackneyed sentiment I could muster after twenty years in journalism, 'then it will be worth it.'

But the words rang hollow when, after raising my glass of wine with a triumphant grin, I looked down at my lunch and remembered I was eating chicken.

So what is the 'Red List'? Well, we have one for the United Kingdom, and there is one for the world – and one thing is for sure, the domestic chicken isn't on either. From the most populous bird on the planet you have to travel a long way down the graph of ornithological abundance before you start entering global Red List territory. But the fact is that more and more birds are sliding down that slippery statistical slope into the red.

The world Red List is all about the threat of extinction. It was first compiled half a century ago by the International Union for Conservation of Nature and Natural Resources (IUCN) to flag up those animals and plants at risk of being lost forever, and is regularly updated. Of more than 44,000 species assessed at the last count, well over a third were judged as being threatened with extinction. And that staggering statistic includes one in eight species of bird.

It is not just the scarce birds that are becoming scarcer – many species around the globe that were once common have found themselves earning the dubious accolade of endangered status. The most startling example of how profusion cannot be taken for granted is that of the passenger pigeon, which plunged headlong down the population graph and into oblivion. At one time this grey-backed, peach-breasted bird boasted numbers that were impressive even compared with today's chicken population. Migrating flocks of the pigeons miles long and containing up to a billion birds used to darken the skies over North America for hours on end. But loss of habitat and hunting on a massive scale for meat during the nineteenth century polished them off. The last one, nicknamed Martha, lived out her final lonely days in

Cincinnati Zoo before dying in 1914, with a taxidermist standing by.

From pigeons to parrots to petrels, the global Red List makes grim reading. And, of the most critically endangered, who could imagine losing birds with such evocative and exotic names as the long-billed tailorbird, cherry-throated tanager, purple-backed sunbeam and Iquitos gnatcatcher?

Reversing the tradition of TV wildlife documentaries that always end with a gloomy message about how humankind is ultimately responsible for the desperate plight of so many species around the globe, perhaps I should get it out of the way now, at the beginning.

We're to blame.

There, I said it.

Habitat destruction and degradation is the biggest killer, with other factors including over-hunting, pollution and poisoning, climate change, and introductions of invasive pests and predators, such as cats and rats.

But while the global picture is one of hundreds of bird species on the brink, the situation in Britain is not quite that dire. We have only a tiny handful of birds that could be considered endangered on an international scale, and half of those are short-stay visitors that don't even breed in the UK. The vast majority of birds regularly found here are widespread across Europe, so that while some might be uncommon for us, perhaps because we are at the edge of their range, they are likely to be more plentiful somewhere else.

It doesn't follow, though, that we are completely in the clear. Our position on the western edge of Europe, within key flyway routes, surrounded by rich seas and warmed by the Gulf Stream, means that we are pretty important for birds. We house globally significant seabird colonies and wintering sites for waders and wildfowl, and act as a vital staging post for birds passing through, providing essential B&B accommodation. Added to that, we boast an extraordinary mix of habitats for a country of our size. Within a single day you could watch eagles soaring over upland moors, herons stalking fenland reedbeds, skylarks rising in song over fields of corn and kingfishers darting along trout-rich rivers. You could see cuckoos calling on heathland gorse, sparrowhawks patrolling deciduous woodland edges, tiny goldcrests picking insects from the cones of conifers and puffins squabbling on turf-covered sea-cliffs. It would be one hell of a long day, but you could do it.

All of this means that we are responsible for a lot of species of birds. And that figure is on the up. In recent history we have experienced a net gain in arrivals over departures, welcoming back former residents and making room for a number of new tenants who have decided to make a home here. Good news – unless the monotonous cooing of collared doves gets on your nerves or the sight of little egrets on our estuaries and ring-necked parakeets in suburban gardens in the South East makes you wonder whether the bird world's sat-nav is on the blink.

However, if you were a landlord checking over the inventory for the last few decades, you would have to conclude that far too much had gone missing. The populations and breeding ranges of a number of our familiar and beloved birds, particularly those of farmland and woodland, have shrunk dramatically compared with the mid-1970s. In some cases they have more than halved since the Bay City Rollers topped the singles chart with 'Bye Bye Baby' – not that the two are necessarily connected. And while the species may not be in danger of extinction in global terms, a worrying number face extinction in Britain. It is concern over the changing fortunes of British birds that is the basis of our very own Red List.

One thing there is no shortage of when it comes to British birds is information. Ours are the best studied in the world, with thousands of volunteers taking part in regular surveys of their populations and distribution. Somewhere within a few kilometres of where you live, someone will be counting birds. And all that monitoring work means the picture is constantly being updated. As soon as you publish one list, it is time to think about starting on the next one.

Our official roll-call of decline began in 1990 and evolved over the years that followed with the introduction of a 'traffic light' system of red, amber and green categories for all our birds – with those in the red category considered the most pressing priority for conservation action. By 2002 the number of birds qualifying for Red List status had risen to forty, including a number of relatively common and widespread birds that had suffered huge declines. Depressingly, out of 250 British species assessed by the various organizations involved, only eighty-five were considered to be doing fine and earned the green ticket.

On the one hand, the Red List is the kind of club you don't want to be a member of. Then again, it can be a lifesaver. Those newcomers making their way up the red carpet can be sure there will be press on the door – and publicity may help ensure vital support and funding. But to be signed up a species needs to meet a few key criteria. Firstly, it has to be considered 'British', or have established links with the UK, Isle of Man and Channel Islands, and cannot simply be some random rarity blown off course onto our shores. Secondly, if it is not considered globally threatened, which 99 per cent of our birds are not, then it must have lost at least half of its population or breeding range over the last twenty-five years, or have undergone a historical population crash from which it has never sufficiently recovered. The fairly generous time spans involved help iron out regular fluctuations in bird numbers and distribution which can happen because of such factors as wet summers or cold winters. And to lift themselves out of the red our threatened birds basically need to claw back the hefty deficits. This may seem like an impossible task, but it has happened. A number of plummeting species have levelled out and enjoyed something of an upswing, including several of our scarce birds of prey, thanks largely to targeted conservation action.

When I decided to set out to see as many of our species of highest conservation concern as possible, preferably in places that were most significant for them, I knew the task would be far from easy. It was August 2007, I had given myself a year, and there were forty species on our Red List. That was my target. And what a mixed bunch of birds lay in store – some were scarce, others common but in decline, some were widespread, others localized, some were resident all year, others were summer visitors, some were bold and eye-catching, others inconspicuous and shy. There was one species of duck, two larks, three waders, four buntings, as well as game birds and thrushes and woodpeckers and raptors . . . and the best places to find them were scattered across the British Isles from Scilly to the Shetland islands, Wales to the West Country, the Highlands to the Hebrides.

I also had a simple, and yet fundamental, question that I hoped to answer along the way. In setting out to learn more about both the birds and birdwatching, I wanted to know why conserving our threatened species actually mattered. When ranked alongside such major worries as international terrorism, global warming and the enduring popularity of *Big Brother*, the fact that some rare brown warbler or other is becoming even scarcer is unlikely to have many of us waking at night in a cold sweat. After all, the dodo has gone, but we're still thriving. In short, when it came to the Red List, why should we care?

CHAPTER TWO

IT WASN'T QUITE THE PROMISED HOLIDAY MY FAMILY HAD been counting on. For a start they had imagined that the accommodation would include an inside toilet. And despite the fact I had booked it at short notice, they had also reckoned on a supply of drinking water and electricity at the very least, and been expecting a shower, and certainly more than one room. Instead, what they got that summer was a week in a converted shepherd's hut on the Isle of Eigg in the Scottish Hebrides.

'Character-building' was how I had described it, though looking around the old stone bothy on arrival I wondered whether some actual building might be required. It was certainly basic. The peat-stained tap water was taken from a stream that ran off the moorland behind and was the colour of black tea, and the heating was supplied by a log burner which divided the single room in half. The toilet was a short sprint through the rain, with too little leg room for the door to shut if you sat down, and the nearest shower was a two-mile walk away down at the dock.

Under the pretext of looking for low-cost and low-carbon alternative holiday ideas I had stumbled across details for the island off the west coast of Scotland. Only my motives were not entirely genuine.

'This hasn't got anything to do with birds, has it?' my wife had asked suspiciously when I was finalizing the booking.

'Birds? No, not at all. Definitely not,' I replied. Then added, just to be on the safe side: 'Not in the slightest. No. No way.'

Of course it had everything to do with birds, though I was sure she wouldn't figure that out. It was a chance to get away from it all without having to climb aboard a plane, I told her.

Ever since moving to Devon we had endeavoured to live as environmentally friendly lives as possible. We drank lots of wine to boost our glass recycling, and we made our own compost with all the root vegetables from the organic veg box delivery scheme we had joined. I cycled to work or used public transport and at one stage owned a moped, which reduced both my carbon footprint and my life expectancy. However, all these efforts counted for next to nothing because of our appetite for travel. We shamefully spoiled ourselves most years with a major holiday abroad, keen to ensure the children saw something of the world before they left home and were too broke to afford to go themselves. On one occasion I felt so guilty after having just reserved long-haul airline tickets that I drove to the nearest garden centre and bought a tree in a token attempt to offset the carbon emissions our trip would generate, then arrived home and wondered whether I needed to buy another tree to offset the drive to get the first tree. It wasn't easy attempting to be green. And looking back over my lifetime I calculated that I had been to twice as many countries overseas as counties in the UK, so a holiday in Britain seemed like a step in the right direction.

The Isle of Eigg was, however, far from a random choice. Not only is it a good location for a certain Red List species I was dying to spot, but it was also the first place I became interested in birds on a family holiday, and I was eager to return thirty years on to see whether it was still as special as I recalled.

Shaped like an inverted comma, five miles long and lying just over an hour by ferry from the mainland, the Isle of Eigg boasts an impressive variety of habitats for its size, and wildlife to match. Seals and otters share the rocky shores, minke whales and dolphins regularly pass by offshore, the meadows, woods and moors are filled with a wide range of plants and insects, and a towering corrugated pitchstone ridge called An Sgurr which dominates the scenery, rising behind the harbour like a shattered temple column, is home to majestic golden eagles. Except that it wasn't eagles that I was most keen to see, much as I would have loved to come across them. The bird I was after was a lot smaller – about the size of a sparrow, was pretty nondescript, with streaky brownish plumage, and had a name that sounded like an insult.

It was raining heavily when we arrived, stepping off the ferry at the end of an exhausting couple of days' travel from Devon involving two train journeys and a stopover in Glasgow, and by the time we made it to the isolated cottage at the foot of An Sgurr, carrying our bags up the muddy moorland track, we were soaked through.

We unpacked in order to dry all our clothes in front of the log burner and sat steaming around the fire listening to the rain hammering on the roof.

'I told you this would be fun!' I enthused, thumbing through the visitors' book and reading out the entries, most of which praised the view of the sea from the outside toilet. For some reason '*Sandra*' thought it important to tell us that while she enjoyed her visit she had spent '*one day in bed with a cold*'.

A week stretched ahead without timetables or plans. Free from the tyranny of our family diary we had nothing to do but do as we pleased. Eat, sleep and walk. And if birds just happened to fly across our path as we explored the island and I happened to have my binoculars and happened to lift them to my eyes to see them better, well, so be it.

When the clouds cleared I put on my walking boots, left my daughters drawing up the final clauses of their treaty regarding alternate occupation of the top bunk bed, and wandered down to get fresh water from a tap at the harbour. I remembered the landscape well despite the passage of time – the rough edges of the island interspersed with sweeps of clean sand, stone walls spattered with circles of lichen, stunted trees given comb-overs by the prevailing wind, and views over the sea to neighbouring isles and the undulating mainland beyond. Points of interest have a tendency to enlarge in the memory, squeezing out backgrounds, so it took a while to readjust perspectives and push familiar scenery back into place. But little appeared to have changed since I had first set foot on the island as a ten-year-old from north London. Back then the Isle of Eigg had offered the freedom to indulge a young boy's primitive urge to hunt – rockpool crabs by hand, mackerel from a boat using feathered lines, and birds on the wing with . . . names. To label them was to claim them, and one by one I had made the species I saw mine, armed with an inspiring and beautifully illustrated book my parents had brought along with us.

It was low tide and the bay beside the jetty was peppered with worm casts and birds. Laying down the empty water containers I was carrying, I sat on a boulder and pulled out my binoculars. My new birdwatching journey had begun. But while I had set out worried about biodiversity, there now seemed to be far too much of it! Waders and gulls and ducks and terns . . . What was what? Were they common gulls or kittiwakes? Arctic terns or common terns? Curlews or whimbrels? Cormorants or shags? Once birdwatching becomes hard-wired into your natural sense of curiosity, you have to look, you want to know. Identification helps impose order on a chaotic world – though the world wouldn't feel half so chaotic if the birds weren't constantly flying about all over the place. Unravelling the puzzle from the clues is the challenge, and I felt like a complete beginner, as new to it all as I had been when I first visited thirty years earlier, staring out across the bay at lots of question marks with wings.

I took a deep breath, and tried to remember all I had learnt about how to birdwatch from the books I had read. The advice seemed to boil down to the ability to stop, look and listen, and to expect the expected. While we all like the idea of spotting something unusual, genuine rarities, the experts cautioned, were just that: rare. So it was better to assume everything was pretty familiar. It was then a case of narrowing down the options. As obvious as it sounds, not everything lives everywhere. What you see depends on where you're looking. You don't get woodpeckers in Ireland or kingfishers in the Orkneys, and you won't hear a nightingale singing in Berkeley Square – though these days you might just look up and spot a city-living peregrine falcon flying past. It also depends on when you are looking. In the summer dozens of seasonal migrants swell the ranks of our resident birds, taking advantage of our long days and plentiful insect life to raise young, while winter visitors from colder climes gorge in our comparatively frost-free fields and estuaries before following milder weather home in the spring. The cuckoo sound you heard in December? Seek immediate psychiatric help.

So once you've worked out where you are and what month of the year it is, you are in a slightly better position to identify the bird in front of you. Many experts advise jotting down details of appearance and behaviour in a notebook, sketching key distinguishing features to refer to later. The trouble is, whenever I have tried it the end result looks like something you might produce in that heads-bodies-legs game where you draw a face, fold over the paper to cover it and pass it on to the next person who adds the torso, and the next the legs. I end up with birds which might have been trapped between two panes of double-glazing: flat wide heads, disjointed legs, circular bodies, wings sticking out at odd angles. No bird I have ever drawn could live without round-the-clock veterinary care.

Once the bird has become bored with being sketched and flown away, you are in a position to put down your binoculars and consult a field guide to make a final diagnosis. Though this offers ample scope for self-deception. Birds regularly change shape and colour to suit. The notes may point to a 'chaffinch', but with a guidebook in hand . . . 'Yes, I'm sure it had a little less colour around the head, and maybe I made a mistake with that dark area on the wings. If I just rub that bit out, and . . . perfect! A snowy owl. I knew it!'

Of course it would be a lot easier to just know what all our British birds look like, saving the trouble of having to make notes or consult guides. But that takes a lot of learning. Supposing there are 250 British species, in order to be able to identify each one accurately in the field you would have to multiply that figure by all the possible variations in plumage dictated by sex or age or time of year. That pushes things up to at least 1,000 pieces of information. Then on top of all the visual cues you have to add in other key facts for each species ranging from the sounds they make, to the places where they live, to the way they fly, to the company they keep, to the similar species they can be confused with . . . the list goes on. Handy as it would be to know absolutely everything, it doesn't matter if you don't, or if you get things wrong – it is fine to learn as you go, the experts reassured, and make mistakes along the way. Which was just as well, as I felt I was about to make lots of them.

I took a pad and pencil from my coat pocket and started to list the birds of which I was certain out in the bay. There were eider ducks with wedge bills shaped like doorstops sitting on a rock out in the water, a black-and-white oystercatcher hammering at a shell with its bright orange bill, and closer to the waterline a couple of ringed plovers were running about in a stop-start fashion like learner drivers – too much on the accelerator pedal . . . too much on the brake . . . And then things started getting tricky. Firstly there were the terns. Daintier than gulls, these elegant long-distance travellers are assembled from thin triangles of white and light grey, with narrow bodies, forked tails, pointed wings, sharp beaks. A group of them were circling and bickering close to the jetty. The only likely candidates for the island were either common terns or arctic terns, but I had forgotten how to tell the similar birds apart. I recalled that one of the species had a black tip to its red bill – only that was not visible from where I stood – and I remembered the other species was lighter with longer swallow-like tail streamers, though without both side by side how could I make a comparison? I ran out of ideas and just stared at them in the hope one would give the game away by calling out its name or scratching its initials in the sand. Then after a few minutes my eye was caught by a large wader probing for worms nearby. Waders are designed to catch you out. They demand the kind of attention to detail that makes birdwatching both tricky and rewarding, and are typically found half a mile away across muddy estuaries silhouetted on the edge of a receding tide so that it is impossible to see much plumage detail without use of the Hubble Space Telescope. Long legs, long beaks – they can look like balls of wool with knitting needles stuck through. Fortunately the bird I was watching was not too far off and I drew what I could, then wrote a couple of suggested names beside the sketch. It turned away as if embarrassed that it might catch a glimpse of my feeble attempts at identification, gazing awkwardly into the distance in the way that shop checkout staff do when you are tapping in your credit card number at the till.

Back in the cottage, arms aching after carrying the water, I got out the two bird books I had packed. One was a typical field guide, while the other was very precious to me. It was a 1969 original edition of the *Reader's Digest Book of British Birds* – the book that had first inspired me as a boy. It wasn't the actual version my parents had taken with us to Eigg, instead it was a copy I had recently discovered by chance on the shelves of a second-hand book stall, and which had helped reignite my interest in birds. It is not a book one would generally turn to in order to pin down the identification of a bird. It is also too large and heavy to take out on a birdwatching trip. And yet despite this it has sold millions of copies and been translated into numerous languages. Unlike guides that have birds painted in exaggerated colours, unnatural poses or side-on in regimented columns facing left to right and right to left like convicts watching tennis, the artwork in the *Book of British Birds* is brimming with life and character. It took years for the publishers to find an illustrator fit for the job – a talented artist called Raymond Harris-Ching who completed the task in a mere ten months and was left exhausted and sick by the end. He has been described as one of the greatest bird artists of all time, and it was his illustrations that for me, along with countless other readers, made birds worth watching. Some seem to have been caught unawares – a mallard duck half asleep with its bill tucked under a wing, a collared dove snoozing on a branch, a pair of merlin disturbed at a kill; while others are filled with action and personality – a black-headed gull seemingly caught in a screaming match with a starling on the facing page, a little owl with shining eyes fixed intently on something approaching from just over the reader's right shoulder.

Even with the two books I still had trouble confirming what I had seen in the bay. I needed professional help. So I arranged to meet up with John Chester, the Scottish Wildlife Trust warden for the Isle of Eigg, the following day. I was told I would recognize him because he arrived everywhere on foot and had the kind of healthy complexion that comes from spending the working week outdoors, so when I saw a tanned man striding along at breakneck speed with a pair of binoculars strung around his neck I knew it was him. The problem was trying to keep up.

'Meadow pipits,' he said without slowing as a group of birds rose from the grass ahead peeping like squeaky toys. 'And that's a willow warbler.'

'What? Where?' I panted, trying to match his pace.

'That sound.'

'Oh yes.'

'And that's a juvenile shelduck over there near the jetty, unusual for this time of year, and redshank by the tide line and curlews further out, and can you see the greenshank by that rock?'

It was the wader I had been trying to identify before.

'Ah, a greenshank. Of course,' I muttered.

'And those?' I said, pointing. 'Are they common terns?'

'Arctic terns.'

'Yes, arctic terns, that's what I meant,' I said, then noticed him giving me a wry smile.

John patiently explained key identification points and I absorbed everything I could as quickly as I could, like a new arrival at a party being introduced by the host to the assembled guests. But I also wondered why birdwatching hadn't become boring for him, since he seemed to know what everything was.

'Well, there are always new species to look out for,' he said, lighting up his pipe as we followed the road from the harbour. 'And you constantly see the more familiar birds in different ways. You keep experiencing them anew.'

'So where should a beginner begin?' I asked.

'The key is to know the common ones,' he replied, 'then you notice when something is unusual. It can come down to what it isn't, rather than what it is.'

When it came to unusual sightings, John had spotted plenty of rarities in the more than twenty years he had been on the island, but I was surprised when he told me one bird never recorded on Eigg that he would jump on his bike and pedal flat out to see was the widely despised and nationally common member of the crow family, the magpie.

To be honest, I would gladly have swapped a few of our Dartmoor magpies for a few of his arctic terns.

My eldest daughter seemed surprisingly keen when I suggested climbing An Sgurr and it took me a while to figure out that she realized her mobile-phone reception might be better at the top. The next morning we set off, with her at the front, taking a path which skirted the western side of the peak and following green dots painted on stones that guided the way. However, after a mile or so we lost track of the paint splodges we were supposed to be checking and continued on along the clifftops to the west of the ridge, missing the turn-off to the summit. At one point we bumped into a flock of sheep with green dye spots on their rumps and wondered whether we were supposed to follow them. Either way we ended up circumventing An Sgurr completely and heading across the purple heather moorland at its base to the ruined village of Grulin.

It was clear, but incredibly windy, and we sought shelter behind part of a stone building and looked up at the ridge where streams of rain water from downpours the previous day were being blown back off the top of the rock face in plumes of spray.

'There! A golden eagle!' my wife cried, gesturing up at a dark shape far bigger than a buzzard effortlessly riding the updraught along the crest of the ridge.

She was right. 'Yes, I was just going to point it out,' I said.

The truth was that while my family enjoyed teasing me about birds, raising their eyebrows with a sigh whenever I mentioned them, they had actually all developed a very keen eye for spotting wildlife. Although they didn't get as excited as I did, they noticed things, and annoyingly this was invariably before I did.

The wind was so strong it was hard to keep the binoculars steady, but we all managed a decent look. It was a magical moment, to be there in that wild and rugged place lying on our backs among the thistles and bracken watching a magnificent raptor circling above, fingered wings weaving sense out of the powerful airstream. It is one of those birds born to be admired.

It is a strange thing to declare of a bird that one feels privileged to be watching it. Of all of them it is generally the masters of the skies that we find the most compelling, that inspire awe rather than simply affection. We look up to them, literally. But there is something else about an eagle, a sense of wilderness, of how the world was before humans evolved. Birds of prey rose from the ground millions of years in advance of early man rising to his feet. As they look down on us from high, you get the feeling that they might just know it too.

To get some idea of just how large a golden eagle is, it is well worth finding a tape measure and marking out its two-metre wingspan on the kitchen floor. Just for fun, if your tape is long enough, stretch it out to 3.6 metres, the record-breaking wingspan of the wandering albatross. Beside it for comparison lay a wine cork, which is roughly the 5cm length of the world's smallest bird, the bee hummingbird from Cuba. Then stand back and marvel, and drink the wine.

'There's another!' my youngest daughter exclaimed, pointing up at a second golden eagle which had joined the first high above us.

'Are they on the Red List?' she asked, trying to wrest the binoculars off me.

I had to disappoint her. While golden eagles are scarcer than quite a few on the list, and have suffered hard times in the past, our population is now considered pretty stable, and the Red List is all about birds in decline rather than species that are simply rare.

When the eagles finally disappeared over the ridge, we walked back to the cottage, stopping when the path neared the clifftops to watch seals bobbing about in the surf below. In a mere 24 hours on Eigg two things had struck me: the wealth of wildlife on our doorstep in Britain, and a sense of regret at not having taken the time to see it. I had encountered wonderful birds travelling abroad: flameback woodpeckers in Borneo, red shining parrots in Tonga, Knysna lourie in South

Africa, standard-wing nightjars in Cameroon, tui in New Zealand . . . but, like unfamiliar foreign currency, it had been hard to feel a true sense of their value. Seeing golden eagles in Britain really meant something.

Despite our best intentions we never did make it up An Sgurr during our week on Eigg. However, I did reach the first high point of my Red List quest. Choosing what to do on such a sparsely inhabited island generally consists of deciding which direction to walk, and on the fourth day we headed north to Laig Bay, turning down towards the sea and following a track between lush hay meadows where cattle lifted their heads from the grass to watch us.

'Quiet, children, we're entering a new habitat,' I said, tightening my grip on my binoculars in anticipation, and they looked at each other, though I didn't quite catch their expressions.

On the path ahead of us was a small party of finches of some kind twittering away in the sunshine and drinking from a puddle. I got the feeling they might be what I was looking for. But they were not going to give away their identity easily, and as I raised my binoculars, a bit slow on the draw, the flock flew off across the fields.

We explored the beach and caught crabs in rockpools and collected pebbles and looked at what the tide had washed up and generally had a relaxing time – or at least I would have done except that my mind was chewing over the sighting of those flighty finches. I hadn't managed a decent view at all, but I also hadn't immediately recognized them as something I had seen before. And that was a good sign.

We left the beach by a path at the northern end and were nearing a chapel when a finch similar to the ones I had already seen flew up from the field to our right and landed on a barbed-wire fence a short distance ahead.

'Wait!' I said, stopping in my tracks, and my wife and daughters instinctively adopted the brace position. I focused quickly on the nondescript little brown bird, which was sitting calmly as if waiting for something. It had a stumpy seed-cracking bill and no distinctive markings that I could discern at all. Another good sign.

'What is it, Dad?' my eldest daughter asked. 'Is it behind that sparrow?'

'That's no sparrow,' I whispered melodramatically, though I still couldn't tell for sure what it was. It had a slightly forked tail, a darkish back and was streaky as if it had been repeatedly jabbed at with a brown pencil.

Then another seemingly identical bird flew down beside it and the first rapidly fluttered its wings in a manner typical of a youngster begging for food. Sure enough the second obliged, cramming a meal into its open mouth. So I knew I was watching a juvenile and an adult. But at that moment I noticed that further up the path ahead two hikers were approaching in vivid yellow and orange waterproof tops so bright that they might be visible from space. They were sure to scare the two birds perched between us, and more worryingly frighten every living creature off the island. I had a few seconds' grace when, just before the two birds caught sight of the dazzling oncomers and took flight, the adult shifted position slightly on the wire, and as it adjusted its wings I saw a flash of pink feathers – a small patch of colour that had previously been hidden where its tail joined its back. Yes! In that instant the birds changed from being nameless quandaries to the special species I had been hoping to see. They were twite.

That's right. Twite.

As the luminous hikers passed they may well have wondered what a grown man wearing binoculars in a quiet corner of a Hebridean isle was doing punching the air in delight as his bemused family looked on. They would have been even more perplexed if they had seen what all the fuss was about. I can't deny it, twite are pretty plain. You may not be familiar with the name, or have seen a picture of twite before, but basically you could take a brown budget starter finch, apply a dash of pink to the rump of the males and a smudge of dull yellow to the bill, and you have one. Sometimes it doesn't seem to take much to make a new species. It was the same with the arctic and common terns I had seen a few days earlier. And yet those tiny variations in appearance make all the difference.

Of course there is a lot more to a species than simply how it looks, but aesthetics plays a large part in our appreciation of birds and, sad to say, the twite seems destined to be one of those birds that gets overlooked. They lack the kind of showy plumage or newsworthy behaviour needed to earn celebrity status. They are small as well, which doesn't help, and they have a name you wouldn't particularly want on a campaign letterhead. But they are here, and they are in trouble, and for me it was as much a privilege to see a twite as it was to have watched the golden eagles. I had seen illustrations of them in bird books many times, and could visualize the painting in the *Reader's Digest Book of British Birds*: a perching male, head tilted down, blushing rump visible, inspecting a tangle of foliage. Seeing them that afternoon was like meeting old friends for the first time, if that makes sense.

The twite is a bird of rough and windy places, of moorland edges, grasslands and coasts. In global terms it is fairly common and doesn't rate as a species of concern, but in the UK, one of its important European strongholds along with Norway, it has retreated northwards over the last century, draining away from the English countryside. As a result, 95 per cent of our twite now live in Scotland, with only a few hundred nesting in the Pennines, where numbers have fallen at an alarming rate. In the winter you can see twite feeding along the south and eastern coasts of England, and a few breed in Wales, but north of the border is the best place for them all year round.

And seeds are what a twite needs. Dandelion, sorrel, thistles, marsh samphire, thrift . . . farmland seeds, grassland seeds, saltmarsh seeds, meadow seeds, seeds from weeds in crofters' smallholdings, in patches of scrub, coastal heaths, along roadside verges, wherever it can get them. Come the spring, most seed-eaters feed their young juicy, easily digestible invertebrates, but the twite is one of the few finches that doesn't have much of an appetite for creepy-crawlies and so it needs to choose its nesting sites within easy flying distance of a decent supply of seed snacks. It would live in a health food store if it could – though despite its quality diet, it only lives two or three years on average, while a herring gull that eats junk food stolen from bins in seaside towns may survive ten times as long. Life isn't fair sometimes.

The trouble is, Britain is not as weedy as it once was – not, that is, in military terms, but agricultural. We have tamed our unruly fields and tidied up our countryside. Intensive farming, the loss of hay meadows and regular mowing of road verges means there are fewer weeds about that provide year-round seeds upon which twite depend. In addition, some heather moorland nesting sites have been damaged by over-grazing and salt-marshes eroded by rising sea levels. If we are not careful more and more areas of Britain could lose the chirpy chatter of this gregarious little finch and the pink splashes of colour that brightened my day on Eigg.

However, all is far from lost. Like many of our small birds, twite can raise lots of young if the conditions are right, and weeds have been making something of a comeback in recent years as farmers are being paid to grow them. Providing for our feathered friends is no longer something that is confined to the back gardens of nature lovers – we are wealthy and well fed enough as a country to be willing to do it on a national scale. Feeding the birds has become government policy.

CHAPTER THREE

AFTER ABANDONING MY FAMILY ON THE STREETS OF Glasgow at night with return train tickets and £3.47 in loose change, I took a taxi to the airport to pick up a hire car. The timing of our holiday on the Isle of Eigg meant that I needed to drive through until dawn to catch the final day of the British Birdwatching Fair in Leicestershire, or 'Birdfair' as it is known, and I was already tired following the afternoon's ferry crossing and train journey from Mallaig.

'So where's that you said you were heading for?' the Glaswegian taxi driver asked as he dropped me off close to the hire car depot.

'The British Birdfair,' I replied.

'Is that one of those speed-dating events?' he said, in all seriousness.

'What? No, I . . . ' I was going to explain, but something stopped me. It's just that I wasn't sure whether the truth was any less embarrassing. Birdwatching may be massively popular, with the RSPB boasting over a million members – more than the membership of our three main political parties combined – but it was not an interest I was comfortable admitting to just yet, least of all to a Glaswegian cabbie. 'Um . . . yes, that's right.'

'Well, I hope you find someone,' he smiled sympathetically, and drove off.

The three-day Birdfair is held every August on the banks of Rutland Water and from its modest launch in 1989 it now attracts almost 20,000 visitors who flock there from all over the country and further afield, not for the birdwatching, but to browse the stands, spend their money and share their enthusiasm. I had never been before, and there were times in the small hours as I shook myself awake at the wheel heading south from Glasgow that I thought I never would. From fuel pump to fuel pump, accent to accent, hot drink to hot drink, I worked my way down the country, taking breaks at motorway service stations and wandering around their empty shops and restaurants, inspecting the limited range of late-night food on offer that slumped in trays under the glare of bright heat lamps as if being interrogated for crimes against nutrition. I just wasn't used to going with so little sleep and I don't drink coffee, and despite swallowing copious quantities of tea there was little else

I could do between stops to keep myself alert besides fashioning makeshift caffeine patches from Typhoo bags taped to my arms. Forced to nap in lay-bys I eventually emerged from the vitamin-D-deficient world of nightshift workers and pulled up at 8am at the Birdfair site near the village of Egleton.

I was there to kill two birds with one stone – not literally, of course. Not only was I hoping to find out a little more about birdwatching, but there was also a resident Red List bird that I had every chance of seeing. Ospreys are now a regular sight at Rutland Water following their reintroduction in the late 1990s, but their national recovery means they are no longer a species of top conservation concern. No, the bird I hoped to see was far smaller and a lot more down-to-earth. It was sparrow-sized. Exactly sparrow-sized, in fact, on account of it being a sparrow. To be precise, it was a tree sparrow – the neater, chestnut-capped country cousin of the familiar house sparrow, and it had suffered a catastrophic decline the like of which must have had statisticians double-checking their figures.

Some birds are easier to help than others. They make the conservationist's task simpler by existing in small populations, living in very localized areas and having specific requirements. Once you have done the field-work you know how many you have got, where they are and what they need, and it's time to scrape together enough cash and volunteers and sort the problem. But others are more awkward. They are relatively common, they spread themselves across vast areas of the country, and they demand national solutions. They include many of our farmland birds, which have had a very bad time of it over recent decades. If you look at a population graph for all the main farm species lumped together it looks like a ski slope black run: a steep drop tapering to the horizontal. Millions of birds have been lost since the 1970s, and while the decline has fortunately levelled off for some, their numbers still remain far below what they were a third of a century ago.

One reason is that finding suitable nest sites became harder as farms modernized. Old buildings were replaced, scrub was cleared and dense crops were planted that left little space on the ground. Far more telling, however, was a lack of food. They need food, and we need food, and at a time when we were struggling to store surplus grain mountains, we left them less than ever before. Unable to scratch a sufficient living in our intensively cultivated areas, hungry parents failed to lay or to successfully raise young, and that soon added up to a catastrophe among those species that normally depend on a couple of broods a year as an insurance policy against losses. Come the cold winter months weakened adults with depleted fat reserves were also doomed, picked off by predators or destined to die of starvation on farms that had, ironically, become more productive than ever.

Rewind to the Middle Ages and our land was largely farmed in strips as part of an open-field system with communal grazing areas that would have suited much wildlife. This was a halcyon era of simple subsistence when the skies were filled with the songs of larks and buntings and rosy-cheeked peasants toiled merrily to make ends meet and coped cheerfully with the challenges of medieval life – like famine, folk dancing and the Black Death. Happy days. But the arrangement came to an end with the process of enclosures which peaked in the late 1700s and early 1800s and saw fields and commons divided up and parcelled off. While bad news for farmers forced from the land and into poverty, the hedgerows planted as field boundaries were a real bonus for birds of the woodland edges that could exploit them. It was not all good news for nature, however, as commons and heathlands were put under the plough, wetlands drained and the drive towards greater productivity gained momentum, feeding our expanding population.

One familiar farmland bird of that time was the tree sparrow. While they favour urban life in Asia, tree sparrows in the UK are rural dwellers, and it is reckoned that two hundred years ago they were doing just fine.

Fast-forward through the Agricultural Revolution to the early twentieth century and our farming industry found itself in the doldrums, undercut by cheap imported food from the United States and elsewhere. But all that was to change. When supply ships bringing in the overseas produce on which we depended came under attack during the war years and rationing became a necessity, the focus shifted towards greater national self-sufficiency. Aided by advances in mechanization and an armoury of agro-chemicals, and later spurred on by a system of subsidies linked to production, intensification shouldered wildlife out of the picture and land that might otherwise have gone uncultivated was turned to profit.

Life got tough for the tree sparrow, as it did for many farmland birds. Herbicides and insecticides wiped out seed-supplying weeds and the invertebrates that fed on them; hedges were pulled up to provide prairie-scale fields for combine harvesters; winter stubbles worth picking over for fallen corn disappeared as cereals were increasingly sown in the autumn to get a head start; improved grain storage reduced spillage; hay making was replaced with early cut grass silage; permanent pasture was re-seeded and treated with inorganic fertilizers to produce uniform grass swards; and mixed farms became monocultures. Numbers of tree sparrows nosedived, assuring them of a place on the Red List.

Sparrows on the Red List? Surely they're too common to be worth worrying about! Well, they are abundant in global terms, and despite a few historical fluctuations they were here. In 1970 their numbers in Britain were in the millions. Twenty-five years later they were down to the equivalent human population of a small city the size of Newport. A staggering 95 per cent of tree sparrows were lost, the largest decline over that period of any of our birds, and at the last count we had 68,000 pairs left.

The tree sparrow is one of those unmemorable birds you assume you have seen. I certainly hadn't encountered one while living in London or since moving to the West Country, from which they have all but disappeared, but thought I had probably come across them during my younger years – and sure enough, up in our attic I found an old list I had compiled in my early teens, and tree sparrow was ticked off. But to be perfectly honest the list was far from reliable. I got the feeling I had probably ticked all the common birds one evening on the basis that it was too embarrassing not to have spotted them. I needed to see a tree sparrow again to be sure.

So where better to go than the most intensively studied colony in Britain at a time when it would be surrounded by 20,000 birdwatchers?

Rutland Water Nature Reserve has remained a stronghold for tree sparrows despite their losses elsewhere, and in the year 2000 a team of scientists moved in to find out why. They discovered that given a range of possible property options, parent birds always chose nest boxes close to the wetland areas of the reserve where there were plenty of invertebrates needed to keep nestlings well fed. The study also found that during the winter they needed a source of seeds within a couple of kilometres' commuting distance of their breeding sites. In short, they want everything on their doorstep: insects, seeds, a hole to nest in, off-street parking, broadband access . . .

When the gates opened for the final day of the Birdfair I joined a steady stream of people making their way onto the main site, and was amazed at my good luck when the first person I came across was the RSPB's Guy Anderson, one of the main people involved in the tree sparrow study. He was manning a display on bird ringing next to the entrance and I introduced myself and went to shake hands, but noticed he had a robin in his.

'Sorry, this is my first time at the fair,' I said. 'I didn't realize I had to bring a bird.'

The robin had just been caught in a mist net and was having its vital statistics taken before being logged, ringed and released. Guy had caught plenty of tree sparrows as part of the study, ringing them with coloured leg bands so they could be identified in the field. But they were canny and difficult to net, he told me.

'It seems lately they have moved elsewhere across the reservoir, though you may well see one visiting the bird feeders,' he said, pointing me in the right direction.

Just off the main track a bench behind a wooden screen with rectangular viewing holes cut in it overlooked a small woodland clearing. In the middle a couple of branches had been planted in the ground, and from these hung a number of tubular seed feeders. There were several bright greenfinches squabbling over the feeding perches, chaffinches and goldfinches waiting their turn, and a rat as fat as a capybara sat underneath gorging on fallen grain.

I assumed that everyone visiting the Birdfair was having a day off from actual birdwatching as I had the bench to myself, but after a few minutes an elderly man with a broad-brimmed rain hat came and sat next to me and we watched the birds with binoculars raised in silence.

'There's a wren by that tree,' he said after a moment.

'So there is,' I said, politely turning my binoculars to find it. And it struck me that there was something charming about that simple observation. The wren is Britain's most numerous bird. Why would you bother pointing one out? You can see and hear them just about anywhere. He would have seen them before many, many times, just as I had. And yet he enjoyed seeing it, I enjoyed seeing it, and we enjoyed sharing in that experience. So what was it about seeing a 10-gram brown bird of modest aesthetic appeal that gave pleasure?

It was hard to say. Did the enjoyment take root in some profound biological affinity with other living creatures? Could it stem from a fundamental desire to connect with consciousness, even across vast evolutionary divides? Was it a case of primitive anthropomorphism? The wren is a loud and perky little bird that lends itself to characterization. Or was it all about the satisfaction of recognition? And if it was purely about the enjoyment of knowing, why could one delight in natural wonders one knew next to nothing about? I don't have a clue when it comes to plants – in fact I once bought a packet of 'Miscellaneous' seeds thinking that was a variety of flower – nonetheless, wandering through a wood or a meadow in bloom is pleasurable, regardless of how little I know about what I am seeing.

I wanted to ask the man beside me why he liked seeing the wren, but it seemed like an absurd question. In any case, just at that moment a bird that looked as if it could be what I was after flew down onto one of the feeder perches. It was hidden from view momentarily, then changed position to feed on the grain and . . . bingo! There it was: a tree sparrow. A handsome little bird, with dark patches on light cheeks and a brown and black back. I couldn't tell whether it was male or female as they both look the same. It tucked into the seeds and after a few seconds was done and flew off.

The man turned to me with a smile: 'Did you see that? It was—'

'I know, a tree sparrow,' I interrupted with a grin.

'I remember when you used to get flocks hundreds strong,' he said wistfully.

I was going to suggest that it could happen again, but his comment deserved a moment's quiet reflection.

More than three-quarters of our land is farmed, and more than a quarter of our Red List birds are farmland species. Positioned at the top end of the food chain, birds are regarded as key indicators of the state of the countryside, and like miners' canaries falling from several million perches across Britain, their huge losses which began in the 1970s, signalled all was not well. However, just when it seemed as if parachutes would never open, plummeting population figures did slow down. And the tree sparrow is one of those that have seen a modest turnaround in recent years.

Set-aside has now been pushed aside, but it undoubtedly helped. It was originally introduced to cut production rather than conserve wildlife, compensating farmers for taking an agreed percentage of their land out of cultivation every year. The benefit was that, managed properly, it provided valuable cover and food for farmland birds. However, increased global demand for wheat coupled with shortages blamed on poor harvests and expanding biofuel production meant that in 2007 set-aside was abruptly set at 0 per cent. Ouch!

While set-aside has all but gone, recent reforms in agricultural policy have introduced important safeguards for nature. To get their pay-outs farmers must, among other things, leave field edges uncultivated and unsprayed. In addition, environmental stewardship schemes reward those who volunteer to go that little bit further. The government has even set a target of reversing the long-term decline of farmland birds by

2020. Giving birds something to chirp about doesn't come cheap, and hundreds of millions of pounds are now being pumped every year into making our farms more wildlife-friendly.

When the tree sparrow failed to reappear I headed along the track to the main Birdfair marquees, and was staggered at the scale of the event. There were dozens of bird art and photography stands to browse, firms selling optical equipment, organizations and trusts vying for charitable donations, new members and legacies, and an incredible 115 travel and tour operators offering to whisk the well-heeled away to prime birding spots around the world. There were talks and quizzes taking place, clothing and crafts and books and bird feeders to buy, and in keeping with outdoor festivals the wash-out summer had also provided plenty of mud.

I felt a bit lost. Did I know enough to consider myself a birdwatcher? Did I look the part? Or would people think I was only there for the free parking? Surveying the crowds around me it seemed that birdwatchers came in all shapes and sizes, and sexes (well, two that I could identify). Older than Glastonbury-goers and younger than a Chelsea Flower Show crowd, the Birdfair visitors were a real mix, and it was comforting to see that a few of the men even looked similar to me – tall and extremely handsome. There were a number of children, and I realized that I could have treated my own family to tickets. How their faces would have lit up with joy! But perhaps they had been spoilt enough in Eigg, what with seeing twite.

As I wandered around looking over the various

displays and chatting to people I began to feel more at ease. I wasn't cornered by gangs of twitchers in camouflage jackets and tested on taxonomy, harangued by angry young conservationists for not being an angry young conservationist, or pursued by earnest old ladies bearing seed cake and collecting tins. Everyone seemed genuinely friendly, and there appeared to be no more misfits than one would find in an average sample of the British population, excluding Crawley. In fact I couldn't help but conclude after an hour or so that birdwatchers were a good-natured lot, and that it didn't matter how much or how little you knew. After a while I stopped opening conversations with an apology, and when I told one person manning an RSPB stand how I was reviving an old interest, he said simply: 'Welcome back!' I was glad I had come.

But I needed more than warm smiles and words of encouragement. I had started my Red List quest with a couple of relatively common birds, and knew things were going to get a lot harder. With four seasons to play with and plenty of travel to arrange, I required information and a detailed plan of action. Firstly I bought a couple of books showing where and when to find British species, and then I collared anyone who looked like a serious birdwatcher and ran the list past them. Not only were people more than willing to help, but their knowledge was astounding, and it was reassuring that they were also coming up with much the same answers as each other.

The marquee selling binoculars and telescopes was by far the busiest on the site, and I practically had to squeeze my way in. Various trade stands for leading brands had their wares laid out on tables, secured with wires to prevent people walking off with pairs of binoculars worth up to £1,000, and telescopes on tripods faced out of the open sides of the tent like rows of rocket launchers. Plastic birds on which to focus had been tied to posts in a neighbouring field, while on the side that overlooked the edge of the reservoir lenses were trained on real birds. Never have a few mallard ducks been stared at with such an array of expensive hardware.

Whatever the hobby, people want to feel properly equipped. It is hard to deny, we love buying stuff. Of course you don't need much to be a birdwatcher, anything in fact, but binoculars do help. And there are plenty of things to consider when selecting a pair, as the salespeople were keen to tell me. What sort of birdwatching was I doing? 'Er, just the type that involves watching birds.' Generally what time of the day? 'Um, any time.' Do I prefer compact and lightweight or heavier and more powerful? 'Well . . . a bit of both I suppose.' How much do I have to spend? 'Oh . . . well, I got this letter through the post the other day addressed to "the homeowner" saying I had been specially chosen as the lucky recipient of up to £1 million in cash if I wrote off for a unique claim number . . .'

No deal, surprisingly.

I had taken my own binoculars along with me for comparison, but they were not exactly the latest in optical sophistication and I kept them tucked away out of sight under my top. They had a magnification of eight, which is fairly standard, but didn't let in quite as much light as they might. They were also fashioned in old-style stepped sections, rather than the modern sleek tubular look. What I learnt was that when it comes to binoculars, bigger is not necessarily better. The trade off is typically between magnification, image brightness, weight and field of view, which seemed like far too many things for me to consider on forty-five minutes' sleep. As it happened my pair didn't compare too badly when I tested them out on a plastic heron alongside other expensive binoculars, and I decided against upgrading. I didn't care what other people thought, they would do fine, I told myself, hiding them again under my zipped-up top.

I also decided that for the time being I would try to get by without a telescope, even though I was blown away by what I could see through them. The clarity and magnification was incredible, bringing birds closer than I thought possible without actually bumping into them. Not only could I count the feathers on the ducks dabbling at the water's edge, I could practically see them changing their minds.

Signing posters in a nearby marquee was TV wildlife presenter Simon King, of the BBC's *Springwatch* and *Big Cat Diary* fame, and when the queue shortened I took the opportunity to have a few words. He has helped popularize British wildlife, from the antics of rutting red deer to nest-cam footage of golden eagles, and has highlighted conservation issues, including the plight of our farmland birds, to huge television audiences.

'Sadly there has been a massive decline among several species,' he said, turning to me once he had sent a final autograph-hunter away with a friendly handshake. 'Such as the corn bunting with a song like rattling keys which was always for me a part of the sound of rural England, and the yellowhammer which I used to hear all the time and am now delighted whenever I encounter.'

So wasn't he weighed down with pessimism about the future?

'I'm optimistic they can all make a comeback,' he said, 'if their preferred habitat is given a chance to recover and favoured food sources the opportunity to flourish. The management of agriculture and principles of conservation must go hand in hand.'

But why, I ventured, should we care? Did it really matter whether we had corn buntings or tree sparrows or yellowhammers?

He weighed up my question for a moment, before answering with the kind of fluency that befits a professional broadcaster. 'It depends whether the only thing one cares about is oneself and one's progress in life. I like to believe the human race thinks in a more philanthropic fashion, that it's not just about oneself, but about one's immediate neighbours, whether human or other life forms. If we don't care for our neighbourhood we're all impoverished as a result. The world would be a grey and shallow and sad place without the charm of these birds and the beauty and music they bring to our lives.'

In bird terms our farmland has certainly become a little greyer and less musical with the widespread loss of two pretty little yellow-plumaged residents: the cirl bunting (pronounced 'sirl') and the yellowhammer.

If you were making a soundtrack for the British countryside, the yellowhammer would be on it. Whether we are conscious of it or not, birds provide the backing tunes for much of our experience of the outdoors. Just as sirens and car horns and the rhythms of hard heels on pavements conjure up busy city life, so the calls and songs of birds evoke a vivid sense of place. It doesn't take much. All a radio sound engineer has to do is look out the tape of gulls yelping to paint a seaside scene, a tawny owl for night, the melancholy cry of a buzzard or curlew to suggest a sense of wilderness. Fade in the flutey song of a blackbird and we are in suburbia or a village, with perhaps the faint sound of a cuckoo in the distance to hint at spring. And for farmland, the medley might include the raucous calls of rooks with skylarks and yellowhammers adding a little ray of sunshine.

The male yellowhammer's song is often described with the phrase *little-bit-of-bread-and-no-cheese* – appropriate for a bird the colour of butter. It sits in a prominent position and delivers this cheery but monotonous territorial message repeatedly through the day for months on end in a show of vocal stamina that takes some beating. The cirl bunting is less impressive song-wise, matching the repeated notes but lacking the yellowhammer's extended wheeze at the end.

These close relatives were once a common sight, feeding along field edges and singing their ditties from the tops of hedgerows. Now the cirl bunting is about as rare on farmland as a barn that hasn't been converted into housing, while the widespread yellowhammer, which looks very much like a miner's canary, provided yet another warning sign that our farmland was becoming less hospitable for wildlife when its population began plummeting from the late 1980s onwards. *Little-bit-dead-and . . .* Silence.

But before we admonish ourselves for our role in their decline, it is worth reflecting on the fact that they, among other farmland birds, largely have us to thank for being here at all. Cirl buntings and yellowhammers love hedgerows and fields, and we have provided both.

The last ice age pretty much wiped the slate clean when it came to British birdlife. Anything that couldn't burrow more than a mile down through the glacial ice sheet to find food wisely opted to make a home elsewhere until things started thawing out 10,000 or so years ago. As the ice retreated, trees advanced across the land until Britain was largely covered in forest, and woodland birds took up residence. And then man set about cutting the trees down, clearing areas for cultivation and livestock, for timber to build houses and ships and for firewood for fuel and smelting, so that by the early 1900s just 5 per cent of the UK was covered by woodland. That figure has now more than doubled, but the centuries of relentless felling was good news for birds that favour open spaces, while the planting of tens of thousands of miles of field boundary hedgerows provided an added bonus for more agoraphobic species like cirl buntings and yellowhammers that need cover within darting distance. What's more, we filled fields with seed-bearing crops and grasses, and were careless enough to spill grain all over the place. You could say that for a while we were excellent hosts.

Living in Devon I was well placed to see both yellowhammers and cirl buntings without having to travel far, and about a week after the Birdfair I had a chance encounter with the commonest of the two buntings thanks to something I had never done since moving from London to the edge of Dartmoor. I went for a walk on my own.

Gibbet Hill stands apart from the rocky moorland tors to the east. Rounded and covered in long grass that turns yellow in the late summer, it can resemble a giant sand dune in the right light. Scattered gorse bushes fringe the base, while at the summit, where wrongdoers and ne'er-do-wells of old were once strung up as rich pickings for the crows and a warning to all, a number of shallow gullies offer shelter from the wind for free-roaming ponies. It is an exposed spot and, lacking a dog or walking poles or binoculars large enough to be visible from a distance, I felt a little self-conscious as I made my way along sheep paths up the side of the hill with no obvious reason for being out of doors alone on a drizzly day unless mad, lost or depressed.

I passed a group of shaggy highland cattle standing knee deep in the grass, and further on a flock of rooks probing the ground gave me one glance and took flight. I think they spotted the half-opened black umbrella I was carrying, which looks a bit like a rook, and assumed I had one of their friends by the scruff of the neck. Then, as I reached the brow of a ridge, a yellowhammer flew past following the contours of the hill – a dash of bright yellow and warm brown against the grey sky. As birds are so often seen flying away, backsides can provide useful clues to identity, and when the yellowhammer dipped purposefully down towards the fields below I saw its telltale reddish-brown rump clearly. I had neither been intending nor expecting to see one, and the pleasant surprise taught me a useful lesson: I needed to get out more.

No sooner had I seen one than I spotted three or four others following behind. Then something else striking caught my eye: two attractive women hikers striding towards me. Judging from their spotless walking gear I knew they couldn't be local, and as they approached along the path I wracked my brains for something interesting to say.

'Nice day,' I commented, like I worked in a post office. It was also about to rain. 'I just passed a lovely flock of yellowhammers,' I added.

They looked slightly baffled, nodded and walked on.

Yellowhammers? What was I thinking? Why couldn't I have come up with: 'Is this the quickest way to the main road as I just remembered I left my fire service uniform on the back seat of my Aston Martin?' It reminded me of an important lesson I had learnt when younger: there are very few circumstances in which birdwatching is considered either cool or impressive.

A while back, seeing yellowhammers would have been regarded as anything but lovely. In some areas they were once considered agents of the devil, and apparently stoned by anyone with the inclination. A few fatalities to well-aimed pebbles is as nothing compared with the mass starvation they have suffered in more recent times thanks to agricultural intensification. But we have lost much more than numbers of birds such as yellowhammers over the decades. Gone too are the stories – the folklore that was once a part of the language of rural life. Given so few of us now have to scrub soil from under our fingernails after a day's work, it is hardly surprising that such an everyday intimacy with nature and all the tales it inspired should have become a thing of the past. But as I read some of the bizarre bygone notions about yellowhammers – that drops of the devil's blood ran in their veins and that serpents hatched from their eggs, which are marked with snake-like squiggles – I couldn't help but feel that today's scientific approach and appreciation of wildlife for its own sake is wanting for a bit of superstitious nonsense.

The tale of the yellowhammer is still in search of a happy ending. With over 700,000 pairs spread across farmland, heath, scrub and downland areas, particularly in central and eastern England, it is still pretty easy to see. But you now have to look twice as hard, as we have half as many as we once did. And while the decline has slowed, it has yet to stop completely. At one stage when other farmland birds were suffering, the yellowhammer seemed to be holding ground, until the late 1980s when it followed suit and was propelled from the green list straight into the red, bypassing amber. Ultimately the same basic effects of changing farming practices were at work: too little leftover grain or weed seeds for adults to eat in the winter – half an eggcup a day would suffice – and too few protein-rich invertebrates to feed to their young in the spring and summer. You could say that neatening up our farms to make a tidy profit messed things up. Though, while it is easy to criticize, how many of us willingly let our gardens, on which we don't depend for an income, run to seed for the sake of wildlife?

The cirl bunting is a thousand times rarer than the yellowhammer, which it closely resembles with the addition of a black chin and eye stripe among males, and is one of our most threatened farmland species. If you look at a map of their distribution, Britain is completely empty save for a tiny wedge of colour along the coast of south Devon. And that is where I headed on a sunny Sunday morning in late August, leaving my family laughing over breakfast that nothing could be nerdier than searching for a 'Cyril' bunting. (Well, if they weren't going to take things seriously I wouldn't invite them along. So there.)

In the 1800s cirl buntings colonized Devon, the northernmost limit of their European range, and gradually spread across southern England. And then from the middle of the twentieth century they beat a retreat, dying back in their thousands as agriculture modernized until just a few dozen pairs remained in the South West, living in coastal scrub adjacent to mixed farmland. By 1989 you could have smuggled all of our cirl buntings out of the country in a suitcase small enough to take on a plane as hand luggage. But thanks to hasty conservation measures in south Devon and the assistance of local farmers, extinction in this country appears to have been averted. Where they were given back weedy stubble and insect-rich rough grassland their numbers increased, aided by a succession of mild winters favoured by this sun-loving species. But they don't move around much in their lifetimes – two kilometres is long-haul travel for a cirl bunting – so they are being reintroduced to Cornwall and other areas to hasten the spread outwards from their tiny heartland once again.

Prawle Point in south Devon is a good place to see this national rarity, and I parked my car nearby and walked down to join the South West Coast Path past wild flower-filled fields which had been planted with the birds in mind. Consulting the notes I had gleaned from books and the internet, I followed directions to go through a gate at the bottom of the lane, walk down into a field beside the rocky shore, turn towards Prawle Point and check the hedgerows immediately on the right running up towards a line of cottages.

Finding myself at the correct spot I looked up from my instructions, and there in a bush opposite me was a cirl bunting. I could hardly believe it. It was a female, with duller plumage than an attention-seeking male – which makes perfect sense for those times when you are trying to remain inconspicuous sitting on a nest. And then I saw another female preening, and a couple of juveniles, and then a handsome male sunning himself at the top of a tangle of brambles. They are among Britain's scarcest resident birds, and yet there they were, exactly where I had been told I would find them, served up within a few paces of the car park. I could have left my engine running.

These Red List birds are easy! I thought. But I was soon to find out just how wrong I could be.

CHAPTER FOUR

SO WHY DO WE LIKE BIRDS? THEY'VE GOT BEADY EYES, scaly legs, pointy beaks and when the fancy takes them they shit on us from a great height. They don't exactly look friendly, are hardly cuddly, and in biological terms we haven't a great deal in common. They evolved from cold-blooded reptiles into fever-temperatured, rapid-pulsed, fast-breathing, hollow-boned, small-brained feathered flying creatures that offload their offspring as eggs and are happy to eat worms. They don't appear to express a great deal in the way of emotion or indulge much in play and, on top of all that, no matter how much we offer the hand of friendship they generally ignore us or avoid us. Why on earth would we give them the time of day?

Well, for a start they mean us no harm. Deaths by wren attack are rare, and childhood obesity has greatly reduced the number of youngsters carried away by eagles. Birds are also easy to see, unlike mammals that are by and large shy and nocturnal, and they don't just appear in the summer, like butterflies, or keep out of view like our resident reptiles and amphibians. Their conspicuousness enables us to observe their behaviour and the patterns of survival and reproduction that reflect our own. And if it is in our empathetic nature to colour the natural world with sentiment and meaning, then birds allow us to do so.

They are also very varied in size and shape and character, sporting a toolbox assortment of bills and a dressing-up box range of plumages, and they present a stimulating sense of novelty. Birds are pleasing to the eye and the ear, inspiring art and poetry and music; can provide good sport for both the hunter and the naturalist; and, let's not deny it, they taste good – not that I'll be recommending recipes for Red List species. Birds are constant companions, from the first ducks we throw bread to as toddlers to the last blue tits we see on nut hangers outside our nursing home windows. Their movement brings a static landscape to life, they keep the picture changing, and with the power of flight they embody freedom. We admire them and perhaps at times even envy them.

Against the odds, we find birds fascinating, enchanting and entertaining. And taking time out to watch them has become more and more popular, aided by the emergence of field guides, advances in optical equipment, the growth of car ownership and an emphasis on leisure pursuits. Evolving from the studies of earnest curates, through the gun-toting years of Victorian collectors to the rise of the 'twitcher', birdwatching has moved with the times and reached the point where upwards of three million people in Britain are reckoned to count it as one of their hobbies.

But in a country where the principal pastimes are shopping and watching TV, devoting an afternoon to wandering around a lake staring at ducks is still viewed with some suspicion. While colleagues at work confidently talk football across a crowded office, I would think twice before bursting through the door with arms aloft to declare that I had just seen a woodpecker. So why has birdwatching become so popular and yet failed to become fashionable?

'Why does it need to be?'

Fair point.

'And wouldn't it be awful if it was?'

Perhaps so.

However much people like to poke fun, birdwatching these days can hardly be labelled a minority interest for boffins, even if binoculars do resemble giant pairs of pebblestone glasses. This is the era of the amateur, when anyone can try their hand at anything – from giving a home a makeover, to running a marathon, to becoming a celebrity – and birdwatching is no different: you buy some kit, you thumb through a book and you give it a go. A remarkable 400,000 people join in the Big Garden Birdwatch every year, taking the trouble to fill out forms noting what they have seen as part of the world's largest survey of its kind. I was returning to a hobby that had grown hugely, and I was beginning to realize that it was an interest I had absolutely nothing to feel ashamed of.

Autumn, I had learnt, was a key time to spot three particularly awkward oddities on the Red List: a bizarre kind of woodpecker and a handsome shrike that no longer nest here – but it is hoped might one day make a comeback – and a visiting species of warbler that never has, and only finds itself on the list because it is internationally threatened. Members of all three species pass through on migration, and to find them means either getting lucky or trusting to other people's good fortune and chasing up their sightings as quickly as possible. In short, I knew I would have to turn 'twitcher' for a couple of months to stand any chance of seeing them.

The term twitcher is frequently wrongly applied to anyone remotely interested in birds. In fact it more correctly describes a certain kind of rarity-chasing enthusiast in the wide spectrum of birdwatchers that encompasses everyone from those who appreciate the company of a few feathered friends on their lawn to experts who take things more seriously and might refer to themselves as 'birders'.

A kitchen window birdwatcher might, for example, remark: 'Ah, a lovely little robin on the lawn.' An experienced birder, spotting something subtly different about it, would exclaim: 'My God, I do believe it's a rufous-tailed robin from Siberia – the second ever sighting in Britain!' and with admirable courage in their convictions spread the word. On hearing the news, a committed twitcher desperate to add it to their tally of British rarities would fake sudden illness at work, cancel a planned anniversary evening out with their partner, jump in their car or on a plane and journey the length of the country to catch a glimpse of the exhausted vagrant before it either expired or departed.

The obsessive name-collecting nature of more extreme twitching has provided an easy target for 'trainspotting' clichés, but as enthusiasts like to point out, seeing scarce birds presents far more of a challenge as, unlike trains, birds are unreliable. (They have obviously never travelled on First Great Western.) Failure is a very real possibility, and that, so I was told, is what gives the pursuit such an adrenalin-charged edge. But where once news of rarities was a haphazard affair, passed along the birdwatching grapevine by those in the know, or relayed through a phone at the long-closed Nancy's Café meeting place in Norfolk, you can now get the latest updates on what is worth seeing instantaneously by pager or online. Equipment has evolved to the point where someone can snap a bird using a high-powered 'digiscope' and download images direct onto the web, with details attached on where it was seen. It means anyone can be a twitcher. You don't even need to be skilled at identification, as someone has already done that for you. All it takes to join in the fun is a small outlay for one of the services that supplies news of rare sightings and a willingness to put in a few miles, whether seeking national rarities or just those of interest on a local level.

While the rarities that get twitchers excited are generally lost and of little ecological significance for this country unless they settle down, the Red List birds I was after belong here. But it is amazing just what does turn up on our shores, depending largely on the time of year and which way the wind is blowing. While there are, say, 250 regular species occurring in Britain, you can more than double that total by adding on the number of oddities from abroad that have taken a wrong turn and ended up here. The official list, maintained by the British Ornithologists' Union, includes such weird and wonderful visitors as gyr falcon, black-browed albatross, oriental pratincole, blue-cheeked bee-eater, Ascension frigatebird, bufflehead, ancient murrelet and gray catbird, as well as dozens of obscure warblers, flycatchers, buntings, thrushes, terns, sandpipers and larks. Perhaps the best-known mass 'twitch' in England happened when a confused golden-winged warbler which should have been enjoying sunny central America turned up in a Tesco car park in Maidstone in 1989, attracting thousands of birdwatchers and doubtless leaving puzzled local shoppers caught up in the crowd wondering whether there was a two-for-one deal on anoraks.

And so to the first bird on my autumn twitching list . . .

It was late August and the air was hot and heavy with insects. The evening sun was sinking behind a stand of pine trees casting long straight shadows across a forest glade in western Norway. At the edges of the clearing where fingers of wind could fidget at the scar in the canopy, older conifers leant against each other, collapsing slowly outwards, while in the centre between fallen trunks birch saplings rose from the earth to stitch up the opening and clumps of rough grass sucked what goodness they could from beneath layers of decaying pine needles. A single mature pine remained standing in the glade, set apart from others like a lone soldier venturing forward from a retreating line. Halfway up its side a neat hole was visible, chiselled out by a great spotted woodpecker. Inside fragments of shell, perhaps a clutch of seven or more, could be seen, though it appeared that the young had flown the confines of the cavity. The pieces were white, visible in the dark and typical of a hole-nesting species, but they were not the remains of great spotted woodpecker eggs.

Outside there was little birdlife about. However, a slight movement could be seen beneath the tree where the sunlight fell on a patch of dry soil. It was one of the clutch that had hatched several weeks earlier. From a distance it resembled a small plain grey thrush, its body held low as it edged forward across the ground in jerky hops, head tapering to a thin pointed bill. On closer inspection patterns in its plumage became visible: light bars on a buff throat, delicate brush strokes of warm brown and grey on folded wings, grey sides stitched with black, subtle variations as if it had been assembled from the feathers of other birds and the wings of moths. Through its eye there was a long dark stripe, while a thick band tapering at either end ran down the centre of its grey back like a stream of melted dark chocolate.

The bird heard a noise and froze motionless, its complex patterning breaking up its outline so that it appeared to merge with the ground beneath it. For a moment it became nothing more than mud-spattered leaves and shadows. And then it shifted forward, probing at the soil for ants, its sticky tongue darting in and out of a nest, gorging fast. It was similar in shape to a small streamlined woodpecker, the grouping to which it belonged, and had the same kind of feet with two toes pointing forwards and two back. Its long tongue was typical of woodpeckers, and it shared its ground-feeding, ant-loving behaviour with one or two other members of the family. But there were features that set it apart. For a start its tail was soft, not stiff like those used as props by the dedicated trunk climbers, and it relied on others to excavate nest sites as its bill was not the powerful wedge needed to hammer holes in solid wood. It was also planning to embark on a journey that none of its sedentary forest-dwelling fellows would ever attempt, a journey that would take it to Africa for the winter. And as the other birds in the forest settled down for the night, it flew up into a tree and waited until the light faded before heading out into the darkness, turning south towards the coast of Norway and open water.

This conundrum of a bird was a wryneck, and in the few weeks it had been alive its training for long-distance migration would have amounted to little more than short flights to feed or roost. But with the wind behind it, the small bird covered ground swiftly, tapping into the fat reserves it had built up in preparation. It undertook the journey at night to avoid predatory hawks and gulls, holding a steady southerly course as it headed out across the sea alone, guided by an internal compass sensitive to the earth's magnetism and by the patterns of stars above. The sky was clear and a ragged strip of moonlight ran across the backs of dark waves beneath. The wryneck passed illuminated trawlers carving furrows in the blackness, and now and again it could make out the shapes of other birds flying above and beside it and heading in the same direction.

After a couple of hours its muscles began to tire, but it had no option other than to press on, driven forward by an overpowering urge to make progress. It had no idea where it was going, or why, or whether it would make it. All it could do was place its faith in reaching landfall in the successes of previous generations passed on within the twists of DNA which dictated its sense of direction. But a storm was brewing in central Europe and at the edge of the weather front the wind shifted and strengthened, nudging the young wryneck from the east. Cruel winds can prove fatal, pushing migrants off course and sapping their strength. Small land birds making a sea crossing cannot stop. In the severest conditions a few out of reach of a coastline may temporarily touch down on ships to rest and seek shelter. Others less fortunate have no choice but to keep on flying until their reserves are used up, until they finally fold their wings, shut their eyes and ditch in the waves, fizzling out like sodden fireworks in the cold water.

It was not a strong wind, but it was enough to push the wryneck west, and high cloud overhead blocked out the stars and disorientated the young bird. On it flew until, as the sky began to lighten before dawn, it spotted a line of grey like a thin film floating on the horizon. The line thickened as it headed towards it, and bands of dull gold and green became visible. It was land: a shingle spit and grassy dunes behind, and before long the exhausted bird crossed the beach and landed in among some low bushes.

For those birds fleeing the threat of winter frosts and famine that survive, the benefits of migration outweigh the risks. However, the wryneck had a sense that it was still a long way from its destination. It didn't know where it was, and something deep within was telling it to keep on moving, though it knew it had to feed and rest first. The rising sun began to warm the ground and it scratched around in a patch of sandy soil for ants and insects, slurping them up with its tongue, the longest relative to body size of any bird. It was hungry and oblivious to two people walking nearby along the coastal path who had frozen in their tracks and simultaneously raised their binoculars with smiles breaking across their faces.

Twenty minutes later and 300 miles away in an office in Plymouth, my mobile phone chirped to life on my desk, alerting me to a text message from the rare bird sightings service I had subscribed to the previous week. It said: *9.37am. Wryneck. Blakeney Point, Norfolk. In low bushes 50yds east of tea room at point. Showing well.*

The wryneck, so named for its ability to twist its head around on its neck in an alarming manner when threatened, was once a fairly familiar sight in England, particularly in orchards and paddocks, but over the last 150 years its breeding population has plummeted to zero. It is not entirely clear why, or what can be done to reverse the situation. Loss of rough pasture and pesticides may have had an impact on the numbers of ants on which it depends, though its decline, which has been less significant in Europe, began here before the introduction of modern chemical sprays. The removal of dead standing trees used as nest sites could also have made life difficult. And there may be other factors at work at its overseas wintering grounds. Either way it has gone, and except for the odd pair found nesting in the Scottish Caledonian pine forests every few years, it is now only seen in Britain as a passage migrant on its way to and from Scandinavia in the spring and particularly autumn, when numbers are swelled by inexperienced young birds heading for Africa.

With the right conditions about 250 wrynecks can turn up in Britain in a year – but that is the equivalent of one of these cryptically camouflaged 16cm-long birds for every 375 square miles of our countryside! However, two factors help ensure they are spotted: they tend to touch down along the eastern and southern coasts, and they do so at a time when birdwatchers are congregating in these areas in the hope of seeing scarce migrants.

North Norfolk was a long way to drive not knowing whether the bird described in the text I had received would still be there, and unless I threw myself to the floor, gasping for air and clutching at my chest, I couldn't get off work. I was stuck, and I wondered how dedicated twitchers in full-time employment managed. Was a bogus heart condition a prerequisite of the hobby? Could I keep up such a deception through the key autumn period for wrynecks? And how bad would I feel when sympathetic work colleagues started running marathons to raise funds for the British Heart Foundation on my behalf?

There was nothing for it but to amend my text service set-up so that it only covered the South West, sparing me the agony of having to read about sightings of this elusive red-listed woodpecker that were beyond my reach. And a couple of days later I got the news I had been hoping for. A text from Rare Bird Alert informed me a wryneck had been spotted within striking distance at Rame Head on the south-east coast of Cornwall. There was an outside possibility it was the very same bird that turned up in Norfolk, still heading south-west, that had come to a new section of coast, seen the English Channel ahead and decided to stop to refuel and re-boot its GPS. I was due to start work at 1pm the next day, so I set the alarm for 4.30am to make the most of the morning.

It had been a long while since I had got up that early. When the bedside clock sounded in the dark, its electrical beeping needling me awake, I leapt up, hair akimbo, thinking the house had been hit by lightning and the smoke alarm had gone off, and made for the door leaving my family to fend for themselves before I realized what it was. A shower and two cups of tea later and I was fully awake and heading west in the car, following my headlight beams down the twisting lanes, narrowly avoiding hitting a weasel along the way. You see so much roadkill on West Country roads: hedgehogs that end up as leathery swirls of matted bristle, pheasants far too beautiful to deserve to be squashed and which usually disappear within a day, the occasional fox whose carcass also vanishes soon after, taken by God knows whom or what, and far too many badgers. Unfortunately badgers, with their grey bodies and white facial stripes, appear to have evolved to resemble road markings. For them 'No Overtaking' is their final message to motorists before death. If they had evolved with white chevrons instead, indicating to bear right, they would probably double their life expectancy as a species at a stroke.

Rame Head juts out into the sea like a fist at the end of a rocky peninsula that shelters Plymouth to the east and looks out over the wide sweep of Whitsand Bay to the west. A disused chapel stands at the point, while further back from the perilous cliffs ponies graze the exposed grassland. There are few places for birds to hide, and according to my latest text message the wryneck had been sighted on the wall of a ruined building a short walk from the coastguard station.

The sun was up when I arrived and I spotted a middle-aged man, top-brand binoculars around his neck, checking his pager.

'Excuse me,' I ventured. 'I'm looking for a wryneck.'

In normal circumstances this would be an insane thing to say to a stranger. But as it turned out he was there for the same reason, having come by bus from Plymouth, and he led me to the area of brambles and tumbled-down stonework where it had been seen the day before.

I didn't really know where to begin, whether to look up at the treetops, into the hedges, down on the ground, and although I had seen pictures in a book I wasn't sure exactly what to expect, so I followed his lead, scanning the area with the naked eye in the hope of detecting movement.

'They're difficult birds to see, they can just freeze and disappear,' he said, lifting his binoculars for a moment to check over the base of a hedgerow.

'Have you ever seen one?' I asked, sounding every bit the novice.

'Yes, but they are such beautiful birds they are always worth a trip.'

It transpired that his bird tally for Britain was a very impressive figure of over 425 species, so if anyone was going to find a wryneck it was him – though our hopes began to diminish after an hour wandering around the field edges without any luck. I was so keen that I mistook the rear end of a rabbit disappearing over a mound for one, and then excitedly pointed out a bird diving into a bush, which ended up being a hedge sparrow, or dunnock.

It was no good. There was no sign of it, and I was forced to give up and head off to work.

So it didn't feel fair when, the next day, another text came through saying the wryneck had been spotted again in the same place we had been looking. I knew I had to take every opportunity that came my way, so after work I headed back to Rame Head, hoping to see a small gathering of birdwatchers pointing it out with their telescopes. Instead, there were two or three people with binoculars wandering around aimlessly. I joined them and also wandered around aimlessly seeing a few birds of interest, but not a wryneck. Not even something I could pretend was a wryneck. I had, in twitching parlance, 'dipped out'.

Now I was under the impression birdwatching was a relaxing pastime, but nothing could be further from the truth when you are on the trail of an unpredictable bird you have always wanted to see and you work during the week, have a busy family life at weekends and it keeps cropping up at the wrong time in the least convenient places. One was next sighted near a golf course at Thurlestone in south Devon, so I searched around at dawn before work but had no joy – only to have to return the next morning following another report, to find it had again either gone into hiding or headed somewhere else. Two days later, sleep deprived and running on cans of high-caffeine energy drinks, I drove before dawn to just about the furthest possible point west from where I live: an isolated coastal valley at Nanquidno, a few miles north of Land's End. Guided by precise directions on the text message I searched around among the ivy-clad boulders and gorse for as long as I could before I had to head back to my office desk in Plymouth by lunchtime. Again, no luck. And then, two days later, I followed up a reported sighting near the secluded Cornish cove of Porthgwarra, just south of Land's End, and racing the clock as ever I ran up a footpath to a dried-up pond where it had earlier been seen. I found the pond – and that was all.

But still the texts kept coming, doubtless sponsored by

manufacturers of Red Bull and forecourt staff at service stations along the A30. Within a few days I was once more heading west, this time to a cycle track above Sennen Cove near Land's End, where I drew a blank, and then the following day I was back at Nanquidno trudging through boggy pasture close to a row of cottages and scanning the stone walls where one had shown itself half a day earlier. By that point I had clocked up more than 1,000 miles, and yet still no luck.

'It wouldn't be any fun if they were all easy to see,' one birdwatcher told me philosophically. But by now I wanted to wring their bloody wrynecks!

Desperate for advice I phoned one of the people feeding me the information I had been chasing – former national Young Birder of the Year Stuart Piner at the Rare Bird Alert service.

'They are tricky as they can show themselves to the finder, and then disappear,' he said, adding that at that time of year in the areas I had been visiting I was just as likely to bump into one when I was least expecting it.

So I tried not to expect to see one. And, on returning to Nanquidno, I still didn't.

But I did bump into an experienced local birdwatcher called John Swann who could see from my exhausted appearance and the desperate look in my eye that I needed help, and who assured me that my binoculars were not at fault or, as I had imagined, somehow 'broken'.

'They can't see wrynecks,' I complained, twiddling with the focus wheel.

He pointed me in the right direction for the most

recent sighting, and laughed when I returned ten minutes later shaking my head at my lack of success.

'Slow down,' he said. 'You have to be patient. I had to wait an hour for it to show the other day. But it is worth it – it's a real birders' bird. It—' He cut himself short, lifting his hand to keep me from speaking. 'Listen!' he said.

'What?'

'Choughs.'

And sure enough a pair of the glossy crows wheeled in from above on fingered wings and landed in the field close by and began probing in the short turf with their bright red down-curved beaks. Almost all of the few hundred choughs in Britain live along the coast of Wales and on the Isle of Man and western isles of Scotland, and despite featuring on the Cornish emblem they had been absent from the county for fifty years, only returning to breed as recently as 2002, so seeing two of England's tiny lone population was a rare privilege.

'Be thankful for the birds you *do* see,' John said with a smile.

Fittingly the word 'jinxed' is believed to have its origins in ancient Greek and Latin terms for wryneck. But I hadn't given up, only I had other birds to track down, the first of which, the aquatic warbler, is so elusive that it is hard enough to find in British bird books.

Warblers are the ultimate 'little brown jobs', and like waders they can be tricky to tell apart. Small, skulking and inconspicuous, they evolved to provide a challenge for expert birders and field guide illustrators, and to intimidate beginners. And somewhat disconcertingly, there are a few on the Red List. Among the scarcest of these – in fact the rarest migratory songbird in mainland Europe – is the globally threatened aquatic warbler. It is about 12cm long, weighs less than a digestive biscuit, has a streaky black and warm buff back and stripy head, and sleeps around. Territorial males are only interested in passing on their genes and don't have anything to do with rearing young, while single-parent females sample the best of what is on offer, producing nests full of chicks from a confusing number of fathers. Scandalous! Despite its name it can't swim, but it does like damp areas. However, large swathes of the insect-rich wetlands, mires and sedge-filled marshes where it breeds have been drained for agriculture, industry and water supplies. Its range has shrunk across Europe and its population has nose-dived. More people attend a typical Sunderland FC soccer match than there are aquatic warblers in the world.

Now there can't be many occasions in the history of international negotiations when representatives from such disparate countries as Belarus in eastern Europe and Senegal in West Africa have got together around a table for talks. But in 2003 that is exactly what happened, and it was the conservation of the aquatic warbler that brought them together. Most of these migratory birds breed in Belarus while the vast majority of them winter in Senegal, and a joint effort was needed to halt their precipitous decline. In Belarus work got under way to restore vital habitat, but the problem was, when it came to taking action in Senegal, no one knew exactly where these secretive birds were concentrated. What followed was a crafty piece of scientific detective work involving the analysis of isotopes in feathers which narrowed the likely sites down, and in 2007 the wintering aquatic warblers were discovered – as luck would have it in a protected area of national park in the north-west of the country.

Given that this long-distance migrant resides so far from our shores, it might seem odd that the UK was one of more than a dozen signatories to a conservation agreement at the 2003 talks, and that it has provided funding for aquatic warbler work. The bird does not live here, and there are no records that it ever has. However, their migration route south takes them on a dog-leg route via France and, like the wryneck, if the winds are heading our way small numbers do get pushed off course every autumn and end up spending a night or two in coastal reedbeds along our south coast. By providing short-stop accommodation we, along with a number of other European countries, have a role to play in their survival.

Only a couple of dozen aquatic warblers are recorded in Britain every year and they don't usually hang about more than a day. But the fact that they regularly come and are globally threatened has earned them a place on our Red List. To see one you need to be in the right place at the right time armed with a pair of binoculars, waterproof footwear – oh, and a 50-metre-long mist net.

Mist netting involves draping a screen of fine mesh

between poles so that small birds flying into it get trapped and can be caught for ringing and surveying. As the majority of the aquatic warblers recorded in this country turn up in nets, I needed to narrow the odds in my favour and once again found myself heading west before sunrise along the A30, though this time my destination was close to Penzance at Marazion Marsh, which has traditionally been England's best location for viewing aquatic warblers.

It was still dark when I arrived, and I parked on the road that divides the marsh from the sea, looking out at the silhouette of the impressive medieval St Michael's Mount perched on a granite outcrop in the bay and listening to the sound of the sea gently brushing sand up the beach. Like an old TV warming up, shapes and colours gradually became clear as the sky lightened, and I crossed over to the grass field beside the reedbed to meet up with a bird ringer from the British Trust for Ornithology called Kester Wilson and RSPB reserve manager Dave Flumm, who were conducting the first aquatic warbler survey at the site for a number of years.

The calm conditions that morning were perfect for mist netting, and Kester donned a pair of waders and headed off into the marsh to set the trap. Then it was just a case of waiting, leaning against a fence watching small birds bobbing to the surface of the rippling, rustling reedbed to warm up and dry the dew from their feathers with the first rays of the sun. A couple of herons, which unusually nest at Marazion in the reeds rather than among the treetops, flew back from the beach, and Dave pointed out a whimbrel overhead, as well as identifying a squealing sound coming from deep in the marsh as a water rail.

Twenty minutes later Kester emerged holding a number of wriggling small cloth bags. Reaching into one he delicately pulled out a warbler. It had a tawny back and a light stripe above the eye and . . . and at that point an over-excited birdwatcher, who shall remain anonymous but who bore an uncanny resemblance to myself, began the sentence: 'My God, is it . . . ?' before he was thankfully interrupted.

'A juvenile sedge warbler, yes,' Kester said coolly. (In defence of the unidentified birdwatcher, this species is easily mistaken for an aquatic warbler.)

He popped it head-down into what looked like a plastic film canister, whereupon it obligingly stayed still to be weighed, then he took a number of measurements and blew on its belly to part the feathers, pointing out pale yellow areas of fat visible under the skin on which it would depend to complete its migration to sub-Sahara Africa. The fat stores were graded using a chart and duly noted before a tiny numbered ring was deftly tightened with pliers around a leg as thin as a pencil lead. Then off it flew, looking very bling with its shiny new bangle.

Two willow warblers were given the same once-over, and another trip to the mist nets furnished a second sedge warbler, a reed warbler and a wren. Three types of warbler, but no aquatic warbler. It was disappointing.

A spell of strong south-easterly winds, of the kind needed to push the migrants our way, might have yielded a better result. But the fact is that aquatic warblers are incredibly scarce here, and even though Marazion Marsh is specially protected and partly managed with these visitors in mind, there had only been two sightings at the reserve since 2002.

Since they are so hard to see, it was a wonder there was such a fuss over saving them at all. It begged the question, would we be any the poorer for not having these little brown birds in the world?

'We've lost so much,' Dave said. 'And it isn't just the big charismatic animals that matter – I would be upset if my children could never see an aquatic warbler.'

Forget my children, I thought, I'd be upset if I never saw one!

Why? Perhaps partly because they are out there, and the more I learnt about them the more they became worth seeing. Perhaps partly because they are rare, which gives them a certain star quality. Perhaps partly because in their own low-profile way they help make the natural world diverse enough to be worth exploring. Compared with beetles and bacteria, there aren't that many species of bird on earth, so every one counts, even if it is, well, mostly brown. I had looked at numerous photos and drawings of aquatic warblers, but it was much like viewing prints of an intriguing painting – I wanted to see the original.

And I hadn't.

I returned to the reserve once more a week later and wandered around on my own in the vague hope of freakish good fortune, but it was futile. As it turned out, they didn't catch any aquatic warblers at Marazion Marsh that autumn, and the closest I came to sharing the same location as one was on a visit to Radipole Lake Nature Reserve, an oasis in the centre of Weymouth, where a single individual had turned up in a mist net one morning that August – the only catch at an RSPB reserve in 2007. Staff helped me find the entry written in biro in the reserve logbook. It was tantalizingly understated. It read simply: *12/8 – aquatic warbler. Ringing am.* They could have added for my benefit: *Sorry, loser, better luck next year!*

One of the things about living in Britain is that you never feel like you have taken full advantage of fine weather. When the summer sun rises into a clear blue sky panic sets in – the feeling that you really should go to the beach and the park and go for a walk, have a picnic, watch cricket, go cycling, have a barbecue, swim, mow the lawn, make salads . . . pack in as much as possible before the rain returns. However, a glorious spell of weather did bless the South West during the early part of that September and I had the pursuit of birds to thank for taking me to places I would never have normally visited. The infuriating wryneck was once again acting as my tour guide to the region, and early in the month I found myself tramping around behind a scenic seafront golf course near Thurlestone in south Devon at dawn, following the text message trail and still having no luck. I felt all my efforts deserved some reward – and it came, though not in the way I expected. What followed was one of the most enjoyable half hours of birdwatching I have ever had.

The sun was just up and apart from a groundsman raking the bunkers at the golf club there was no one about. I had parked in the empty 'Members Only' car park (after all, who would have suspected that the club chairman drove anything other than a second-hand Ford Focus?) and was taking a look at a marshy area opposite. It was far from remarkable, a few shallow reed-fringed muddy pools set in the centre of flat rough pasture – not the kind of place that would earn a prominent billing in any eco-tourism guide. But as so many of our wetlands have disappeared, every last fragment is valuable. From the large-scale reclamation of the fens, to the draining of flood plains for agriculture and housing, Britain's reedbeds and grazing marshes have evaporated over the centuries like puddles in the sun. The rivers that feed them have been straightened and hemmed in and sapped of strength to supply water to our expanding conurbations, and many of our lush flower-rich wet pastures have been lost to more intensive farming methods.

Reedbeds are particularly fragile and transitory habitats, susceptible to getting clogged up and overtaken by willow scrub or swamped by rising sea levels, and take a lot of looking after. Fortunately the scattered patches that remain in the UK are very well protected. When it comes to wetland conservation we lead the way, with far more areas than any other country safeguarded under an international treaty called the Ramsar Convention. From the Ouse Washes in East Anglia to the Caithness and Sutherland peatlands in Scotland, more than 140 of our wetland nature havens are listed as of global importance. In addition most are

Sites of Special Scientific Interest, plenty are designated national or local nature reserves, and quite a number are Special Protection Areas for specific bird populations.

The small marsh on private farmland that I was looking at was none of these. While a useful coastal staging post for migrating birds, and recognized on a county level as a wildlife site of value, it had no impressive letters after its name and ranked on the bottom rung in the hierarchy of legal protection. Still, it appeared to be in good shape and was free of shopping trolleys and car tyres. There were areas of weed which had been fenced off, and the main field looked to have been spared the spray-gun.

I skirted the outside of the fence and as the sky lightened I noticed birds at the edge of the water appearing in the low mist as if they had emerged from the mud. They were tiny brown-backed waders, perhaps a dozen or more, frenetically stitching the slime with black slightly down-curved bills and creating footprint patterns in the soft bank like overlapping arrows from prison shirts. Waders normally make me nervous, but I was under no pressure to get them right, so rather than jump to conclusions I took my time and decided they were dunlin. A flock of small ducks then took to the air, circled and landed again and I saw they were teal, and tucked away in a wedge of grass that jutted out into the water I spotted four common snipe pushing their long touch-sensitive bills into the mud to feel for invertebrate life beneath. As I drew closer and knelt down in the grass my attention was next drawn to a grating call from a bush nearby, and out popped a sedge warbler. Waders and warblers named with confidence? I was on a roll! Not only that, I felt like I was really birdwatching, and there was something satisfying about having a go without any help. It was about observing and trying to understand, and for a short while the hurrying in my head slowed and I had the unfamiliar sensation that I had time to spare and there was nowhere else I needed to be other than where I was.

How I had overlooked them at first I have no idea, but in the centre of the pool, nearly up to their bellies in deeper water, were three much larger grey-brown waders. Unexpectedly large. And they were truly striking birds, with elegant long necks and impressive elongated bills that must have stretched to such lengths in an evolutionary race to keep pace with their growing legs. Those ancestors that couldn't touch their toes had presumably died out. They had pale reddish hues in the soft plumage of their heads and chests, and a noticeably darker end to their straight bills. They were godwits, and the black-tailed variety are on the Red List. The trouble was the slightly smaller bar-tailed godwit is very similar in appearance and I couldn't be sure which species I had stumbled across. As the names would suggest, one of the clues is in the tails: a barring at the end of one, and a conspicuous black band at the end of the other. Another defining feature is that the black-tailed godwit has white wingbars in flight. But unless they took off I could see neither their tail nor wing markings.

I would have remained stumped, except that one of the trio conveniently kept flashing its wings open slightly at every step, and I realized that the unfortunate bird must have broken its leg – one of the drawbacks of having calves no thicker than drinking straws. As it limped forward, lifting its wings momentarily to ease the weight on its injured limb, its markings were plain to see: white wingbars and a white tail with a broad black band at the end. They were black-tailed godwits: one of our rarest breeding birds.

I had never been particularly attuned to the seasons. I had never really needed to be. But at that moment I could appreciate why so many birdwatchers look forward to autumn. After a relatively quiet period at the end of summer when bird song peters out and juveniles and moulting adults try to keep a low profile, early autumn heralds a period of movement, changes and surprises. As the tide of birds that washes over us in spring turns and retreats, swelled by huge numbers of young, billions of birds across the northern hemisphere flood into warmer regions following established flyways and navigating by the sun and the stars, polarized light and the earth's magnetism, sight and smell and memory and who knows what else. They include insect-eaters heading for the bug-rich tropics, strong-flying waders seeking ice-free waters for the winter and ocean-roaming seabirds freed from the constraints of having to nest on land. Some migrate by day, such as swallows that feed in flight and broad-winged raptors that need to ride thermals, while the majority travel during the cool of night and stop to rest and refuel during daylight. Many of our stay-at-home resident species also opt for a seasonal change of scenery, making short-haul journeys to new feeding grounds along the coast or more southerly counties, shifting downhill from exposed upland areas and putting aside the territorial differences that kept them apart in the summer to gather in winter flocks. It is a time of year when even some cagebirds instinctively turn on their perches to face south.

All of this means that strategic sites become busy flight terminals where migrants touch down and depart on a daily basis, and beside the smallest patch of marsh you can find treasure scattered in the mud. I had got lucky, and it had saved me having to spend days at wetlands and estuaries desperately scanning new arrivals while holding up a square of card saying 'Black-tailed godwit'.

Godwits were, apparently, a tasty delicacy in days gone by, and there are references to them being served up from Tudor times through to the 1700s. There is certainly far more meat on these broad-chested waders than some of the tiny songbirds which ended their days on a pewter plate, but by the mid-1800s you would have been hard-pressed to find one on the menu in the spring and summer because, well, there weren't any around. A combination of hunting coupled with the draining and ploughing up of wetland nesting sites meant numbers of black-tailed godwits dwindled to the point where they were not only uncommon as winter visitors, but they became totally extinct as breeders in this country. And that is the way it stayed for the best part of a century.

To the delight of many they made a comeback in 1952, nesting in the damp flat grassland of the Ouse Washes. At first it was a carefully guarded secret – and I'm guessing a close watch was kept on Tudor-themed restaurants in the area – but soon the news spread, as did the birds, which gradually got a toehold in other protected marshland reserves. As comebacks go it was a modest one, and has pretty much stalled, while their numbers in Europe have also gone into reverse. However, they are thriving in Iceland of all places, and the three birds I was looking at had very likely flown over 1,000 miles from there to spend the winter in Britain or a bit further south.

After my aquatic warbler defeat things were looking up. But the great half-hour of birdwatching wasn't quite over. As I headed back to my car I spotted something unusual perched on a length of barbed wire fence beside the golf course. It was brownish (so that narrowed things down!), the size of a large greenfinch, with a faintly rufous back, and in the seconds before it flew down to the ground out of view I saw it had a darkish patch through the eye and the feathers on its lighter underparts looked all wispy at the sides. Weird. A rufous wispy wire-percher? Is there such a species? And if not, should there be?

I had a strong suspicion that it was a significant find – that it was one of the three scarce visitors I needed to see that autumn, and when I checked my field guides back at home the details added up: the colouring, the bill, the light shadow around the eye, the crescent markings on the underparts (the 'wispy' effect), the choice of perch and the posture. It was a young red-backed shrike – a red-listed species I had been relying on someone else locating for me. I had out-trumped the twitcher texts! Though I was soon cut down to size when I found out on a Devon wildlife website that some clever clogs had seen it two days before me.

Just like wrynecks, red-backed shrikes drop by along southern and eastern coasts in autumn and spring. Also like wrynecks they were once widespread but began an unstoppable decline in the nineteenth century and no longer make their home in Britain. As with wrynecks, no one is exactly sure why. They like heaths and commons, scrub and thorny bushes, hot dry weather, and grassy areas that can supply them with large insects such as grasshoppers, beetles and bumble bees. While pesticides, the plough and the intensification of pastureland have all reduced suitable habitat, breeding pairs disappeared from good sites as well as bad, so that by 1989 there were none. The only red-backed shrikes that now nest here are very occasional birds aiming for Scandinavia in the spring that miss and wind up in Scotland, and the expert opinions I read were united in their pessimism about prospects for the species ever recolonizing Britain in the future, especially given that they are thinning out in neighbouring countries.

Judging by the fact thousands of birdwatchers travelled to Norfolk in 1988 to see our last nesting pair, losing red-backed shrikes matters to a lot of people. Adult males are stunning small birds, with a light grey-blue head, striking black eye band, orangey-brown back and pink-tinged breast. They were charismatic additions to our countryside in the summer, flying all the way here from southern Africa where they are still a common sight perched along roadside fences and telegraph wires. Acting like miniature falcons they swoop from lookout posts onto prey as large as frogs, mice and lizards and tear them apart with their hooked beaks, and their grisly habit of creating a larder by impaling spare food on thorns or barbed wire has earned them the nickname 'butcher bird'. They also lay attractive eggs of varied subtle hues – and this, coupled with their rarity, sealed this protected species' fate in Britain when numbers were approaching critical levels. The only red-backed shrike clutches you will now ever find in this country are devoid of life: labelled empty shells decades old plundered from nests and stashed away from the authorities in lofts and lock-up garages as part of illegal hoards, with small drill holes visible in the sides from which the contents have been extracted. Egg collectors have blood, not yolk, on their hands.

It is because of the threat of egg collectors – a diminishing yet dogged few prepared to risk jail simply to add the clutches of rare birds to their private stockpiles – that if any red-backed shrikes do settle here, you and I are unlikely to hear about it. The location will certainly remain confidential, shared between a few trusted conservationists and members of a select body called the Rare Breeding Birds Panel, and kept on file under lock and key.

I was thrilled to have seen one passing through, even if a duller-plumaged juvenile, and was pretty much on schedule with my sightings. I had every reason to feel cheerful, but . . . well, this Red List business could feel a bit depressing. Shrikes gone, wrynecks gone, aquatic warblers disappearing fast, yellowhammers and twite declining. Just as well I don't work in the field of conservation otherwise I'd spend my days moping around in a state of despair, listening to The Smiths and watching daytime TV with the curtains closed. However, it is fortunate there are people out there who are determined to make a difference. Some of them even get paid to do it. Thanks to their lobbying and tree planting and nest-box making and pond clearing and willingness to tramp across bogs and wade through mires, both inside and outside the Houses of Parliament, birds such as tree sparrows are managing to scramble upwards a little from the bottom of their steep slope of decline, breeding black-tailed godwits are back and the cirl buntings I saw are slowly gaining ground.

CHAPTER FIVE

'*THE LODGE, SANDY, BEDS*' IS AN ADDRESS FAMILIAR TO many as the nerve-centre of British bird conservation. Standing in the middle of a woodland and heathland nature reserve and surrounded by immaculate lawns and formal gardens, the 140-year-old former residence of Viscount Peel is a large and impressive building, solid and confident, with tall chimneys and gables, wisteria on the walls, an arched entrance and a magnificent cedar tree at the front. It appears one of the most idyllic locations possible to call a workplace. But that is what The Lodge is. Since 1961 this mansion just off the B1042 in Bedfordshire has been the headquarters of the RSPB.

I couldn't have picked a better day for my first visit. It was a warm September morning, there wasn't a cloud in the sky or a breath of wind, and as I wandered from the visitor car park through a stretch of woodland to the main entrance I was unable to imagine a single reason for any member of the natural kingdom present to feel anything but content – even the trees, and you know how they like to moan. There were grey squirrels rummaging in the leaf litter, butterflies circling in shafts of sunlight and birds calling from the canopy – I hadn't a clue what they were, but didn't particularly mind. No, it didn't feel like a day for bad news, but that was what I had come for. I needed to find out a little more about where things were going wrong for our birds, and had arranged to meet RSPB head of species conservation Julian Hughes, one of a number of people responsible for compiling the British Red List.

Far from looking like a bringer of grim tidings, Julian greeted me in the foyer with a cheerful handshake and took me to an upstairs room decorated with wildlife posters where both he and Grahame Madge, a conservation expert in the press office, enthusiastically discussed the birds I had seen so far – and those that had eluded me.

'Ah, the aquatic warbler,' Julian said, giving me a sympathetic smile. 'Yes, I saw one of those years ago at Cley in Norfolk. It had been raining and the willows were full of birds, and I remember it looked almost orangey among them.'

Couldn't he conjure one up for me? He was an RSPB head of department after all. Surely he and Grahame could pull a few strings!

The room we sat in may have been fairly small, but

in effect their work space extended across the UK, and as they advised me on key habitats and species it struck me how familiar they were with where things belonged, much in the same way that I know where to find the paperclips in my office. 'The best spot for that bird is probably on such-and-such island during the summer . . .' 'Well, if you want to see them try such-and-such reserve over the winter . . .' With conservation battles being waged up and down the land, senior RSPB staff obviously need to know what's going on and where, but it brought home to me just how much birds connect us with our surroundings. In learning about them, watching them or working on their behalf you can't help but develop a special intimacy with the geography of our country.

And so to the bad news . . .

'The fact is that while there have been conservation success stories,' Julian told me, 'the list of birds of conservation concern has got longer. Clearly our goal – not just that of the RSPB, but society in general – should be an empty Red List.'

Five species made up enough lost ground to come off the list when it was last revised in 2002, including the osprey and red kite, but nine new additions somewhat spoilt the party. And the headline news, Julian explained, had been the addition of once-common farmland birds to the tally, drawing the public's attention to the fact that our widespread species could no longer be taken for granted. These were not species for which nature reserves were the answer, and the loss of set-aside could prove devastating.

'Society has to ask what our land is for,' Julian said. 'Given that so much of it is farmed and that we subsidize agriculture to the tune of billions of pounds a year, what do we, the public, expect in return for the cash? Clearly food, but also biodiversity, and access, and a whole range of other things. We can't expect farmers to make those decisions, it's up to policy-makers.'

It is easy to think of the RSPB as a cuddly well-meaning charity for bird-huggers. But the character of this campaigning organization is much more tough and tenacious than its dainty avocet logo would have one believe. It was born fighting, coming into existence in 1889 when a group of women from Didsbury, Manchester, got together to oppose the use of bird feathers in the fashion industry, and it is now the largest conservation charity in Europe. It owns and manages reserves, undertakes research and oversees recovery projects, tackles wildlife crime, restores and protects key habitats, and works with landowners and decision-makers. The RSPB means business. So much so that Grahame told me it had even gone into business, putting what it preaches into practice by buying a large arable farm in Cambridgeshire and running it commercially, but with nature in mind. The result has been that both birds and farm income have profited.

There are, of course, many other factors besides farming policy that impact on bird populations. The expansion of urban areas has destroyed valuable habitat, and for those birds uncomfortable in human company our congested country presents increasingly limited options for privacy – especially with birdwatchers popping up all over the place! Three million new homes are to be built by 2020 to tackle a shortage of affordable housing, requiring both land and, perhaps as significantly, fresh water supplies. And new roads have added to the fragmentation of habitats, splitting up populations of birds and paving over greenery (I have seen them named 'Buzzard Close' and 'Heron Way' with no sense of irony). Densely packed plantation forestry has covered valuable tracts of moorland and heathland, and then there are the effects of over-fishing on seabird populations and climate change to consider. All in all, while society is more environmentally aware, the need for the RSPB, they told me, had never been greater.

After lunch in the canteen I walked to the visitor centre at the top of the main driveway and examined a chalk board on the wall which, much like a restaurant specials menu, listed a tasty selection of that day's sightings in The Lodge reserve. Halfway down the board I spotted that someone had spotted two spotted flycatchers – which is easier to do than to say. This is a characterful little summer visitor that comes to Europe during the hottest months to breed before heading all the way back south of the equator for the winter – a huge distance for a bird with wings the size of playing cards. It is also on our Red List.

The problem was I hadn't brought my binoculars with me as I hadn't been planning on doing any bird-watching or expecting the RSPB to throw such a surprise my way. I was also pushed for time and could only manage one quick circuit of the reserve before I needed to drive home. With no idea where to look, I headed off through a section of oak woodland, striding too fast to notice much, before following a path around an overgrown quarry to the edge of an open area of heathland, where I checked my watch and caught my breath. It was a lovely place to rest for a moment. The heather and bracken were bathed in sunshine and above the clear blue sky was criss-crossed with aeroplane trails like dissolving sticks of spaghetti. I could hear a green woodpecker laughing (they were beginning to give me a complex), and saw a couple of blue tits feeding along the woodland border. I checked my watch once again and started down across the heath when something unusual caught my eye and I stopped. Up ahead a small bird flew out from the branch of a low tree, caught something mid-air with impressive agility, then returned to its perch. Unfortunately, unlike on television, wildlife doesn't behave in close-up or slow motion or, more usefully, come with a commentary telling you what you are seeing. Without binoculars I had to move closer, but as I stepped forward down the sloping track I slid slightly and grabbed a branch to steady myself, which bent, flicked back as I let go and frightened the bird away. It was one of those moments when I found myself instinctively searching for some virtual computer 'undo' command to reverse my blundering. Wouldn't things be so much easier if the 'CTRL + Z' keystroke applied to real life, allowing you to instantly rewind errors, such as mistaking a work colleague's weight gain for pregnancy or throwing your wife's favourite owl pellet collection out with the recycling? Just think of the friendships and marriages that could be saved were it possible!

Now I am pretty certain the bird I saw was a spotted flycatcher. Sure, it was the world's worst sighting, but it was probably enough. There are times when you don't need that much information to make a judgement call, just a general impression − something referred to by birdwatchers as 'jizz'. It's not another term for cheating, it just means that, even at a distance or in silhouette, a few key characteristics may be all it takes to distinguish some species − much like recognizing sentences from mobile phone text abbreviations. In the case of the spotted flycatcher these can come down to its size, upright perching posture and signature behaviour of darting out from a lookout post to catch flying insects before commonly landing back at the same perch. It is this entertaining aerobatic performance that makes it a popular bird, despite the fact it is not much to look at being, well, light brown. If it makes things sound slightly more interesting it does veer towards the grey end of the brown scale, and has white underparts and faint streaks on its breast.

The spotted flycatcher is a perching bird or 'passerine', part of a classification grouping accounting for more than half of all species in the world and which are often referred to as songbirds even though not all sing. The spotted flycatcher does sing, but its squeaky tunes are about as exciting as its plumage. However, it does endear itself to people by frequently choosing to nest in alcoves in walls, amid ivy on the sides of houses or in open-sided nest boxes, and by putting on a show in parks, gardens and woodland clearings with its aerial sorties to snap up passing bugs, butterflies and, as its name suggests, flies.

Obviously it needs to be nice and hot to get flying insects up and about, so spotted flycatchers don't thrive in the wet, when they have to grub about in the canopy for measly aphids. On the other hand too little rain in northern Africa can spell disaster for these trans-Saharan migrants that rely on well-stocked pit stops to keep them going. Insects need plants and plants need water, and the persistent droughts that have spread human misery across the semi-arid Sahel belt are believed to be one of a number of reasons why the British population of these widespread and fairly numerous birds has tumbled by over 80 per cent since 1970. Conditions on their wintering grounds and pesticide use closer to home may also be playing a part.

So how do we know they have fallen by that much? And, come to that, how do we know enough about any of our bird populations to decide which need help?

To find out I visited East Anglia to meet another member of the Red List team, Dr David Noble, who is head of census at the British Trust for Ornithology, which is based in a converted medieval nunnery in Thetford, Norfolk.

My trip began with an embarrassing awakening on the A11. I had driven through the night after a late shift at work and as dawn broke I pulled over into a deserted lay-by just outside Thetford for a snooze, having come prepared with a borrowed duvet and conveniently finding an elasticated airline mask in the glove compartment to shield my eyes from the rising sun. However, an hour later I was woken by the sounds of people talking and lifted up the patch to find the lay-by crammed with lorries, a busy mobile truckers' café serving breakfast alongside my car, and a crowd of HGV drivers standing around smoking while I was in full view stretched out on the reclining front seat covered in a flowery duvet and sporting a powder blue British Airways eye mask. It's not easy to emerge from the car with much masculine dignity in such circumstances, and ordering a bacon butty and asking for six sugars in my tea wasn't impressing anyone.

When I eventually turned into the tree-lined driveway that leads to the headquarters of the BTO, a number of members of staff were heading the other way. Not necessarily because I was coming, but because a rare Asian brown flycatcher blown onto our shores had been spotted in Yorkshire. As reasons go for taking a day off at short notice that takes some beating, and it made me wonder whether work rosters were drawn up on the basis of wind direction. Fortunately David was in, and he explained how the charity supplies many of the key facts and figures from which the state of our species can be assessed, helping to shape policy and guide conservation priorities.

The BTO is an independent scientific research trust which has been gathering data on the populations, movements and ecology of our birds since it was established in 1933. But with only a few staff it relies on thousands of volunteers to carry out the stocktakes, which range from regular surveys of wetlands, waterways, woodlands and gardens to detailed and time-consuming projects mapping the distribution of species. On top of this, hundreds of trained volunteers help with the ringing of hundreds of thousands of birds every year, most of which are never seen again. Only a very small percentage of the aluminium rings are ever recovered – though I would suggest putting cats through metal detectors might boost results.

One of the BTO's most important surveys has been the Common Bird Census, which was launched back in the early 1960s at a time when alarm bells were sounding over the effects of the insecticide DDT on bird numbers. In recent years it has been replaced by the Breeding Bird Survey which has spread the net wider and now monitors over a hundred species in 3,000 randomly selected kilometre squares across the UK. The combined results of both studies mean that people such as David can plot many of the trends on which our red, amber and green lists are based.

'The data we gather is far from information for its own sake,' he said, showing me illustrative graphs of farmland bird numbers on his computer screen. 'It's influencing policy across the UK and in Europe.'

But while we know a lot, there is still plenty to find out. Birds are not that easy to count. For one thing they don't keep still. In addition, some are hard enough to spot, let alone survey. Take the water rail – a secretive wetland dweller that looks like a long-billed brown and grey undersized version of a moorhen and is more often heard than seen. It is the kind of species that doesn't want to be studied. So, you might ask, why bother?

'You see water rails so rarely a decline is not necessarily going to affect many people's quality of life,' David said. 'But if they are disappearing it may well indicate something is going wrong with their habitat, which has wider consequences.'

The detailed surveillance of our birds by the BTO, RSPB and other organizations has enabled us to learn a great deal about the health of our countryside. So if any birds out there are wondering why they are being followed around by people with binoculars and clipboards, they can be reassured it is for the greater good. And if they have any information they would like to volunteer, now is the time to come forward.

You know you've crossed the line from enthusiasm into obsession and borderline insanity when people stop asking you how you are because they're afraid you might tell them. I would therefore like to apologize to anyone who asked that question of me during September 2007, because they would have got an answer along the following lines:

'Me? Oh fine a bit tired what with all the driving you know how it is well perhaps you don't know but I've been trying for weeks to see a wr . . . wry . . . I can't quite get the word out right now too painful but anyway I was up at 5am this morning at Land's End and there's never enough time and it was lying low or had flown on though it rained in the night which can keep them in one place whether it is the same one moving around the area I'm not sure but . . . sorry I didn't notice the queue, how much do I owe you?'

'Pump number three? Unleaded? £30.'

I had become more and more desperate to see a wryneck as the weeks passed and the window of opportunity narrowed. Whenever my mobile phone alerted me to a new text message of a sighting I was inevitably just turning up for work and unable to follow it up, arriving home with no chance to make it further than the end of the lane before dark, taking my daughters to one of their various activities, or being reminded by my wife that we were late for some arrangement or other that I hadn't made or even remembered involving people whose names I couldn't recall. Life was so busy it sometimes felt like I was fighting my way through a full wardrobe, and whenever I could squeeze daylight between work and family commitments it inevitably meant chasing up text messages several days old around the West Country with little chance of success. After a while I didn't know which I most wanted to hurl off the tip of Cornwall into the Atlantic: my work diary, the family diary or my mobile phone.

I needed to get away from it all. So where better than the Isles of Scilly – after all, they never get wryneck there, do they?

The archipelago of Scilly has more letters after its name than a professor of medicine. AONB, SPA, SAC, RAMSAR, SSSI . . . they give some idea of how valuable the islands are for wildlife. Warmed by the Gulf Stream, surrounded by rich seas and with habitats ranging from rocky uninhabited outcrops to sheltered woodlands, small marshes, sandy beaches, heaths and grassy downs, the scenic isles provide a haven for flora and fauna. There are unique species, such as the Scilly bee; plants found nowhere else in Britain like the dwarf pansy and orange birdsfoot; and impressive marine visitors include basking sharks, giant sunfish and leatherback turtles. More than 65 species of bird breed on the islands, which are a haven for seabirds such as petrels and puffins, but that is as nothing compared to the range of migrants, lost or otherwise, that drop in. Breaking the surface of the ocean 28 miles south-west of Land's End, the cluster of islands a few miles across provide the first glimpse of land for many tired migrating birds swept off course over the Atlantic, and they have earned a reputation as one of the premier places in Britain for rarities. So much so that when the annual influx of holidaymakers departs at the end of summer, a second invasion dressed in muted greens with binoculars strung around their necks follows in the autumn, providing a welcome late-season boost in tourist revenue, on which the isles' economy largely depends. A staggering total of over 425 species of birds have been recorded on Scilly, and the numbers of expert birdwatching eco-tourists – forgive me, 'beako-tourists' – who descend, mainly in October, ensure that more and more obscure vagrants are added to the tally.

When I boarded the Scillonian ferry at Penzance on 15 September I was a couple of weeks ahead of the main birding crowds, but there were a dozen or so young and fit-looking early arrivals chatting excitedly on the deck with telescopes attached to tripods strapped across their backs. An open book of possibilities awaited them, in particular American birds sucked up by airstreams and dumped 3,000 miles from home among the bushes. But I wasn't going to be tagging along. I was after a species far more familiar in Britain, and one which abounds on Scilly, where it has become remarkably tame.

While certainly handsome, with warm brown plumage, smart dark arrowhead spots on its breast and the kind of simple proportions one might draw if asked to sketch the basic outline of a bird, the species I was expecting to bump into is far better known for its voice than its looks. Voted the nation's favourite songster, its exquisite refrains, as refreshing as cool water on a hot and dusty day, seem to clear the air of other noise. The intricate phrases demand attention, and it sings them loud, from a prominent position and repeats many for good measure – which is one of the key clues that identify it as a song thrush, that much-loved darling of the garden that has sadly taken its place on the Red List.

Some birds are born with a fixed tune in their head, but the song thrush is among those gifted singers that possess the ability to learn. Over time it builds an extensive repertoire of riffs and can call on dozens of phrases to construct its music, augmenting its range by mimicking whatever sounds take its fancy. The resulting compositions are so inventive and unpredictable that it is tempting to consider them the melodies of a free creative spirit rather than the trillings of some biological automaton, for while they may have brains the size of pecan nuts, as yet we simply don't know what these avian maestros are going to sing next. In fact so beloved are they that back in the 1800s before portable CD players had been invented, British settlers even introduced them to New Zealand and Australia so that their songs might remind them of home. From what I gather, however, all the thrush's acoustic embroidery merely serves to dress up two very simple messages: 'go away' and 'come here'. 'Go away, rivals, this is my territory' (much the attitude of those colonial settlers) and, 'Come here, potential mates, and join me.'

Now I'll let you into a secret: I have seen a song thrush before. So why bother travelling to the Isles of Scilly? Well, song thrushes are ten times more common on Scilly than on the mainland and I was interested to find out why. They also provided me with the perfect excuse to visit the renowned birding hotspot for the first time, and I was really looking forward to it. Strange then that as the ferry eased away from the dock in the morning sunshine and began its course across the flat-calm bay I was suddenly gripped by an overwhelming desire to throw myself overboard and swim back to shore.

I should explain that I had not driven direct to Penzance to catch the boat, but had got up at an excessively early hour and taken a detour along the way. A wryneck – or rather *the-bird-whose-name-cannot-be-spoken* – had been seen yet again among the now familiar stone walls at Nanquidno near Land's End, and, chasing yesterday's news as ever, I took the opportunity to drive to the coastal valley at dawn for a quick look before a half-hour sprint to Penzance to catch the ferry. My search was, as ever, fruitless, so it was doubly unfair that minutes after the boat got under way my mobile chirped in my pocket with the message that one had just been seen in the very spot I had been searching an hour earlier. Worst of all was the knowledge that had I immediately abandoned my possessions, plunged into the sea, dodged the life-rings thrown by well-meaning passengers, made it to the dockside, clambered up the steps, dashed dripping wet to my car and driven at full speed I would probably have found the anonymous texter with mobile still in hand and sights trained on the bird. A wryneck would finally have been mine! Instead I was sailing away from it for the weekend, and had no possibility of leaving the isles the following day, a ferry-free Sunday, without either private charter transport or the help of the air ambulance.

Song thrushes proved somewhat easier to locate, and turned out to meet me near the jetty on St Mary's. In fact I found them so friendly that when taking photos I actually had to step back several paces to fit them in the viewfinder. They obviously had nothing to fear from people on Scilly. But how had they come to be so numerous?

The person to ask was Will Wagstaff. If you see a small crowd of people wandering along the tracks and paths on the main islands, there is a good chance Will will be at the front. Ever since moving there in the early 1980s he has led guided wildlife tours, and is chairman of the Isles of Scilly Bird Group. I caught up with him after attending one of his regular nature talks in a church hall close to my B&B in Hugh Town, the main settlement on St Mary's.

He summed up in a sentence: 'There's a lack of predators here, it is relatively frost free, there are plenty of places to nest and sufficient food available.' Basically Scilly ticks all the boxes for thrush requirements.

Winters hit thrush populations hard, but the isles' maritime climate means that there hasn't been a serious cold snap for over twenty years. This mild weather is also ideal for growing flowers, and small fields given over to nurturing early blooms for market have been protected against the wind with tall hedges, which are perfect for cover-loving thrushes. There are also no foxes, weasels or stoats to trouble them, few sparrowhawks, and the patchwork of mixed farming fields provides a range of habitats in which to forage for worms, fruit and, during dry summers when worms are hard to find, snails whose shells they famously smash open on 'anvil' stones.

On the mainland it is another story, where numbers totalling just over one million pairs are half what they were in the late 1960s. Young birds have had trouble getting enough food to live through their first winter, especially on farmland where more intensive approaches and improved drainage makes it harder to find worms and other delicacies. Parks and gardens have now become a refuge for many of our thrushes, though even there the use of slug pellets mean they are far from chemical-free sanctuaries. However, despite a gloomy few decades, numbers have been heading up in recent years. While it would be nice to credit conservation work, sometimes these matters are in the laps of the gods, and a few wet and wormy summers are thought to have made the difference.

Walking around St Mary's I bumped into a number of birders who were on the trail of vagrants and checking their pagers every couple of minutes.

'There's a spotted sandpiper at Porth Hellick Pool and a citrine wagtail about,' one of a small group told me, and I nodded as if I had actually heard of them before.

'I just saw a song thrush on the path, back there by the crossroads. Well worth checking out,' I replied enthusiastically, and the group thanked me with strained smiles and moved off.

As it happened I was on my way to Porth Hellick, so I decided to visit one of the two hides, though not to see the lost spotted sandpiper from America, because to be honest I was happy enough just trying to see British species.

I hadn't been in a bird hide since I was a teenager, and it felt very strange to find myself once again lifting a latch and stepping inside the dark resinous-smelling shelter. The close confines of these squat boxes with their wooden floors raised off the ground seem to amplify sound, and I tiptoed as quietly as I could to take my place on the bench beside two other birdwatchers.

Raising the wooden observation flap in front of me I was greeted with a tranquil scene: a small shallow pool bathed in sunshine, sheltered from the breeze by dense reedbeds and dotted with a manageably modest number of birds. 'Anything about?' is the accepted opening question, only I didn't dare break the silence to ask, even though it would have made things easier. All the earlier talk of weird and wonderful scarcities had knocked my confidence. There was a heron. But was it just a normal grey heron? And there were smaller waders that I recognized, only in a place such as this surely they were going to be something bizarre. I couldn't trust myself to get anything right, and I was glad of my dated binoculars which hung like an 'L' plate around my neck ensuring neither of the other two in the hide would think me an expert and engage in conversation about superciliary stripes and sexual dimorphism. As if to underline that fact I pulled out a bird guide and started looking everything up.

Enjoyable as it is to see a heron hunting in the shallows or a dunlin working the mud, I can only watch them going about their business for so long. Nothing else turned up, not even anything resembling a sandpiper, spotted or otherwise, and after ten minutes I was itching to leave and see the rest of the island – except that you can't just breeze in and breeze out of a hide without it appearing like window shopping. There is an undefined minimum time period required before it is acceptable to move on, much as there is when viewing a painting in a gallery, and I hadn't yet crossed that threshold. My early exit strategy involved looking at my watch, uttering a gasp of surprise that one might if, say, late for a dental appointment, and with a polite nod treading softly to the door and out into the open air.

The patience of the other two in the hide would surely be rewarded, but covering ground also has its benefits. As I marched up to the northern end of the island I reassured myself with the notion that one of the fundamental reasons for the success of the human race, apart from opposable thumbs and large brains and so on, is that as a species we are easily bored. Our restless nature has led to creativity and conquest, and as if to prove that point I got decent views of two

spotted flycatchers half an hour later in the woods at
Bar Point.

When I returned to my B&B I noticed a public chalk-
board for bird sightings behind the neighbouring Pilot's
Gig Restaurant, and below the list of obscure warblers
and wagtails and waders I added: *2 Spotted Flycatchers, St
Mary's*. No one would be going out of their way to see
them, but with that token act I somehow felt that as a
birdwatcher I had finally arrived.

But what was that faint word chalked on the list from
a few days ago? Surely not!

I would have dwelt on it no further . . . only I had no
choice. The next morning I joined a boat excursion to
see seabirds with Will as guide, microphone in hand:
'Curlew on our left, sanderling to our right, egrets
straight ahead . . .' But halfway across the bay my mobile
bleeped and I nearly leapt to my feet, grabbed the
boatman beside him, held a copy of the *RSPB Handbook
of British Birds* pointed at his head and demanded: 'Driver,
turn this boat around!' A wryneck had been spotted a
fifteen-minute walk from our departure point, and we
were heading off in a direct line away from it towards
the island of Tresco. It was exactly as had happened at
Penzance. Boarding boats was becoming a very bad idea.
So instead of exploring Tresco I remained on the vessel
for its return leg and Will pointed me in the direction
of Buzza Tower, a circular hilltop landmark overlooking
Hugh Town where it had been seen, and I ran all the
way up and found . . . nothing. The wryneck had gone.

Now generally I am of a stable mental disposition. I
suffer from a blind faith in health advice and a mild fear

of poetry, but apart from that my therapist and back-up psychiatric team assure me I am perfectly sane. So I would like to take the opportunity here to make that clear to the couple I overtook at speed on the footpath to the tower who a few minutes later found me creeping up on a bush then standing on a stone bench and staring forlornly at a patch of grass before clasping my head in my hands with a wail of despair.

If you saw a group of a dozen people standing on a head-land scanning the sea with high-powered telescopes on tripods you would imagine some newsworthy disaster was unfolding offshore. Sidling up alongside to listen in you might instead be surprised to hear something along these lines: 'Arctic skua . . . two o'clock . . . passing sun, left to right . . .' Given that an arctic skua is a seabird it would be clear you had stumbled across a group of birdwatchers. But how much sadder could you get than spending time staring at the ocean for passing birds? Tragic, I would have said, until I joined in one morning and had one of the most memorable views ever of a bird, lasting precisely two seconds.

To see offshore seabirds means either taking a boat trip or standing at a good vantage point and waiting to see what flies past. I had heard that the latter 'seawatching' option could be tedious and required far more patience than I had managed in the Porth Hellick bird hide. However, I decided to give it a try after learning the time was right to spot one particularly significant species which, while not British enough to qualify for our Red

List, was being seen within viewing range of our coasts: the balearic shearwater. Its name may be unfamiliar, but this is no twitchers' oddity.

Skimming the peaks and troughs of waves on stiff outstretched wings, shearwaters are an inspiring sight. Smaller and darker than most gulls they are in their element in strong winds, cutting through the sea spray just above the surface of the water and banking from one wingtip to the other. Like albatrosses, these ocean travellers at home in a world of unbroken horizons and vast distances embody a sense of freedom. They are well worth seeing, and I was familiar with the manx shearwater, which nests in Britain, returning to its clifftop burrows at night to avoid predatory gulls and skuas. However, I knew nothing about the closely related balearic shearwater, except that it is a dirtier brown version of our black-topped, white-bellied manx shearwater, and that it has become an increasingly regular offshore visitor during the autumn, particularly in the western approaches to the English Channel.

While it is always nice to see a shearwater, even if it is just passing through our territorial waters without stopping, why bother taking a detour to see this particular autumn holidaymaker from the Med?

The reason is simple: it is one of the most critically endangered birds in the world, and at its current rate of decline could be gone by 2050. Not even tigers, polar bears or pandas qualify for critically endangered status, and unless you are interested in obscure seafish and freshwater mussels you won't find any other animal in the UK ranked at this maximum priority alert level. Only three other birds classified as critically endangered by the IUCN have ever touched down in the UK: the eskimo curlew – a formerly abundant New World species last spotted here in 1887 and now considered extinct; the slender-billed curlew from Siberia – on the brink of extinction and confirmed as being sighted just once here in 1998; and the friendly sounding sociable lapwing from Russia and Kazakhstan which drops in very occasionally. So the fact that we are lucky enough to get at least 10 per cent of the few thousand balearic shearwaters in the world racing past our shores every year is good grounds for trying a bit of seawatching.

In the summer it nests in a tiny touristy area of the Mediterranean, where it is threatened by cats and rats and development, and out at sea it faces other hazards as trawlermen give with one hand, by chucking fish waste overboard, and take with the other, drowning unfortunate birds that get hooked on long baited lines before they sink. On top of that global warming is thought to be shifting the fish shoals on which they feed further north, adding to their woes but conveniently bringing more and more of the scarce shearwaters close to our coast. One day they may indeed be regarded as having strong enough ties with our islands to join the UK Red List.

In trying to spot one I could have visited a team of volunteers who were at the time engaged in an exhausting three-month dawn-to-dusk count of the birds – but they were stationed near Land's End and I couldn't face yet another trip down the A30, so instead I travelled to the next best place for them: Portland Bill in Dorset.

Of course identifying birds out at sea requires more than binoculars. I needed a telescope, and a friend from my village kindly came to my aid and lent me one. Only it wasn't a birdwatching telescope. He had bought it to give his young daughter a lesson in astronomy, and unlike field 'scopes' in inconspicuous green it was moulded in bright blue plastic. It also didn't have a tripod, but I managed to screw it onto a particularly thin-legged wobbly one I had been given free when I bought a camera years before. I'll be honest, the resulting combination was not a high-spec optical outfit. So when I turned up at the tip of the Bill at dawn on a clear but windy day in late September, I was quite glad there was no one else about.

After half an hour struggling in the wind to get a steady view of anything in the telescope, and failing to see much more than a couple of gannets through my binoculars, I was beginning to get frustrated and was on the verge of giving up. I did see birdwatchers wandering across the grass towards me, but they seemed to disappear when they reached the headland café and I assumed they were having breakfast. When I did eventually drift over that way, however, I discovered a dozen of them, all men incidentally, lined up sheltered in the lee of the café behind tripods, chatting quietly to one another with eyes glued to their telescopes scanning the rough open water. So I took my place among them, wedging my tripod against a bench so it wouldn't fall over, and stared out at the wrinkly grey sea hopefully. It felt a bit like looking for fleas on elephant skin.

And then someone spotted an arctic skua, the clockface directions filtered down the line and everyone was on it within seconds. But I just couldn't find it. Left a bit . . . right a bit . . . waves . . . more waves. I was lost at sea.

More seabirds were pinpointed and again I struggled to see any before they disappeared out of range. It was quite incredible the speed at which those around me not only identified distant birds, but also managed to all latch on to the moving targets.

Twenty minutes later and the call that I had been hoping for came. 'Balearic shearwater . . . one o'clock . . . below tanker on horizon . . . moving right . . . showing now . . . showing . . . '

Like boat oars the telescopes all moved into line and to the right as everyone found and tracked it. But one stood out, a bright blue telescope rowing the wrong way. I needed help, and fast. Putting pride to one side I ditched my gear and asked a birder in his sixties beside me whether he would mind me looking through his telescope. Thankfully he was happy to oblige and quickly and cleverly lined up his lens anticipating the bird's continuing flightpath.

'Right, look now,' he said, shifting swiftly to one side.

I moved into place and looked through the eyepiece. The view was crystal clear, a circle of distant foam-flecked waves. Then from the left the low-flying shearwater appeared, carving into the prevailing wind, its brown back showing, switching wingtip in an instant to reveal a light underside smudged with brown, exactly as I had seen in a book, before it passed out of the circle of view.

It was a wonderful sight. Fleeting, but one I will never forget. I really owed that birdwatcher.

When things tailed off I made my way home, desperate to tell everyone I knew about the sighting even though I was aware none of them were the slightest bit interested.

'You drove all that way to see a bird?' a friend out shopping asked as we chatted in the street, their expression a mix of incredulity and pity.

Well, it felt like more than that, but how to explain? Yes, at its simplest level birdwatching is just about seeing and naming, whether you chance upon species or go out of your way to find them. Then there is the satisfaction of learning and sharing – even though my friends and family were less keen on the sharing side of things – and of feeling that little bit more in touch with the natural world. But there is something else as well. Something endured beyond the fleeting pleasure of 'ticking off' a balearic shearwater, and I wasn't sure exactly what it was. All I know is that when I woke the following morning I wanted to see another one.

'It was worth it,' I replied to my friend. 'And you know if you asked me whether I'd prefer to spend a morning on some rain-sodden, windswept headland looking for birds at sea or lazing around at home watching telly I know what the answer would be.'

With a smug grin I left the choice hanging, turned on my heel and headed off.

And the answer?

Well, it depends what's on TV.

CHAPTER SIX

'IT STINKS!' THE ELDEST OF THE TWO CHILDREN LAUGHED, pointing at the display.

His younger sister joined in with a naughty giggle: 'It stink! It stink!'

'Shhssh!' their mother snapped, looking at the stuffed dodo behind the glass. 'I said "ex-tinct". It's extinct.'

Still, I thought, if they were commenting on its demise then her children did have a point, even if not the one intended.

The family moved on and I took their place in front of the exhibit.

The Natural History Museum in London has a corridor dedicated to birds, and as part of the display a section near the entrance houses species that no longer exist anywhere but in museum collections. Standing in the centre are two dodos, the heavyweight big-beaked flightless fruit-eaters that enjoyed a predator-free existence on Mauritius before hungry human invaders with carnivorous pets in tow turned up and wiped them out by the late 1600s. Above them a pair of preserved passenger pigeons, one with head bowed, perch on branches fixed to the rear of the display, their plumage a mix of delicate grey and brown and reddish hues. To the right, huia, metallic black with long down-curved beaks, that were last seen in the wild in New Zealand in the early 1900s, and beside them striking red-headed imperial woodpeckers from Mexico and green and yellow Carolina parakeets, all now gone.

Just beneath the fat frowning dodos at the edge of the display was the reason I had come to pay my respects: Britain's only extinct species – the great auk. Looking much like a large razorbill, the stuffed seabird stood upright a couple of feet tall, webbed toes spread on the board, tiny flipper-like wings folded against its sides and glass eyes staring blankly out from the base of its long dark bill. It was about as well camouflaged as it is possible to be for life on the open ocean, with a white belly making it less conspicuous to predators below and black upper half doing the same for aerial hunters above. In fact with its ying-and-yang plumage and stubby wings it looked every bit the typical auk, our strong-swimming northern-hemisphere equivalent of penguins – except unlike other auks this particular member of the family was unable to fly, which had made it easier to catch. And catch it we did for meat and feathers and fat and fish bait, hoovering up the scattered colonies across the north Atlantic until there were none left. The last great auk in British waters was killed on St Kilda in 1840, and soon after sightings elsewhere tailed off to zero.

The great auk is one of 153 birds documented as having become extinct worldwide since 1500, with flightless and island species generally the worst hit. Was this figure worse than I expected or better? I wasn't sure. Of course extinction is a necessary consequence of evolution, and those species lucky enough to have made it this far are only a tiny fraction of what has ever been. But that said, current levels are considered far, far higher than would be expected through natural rates of loss, and thousands more birds and mammals and reptiles and amphibians and fish and insects have now joined the queue to become history.

So who cares? If someone told you that you'd never encounter a thylacine or quagga, you might be thinking: 'Phew, I never did like chemistry or physics.' And, like me, would you struggle to know where to turn in an encyclopaedia to cross out a pygmy elimia or a longjaw cisco? They are among those animal species lost forever within the last 150 years – a kind of zebra, a carnivorous marsupial, a snail and a freshwater fish. They are not names that often crop up in conversation. Yet a few losses have lodged in our collective consciousness, and on the day I visited the museum, the dodo, that A-list celebrity of annihilation, was certainly drawing the biggest crowd in the bird morgue. Morbid fascination, but also a tiny bit of proof that we do care.

And should we care? We might feel a tad guilty so many species have disappeared on our watch, but does it really matter in the long run?

Er . . . yes.

There are 10 million bricks in the Empire State Building – roughly the total number of plant and animal species estimated as existing on earth. Remove a few bricks picked at random and the skyscraper holds steady. But take out too many and the structure becomes unstable and eventually collapses.

As things stand over 16,900 species that we know about currently face extinction. That is a lot of bricks. And that is precisely what worries experts like Craig Hilton-Taylor. He is the manager of the IUCN Red List, which evaluates the wellbeing of the world's flora and fauna, and I called him up to ask whether we were all doomed.

'When it comes to extinctions we just don't know how far we can go,' he said. 'There is some degree of redundancy – you can lose some species and not affect the system, but you could get to a point of no return, and we don't know where that point is.

'There has certainly been good news in recent years in terms of the political will to conserve biodiversity. However, we are not seeing that being capitalized on, and while there have been success stories with some species, overall the list of those at risk just grows longer and longer.'

The term 'biodiversity' may sound like the name of a washing powder for mixed coloureds, but it describes the vital variety of natural life upon which we depend for everything from food to building materials to fuel to medicines. Biodiversity gives us pests like lettuce-munching larvae, but also pest controllers like great tits, a pair of which can get through over 7,000 caterpillars in three weeks feeding their young. Take birds out of the equation and we would soon feel the effects. In India populations of vultures, poisoned by veterinary drugs in the food chain, have collapsed, leading to an explosion in numbers of feral dogs that have taken up the birds' role of animal-carcass scavengers. This, in turn, has resulted in a disturbing rise in cases of rabies and, it is estimated, thousands of human deaths. It is obviously in our interests to maintain the planet's complex web of life, and in recognizing this the international community has set itself a goal to slow, or in Europe's case halt, biodiversity loss by 2010. This target nails a deadline onto the objectives of the Convention on Biological Diversity which was agreed at the 1992 Rio Earth Summit, and there has been progress in some areas as more land than ever before is now protected and water quality has improved in many countries. In doing our bit towards conserving dwindling species and meeting the 2010 target the UK has drawn up its own Biodiversity Action Plan for habitats and species in need of help, which includes a priority list for birds broadly similar to the national Red List.

Biodiversity provides us with more than simply life-support services though – the natural world enriches our lives culturally, spiritually and aesthetically (excluding naked mole rats). And we like the diversity. After all, how many people visiting a zoo spend the entire day in front of the first cage they come to? Lose a few species, board up a few enclosures and we might not notice, but gradually the losses would begin to tell. We would miss them. And while I may not have seen a live great auk or any bird now wiped off the map, I can imagine what it might feel like to lose something familiar, having experienced the extinction of one majestic sight in the skies over Britain that is now just a memory and a museum piece. It may sound like an odd example, but I'm talking about Concorde. Today when you hear the roar of aeroplane engines overhead and look up it is always something else.

Unfortunately, it is widely acknowledged that as things stand the target to reduce biodiversity loss by 2010 is unlikely to be met and looks like remaining out of reach well beyond the end of the decade if climate change, a spiralling human population and an unsustainable demand for resources continue to squeeze species and ecosystems. But all is not lost. While conservation success stories may be outnumbered by bad news, they do show just what is possible. Southern white rhinos are back from the brink along with Mauritius echo parakeets that at one stage numbered just ten, and if the dodo were alive today and under threat again I like to think we would manage to save it – for its own sake and not just ours.

So far the Red List birds I had seen included a rock lintie (twite), scribbler (yellowhammer), copper head (tree sparrow), miller (spotted flycatcher) and a throstle (song thrush). Yes, many of the evocative old names are going the way of the birds! Standardization in field guides and as a result of improved communications means that a rich heritage of regional terms is gradually dying out. If you were travelling the country looking for chaffinches you could prepare by learning a staggering forty-five recorded names ranging from chink chaffey in Hampshire and pink twink in Devon to fleckie wings in Lancashire and charbob in Derbyshire, but the chances are most people wouldn't know what you were talking about. Of course should you find yourself without a dictionary of local terms in some time-warp village in the back of beyond inhabited by lobe-tugging mouth-breathing roadkill eaters you could always adopt the trusted method when making yourself understood abroad and just say 'Chaffinch' very loudly and slowly several times while flapping your arms.

Just as well I wasn't searching for chaffinches.

The next bird on my list was one with quite a few different names, though many share similarities which date back 1500 years, so that an Anglo-Saxon ornithology club branch meeting on 'sparwa' would make sense as the bird we now call a 'sparrow'. However, while that early get-together might well have been discussing how to get rid of them, one today would be fretting about how to bring them back.

House sparrows have been following us around for thousands of years, making their homes in our homes and scrounging the scraps from our table. They may not be quite as common as wrens, chaffinches, blackbirds or robins, but their attachment to us means they are the bird you are most likely to see out of your kitchen window, which makes them the most surprising candidate for conservation concern. And yet an astonishing six out of every ten of these sociable, resourceful and chirpy companions have disappeared since the mid-1970s, with the declines highest in urban areas. In the centre of London you are about as likely to see Concorde fly past as these little birds – so I set myself the challenge of trying to find one in the heart of the capital, where every sparrow matters.

After visiting the Natural History Museum I met up with London RSPB manager Paul Forecast, who keeps a close eye on 'cockney sparrow' populations.

'If you'd asked twenty-five years ago whether we would be working on house sparrow recovery projects I would have laughed,' he said. 'But there has been a catastrophic crash in numbers and at the moment it's like a game of Cluedo trying to figure out exactly why.'

He showed me a map of house sparrow populations in London and the shaded areas where they are now found resemble a doughnut, with an empty hole in the centre. 'I have been working here in Westminster for several years and I have never seen one in the area, and I have been looking,' he said.

The plight of the humble house sparrow has been the subject of numerous studies, with thousands of willing volunteers helping to keep tabs on numbers, and concerns have even been raised in the House of Lords and a newspaper reward offered for research that finally unravels the exact cause of the decline. The finger of blame has been pointed at cats and sparrowhawks and magpies and cars and roofers and gardeners and homeowners, but the murder-mystery still remains unsolved. Further research is now examining the effects of inner-city traffic pollution and assessing how much a shortage of grubs for newborn chicks in the spring and seeds in the winter is having an impact.

'It is very much a work in progress,' Paul said. 'There are a number of factors which we do not fully understand, but I don't think we are that far away from an answer, then the next stage will be to put things right.'

There was a time when there were so many house sparrows we couldn't kill them fast enough. We trapped them as crop pests and a domestic nuisance, we put a parish bounty on their heads with pay-outs for bundles of a dozen, we formed clubs to shoot them, we ate them in pies and netted them at London Zoo to feed to the animals. It has been calculated that we exterminated over 100,000,000 house sparrows between 1700 and 1930, without really making much of a difference. So it is ironic that after the slaughter ended their numbers started to slide, shedding millions and reaching the point where we would welcome a few more back. London Zoo now puts up nest boxes for them.

From Paul's offices near Victoria station I travelled to Kensington Gardens to try to find one. I knew the odds were stacked against me as numbers recorded there had dropped from 2,603 in 1925 to just eight by 2000, and I was told I would be lucky to find any at all now – which proved accurate advice. I then walked to Trafalgar Square, where I had no luck, and made my way to Leicester Square where I remember the plane trees used to fizz with roosting starlings in the evening, but the only birds about were scraggy pigeons. With no house sparrows to be seen and the light fading fast I was forced to give up for the day and instead found myself drawn to a large crowd of celebrity twitchers outside the Odeon West End waiting for stars to arrive for a film premiere. As the first limo pulled up beside the red carpet and someone famous stepped out into a lightning storm of paparazzi flashes, the crowd of on-lookers surged forward to catch a glimpse and up went arms holding mobile phone cameras aloft like dozens of eyes on stalks, accompanied by desperate cries of 'Jamie! Jamie!' 'Over here! Over here!' A few minutes later and another celebrity rolled in and a pulsing anemone of hands reached out for a touch as they skirted the crowd. 'Michael! Michael!' Then: 'Jennifer! Jennifer!' And as I stood among the throng I felt like a bewildered bird-watcher on their first field trip. I hadn't a clue who any of the stars were.

I'm not completely out of touch, I distinctly remember having once seen a film before, but I was at a loss to recognize a single one of these famous faces so familiar to those around me. However, I think birdwatchers could learn something from the star-struck autograph-hunters. Instead of keeping as quiet as possible when observing rare and interesting species, I suggest it would make identification far easier for all if birdwatchers waved their mobile phones at them and screamed the birds' names at the top of their voices.

Anyway, from the red carpet back to the Red List, and the next morning I set off once again into central

London. The trouble was I had arranged to meet up with a friend who has no interest whatsoever in birds, so, knowing I needed to look around a specific area on the South Bank, I suggested a stroll beside the Thames. We headed over Westminster Bridge and along past the London Eye and the buskers and skateboarders to Gabriel's Wharf, and as he veered towards the cafés I managed to steer him past and across a small area of grass set back from the river to a sunken garden flanked by thick hedges and trees.

And that's when I heard it.

Chirp. Chirp.

Music to my ears.

'Brilliant!' I exclaimed. Usually the fact that a small bird *isn't* a house sparrow is what makes it interesting – but not any more.

'What?' My friend looked puzzled. 'Anyway, why are we standing here?'

'We just need to find him now,' I said, creeping up towards the bushes where the sound was coming from.

'Er, whom exactly?' he asked anxiously.

By the time I had explained what I was after we had circled a thorny hedge and there in the centre I caught sight of a lone male house sparrow with grey cap and black bib. While there may have been others about I couldn't see any, and although I was pleased to have found even one it did make for a sad spectacle: London's most central sparrow chirping away on his own for all he was worth.

*　　*　　*

For those who complain that too many of our birds are small and brown, let me say that this is probably a blessing. Imagine that instead of blending in they were all vivid orange or pink or scarlet or yellow. Flocks at our bird tables would look like flying scoops of pick'n'mix sweets, our lakes would be awash with birds bright as floating segments of tinned fruit salad and our treetops would be sprinkled with plumage colours from a cake decorator's palette. After a while it would be hard to stomach.

I make the case because the red-listed reed bunting is small and mostly brown and I don't want anyone to hold that against it, as it has had a hard enough time in recent years as it is.

The next stop on my capital sightseeing tour was the London Wetland Centre in Barnes, which was created by the Wildfowl and Wetlands Trust on the site of former reservoirs and is home to marsh-loving reed buntings among plenty of other species. If you like your birdwatching with a gift shop and restaurant attached and children's activities laid on, then this is the place to come. And I'm not getting snobby and purist about things – it was quite a relief to open the book of visitors' sightings in one of the hides and see that all levels of ability were catered for, as entries included such rigorous scientific records as '*swan*' and '*sheep*'.

In the centre of the wetland area is a three-storey observation tower which overlooks expanses of water, grazing marshes and housing blocks beyond, and I made my way there and settled in on the top floor for a bird's eye view. There were herons pacing around, beautiful lapwings with glossy bottle-green backs gleaming in the autumn sunshine, handsome wigeon, and a jack snipe which was causing plenty of excitement among the more experienced birders.

Before long I spotted a small flock of reed bunting feeding among the dry seedheads of waterside plants. In the spring and summer the males have a striking black head with a white collar and white stripe behind the bill, but after moulting in the autumn these features are largely obscured by buff feather fringes which need to wear away during the winter months to look their best for spring. Given that the birds I was looking at had recently moulted they made for a poor imitation of the pictures I had seen in field guides. However, even though there wasn't much to go on I knew they were reed buntings and not sparrows or something else because of their subtle cheek markings, chestnut shoulders, longish tails with white outer feathers – and because the man next to me said they were.

You can't always trust other birdwatchers to be right, but chat for a while and you soon get the measure of their expertise, which was well worth doing as people around me were making plenty of mistakes when it came to the finer points of identification. ('It's a swan!' 'No it isn't, I'm sure it's a sheep!')

Like all our birds, reed buntings depend on us to be benevolent caretakers, and in many ways we have helped them, even if not always intentionally. We may have drained wetlands and neatened river banks and filled in ditches, but we have also given them reservoirs and flooded gravel pits and expanded our reedbed reserves.

In addition they have shown themselves to be adaptable, colonizing drier habitats so that nowadays you can find them anywhere from marshes and scrub to young forestry plantations and fields of crops. And fortunately their numbers are now edging back out of the red after enduring a dramatic downturn during the 1970s, 1980s and early 1990s. They have even begun coming to bird tables. In fact upwards of eighty species have been recorded at garden feeders in Britain – a staggering list which includes such birds as kingfishers, dippers and goshawks. Just what are people putting out as food?

I had not been allowed to forget the second promise I had made to my family in exchange for devoting a year to birdwatching. Sure, I had fulfilled my side of the bargain when it came to arranging a holiday, of sorts, but there was the small matter of a puppy.

I had never really wanted to have a dog for many reasons. There were the food bills and vets' bills as well as the promise of having to carry around warm bags of excrement, of course, but also the fact that people who own them always seem to discover dead bodies. Whenever you read in a newspaper that a corpse has been found in a wood or washed up on a beach with the tide, it invariably says that it was first stumbled across by someone walking their dog.

However, no one was listening to my protests. I tried to convince my children that it would be hard work, that they would have to get up early and walk lots. A dog is for life and not just Christmas, I told them, unlike a turkey. But they didn't want a turkey, they wanted a dog, and they didn't want an old one with just a week to live as a compromise solution either. No, they wanted a puppy with years of love and friendship and body-discovering ahead of it. So I finally relented and off we went and got a springer spaniel and brought a little bundle of chaos into our home.

A springer puppy is like a furry slipper with a firework inside, whizzing all over the place, bouncing off the walls and leaving fragments of shredded furnishings in its wake. Our new arrival, Oakey, chewed chair legs and shoes and socks and the cat, and he ate enough magnetic alphabet letters on the fridge to crap whole sentences. In an attempt to prevent him from devouring everything we bought lots of treats from the pet shop, such as boiled bones, dried hide, pig ears and snouts, which he distributed about the garden before coming in to pee in the hall. The outside looked like a crime scene, while inside the carpet was very clean in lots of small scrubbed patches.

His behaviour got progressively worse, and when I caught him hot-wiring the neighbour's car we decided to take him to puppy training, where we were given a booklet which included lots of useful tips on obedience and also a section on the importance of socialization. It said that not only was it important for puppies to get used to other dogs, but also strangers *who differ significantly in appearance from family members* – so odd-looking people in the area who at that time found themselves approached out of the blue by a family with a puppy now know why.

Springer spaniels may have traditionally been bred to flush out birds for the gun, but there was no way I was going to let him near the two game birds next on my list: the black grouse and the grey partridge.

There was a time when I could have saved myself a journey and seen black grouse in Devon, but they have drained northwards over the last century so that in England they are now mostly confined to the North Pennines, with a small population in Wales and the majority in Scotland. It meant I was forced to get in my car and head for the hills, leaving puppy mayhem behind.

I hadn't been driving more than twenty minutes when I spotted something very unusual up ahead flying across the road. Not a black grouse trying to make things easy. It resembled a huge heron, with broad grey wings and trailing legs, but unlike a heron it flew with its neck and pointed long beak stuck straight out, and as it passed over in front of my car I saw clearly that it was a crane.

A crane?!

It may be called the common crane, but it is anything but common in this part of the world. I was aware that they had been driven to extinction as a breeding species in Britain several centuries ago, that they were making a tiny comeback in Norfolk and that a few passed through on migration to and from northern Europe, but I had no idea whether they cropped up this far west. So I was surprised when, on contacting the Devon Bird Watching and Preservation Society to find out, I was immediately sent a special form with lots of probing questions about the sighting. I duly filled it in: *Previous experience of species*: none. *Other observers*: none. *Species present nearby for comparison*: none. *Optical aids used*: none. I wasn't picking up many credibility points, but there was room for an account of what I had seen and I was later informed that my record had been accepted – and that only sixty-four have ever been witnessed in the county since records began in 1826. Golly!

Much like a crane I was walking tall for days after. I felt like a giant among West Country birdwatchers – though I didn't actually know any to show off to, which was a shame.

Following the initial excitement my journey north became a tedious slog, punctuated by glimpses through the roadside scrub of combed ploughed soil and wide harvested fields with scattered round bales of straw resembling rolls of unlaid carpet. Like grey rivers, motorways can drain the colour out of the neighbouring countryside, and it was a relief to finally turn off onto an A road and head into an expanse of green with the Pennines in the distance and a scenic route to Upper Teesdale ahead.

The North Pennines is designated an Area of Outstanding Natural Beauty – not for the attractiveness of its residents, but for its stunning landscape of heather-covered hills, fertile dales, tumbling streams, traditional hay meadows and scattered woodland. It provides an ideal mix of habitats for black grouse, which prefer places that are neither too open nor too enclosed and thrive on the fringes of open moorland, pine forests and upland pastures.

Conservation measures mean the grouse are clinging

on here, but their decline across the UK over the last century has been nothing short of catastrophic. The plummeting graph of estate bags for this quarry species since 1900 resembles the trajectory of a bird shot on the wing, and voluntary hunting bans are now in place. A recorded day's hunting which bagged 250 back in 1860 would today wipe out a quarter of the English population. But shooting is not the culprit in the black grouse story. Habitat loss has been the real killer as the soft-edged mosaics of heather, grasses, young trees and shrubs that these birds need have been overgrazed by sheep and deer, drained for farmland or buried under maturing forestry blocks. And as numbers have declined the impact of predators, wet summers and even fatal collisions with cars and fences has become more and more significant.

The situation is so desperate that conservationists and the shooting lobby have put aside their differences to work together with enlightened landowners on recovery projects to steer this threatened grouse's population back into the black. And if ever there was a species worth saving it is this one – not that I'm saying aquatic warblers aren't just as important, or twites for that matter, or tree sparrows or . . . well, you know what I mean. It's just that the black grouse is such an impressive bird in so many ways. Not only do they look good, and fly fast, and sound unique, but the glossy black males' displays are among the most astonishing sights in the bird world. And I was lucky enough never to have seen them before. Lucky because it meant I had a treat in store, and I could hardly get to sleep that night.

I met Phil Warren at dawn outside my hotel. He was wearing a tweed jacket, owns pointer dogs and represents game hunting interests. He is not someone one might immediately think of going birdwatching with, but as Game and Wildlife Conservation Trust lead officer for the North Pennines Black Grouse Recovery Project, Phil knows just about everything that the local birds are up to and is exactly the sort of person you want by your side when looking for them.

My experience of shooting to date had amounted to a press day with the military which involved firing a machine gun, and an afternoon learning how to use a 12-bore on my grandfather's farm. While I am now capable of overthrowing a small regime or holding up a bank, I have never shot at a game bird, not even in self-defence. But I have nothing against those who do, and would far rather eat a pheasant, grouse or partridge that had enjoyed the freedom of the outdoors before meeting its end than a battery-farmed chicken. More than that, it seems obvious that those who have a personal or financial interest in shooting will do everything they can to ensure there is plenty of game about, and are often best placed to make sure that there is.

It was a clear, crisp morning – perfect conditions for what I had come to see, and as Phil drove me out onto the moors he was confident about my chances of success, even though spring is the peak season and it was October. I had drunk too often in the saloon of false hopes, and wasn't going to jinx my chances with anything nearing optimism.

I babbled away about my trip up and seeing a crane

and having supper opposite a couple who said absolutely nothing to each other throughout the entire meal, and he smiled and nodded in the right places, but his attention was fixed on the rolling landscape before us. Then, as I was nearing the conclusion of an anecdote involving our new puppy, a carnival parade and a claim for compensation, Phil pulled up on the verge and cut me short, winding down the windows and pointing down the slope beside us at an area of short grass and rushes.

It was an incredible sight. The exposed patch of flat sward on the side of the valley was crowded with male grouse pacing and posturing in the low morning mist with blue-black necks puffed up, red eye wattles gleaming, wings held low, and lyre-shaped tails cocked and spread beneath raised fans of white feathers. Pairs of them jousted, pacing back and forth with ritual moves akin to sumo wrestlers sizing up their opponents, and they filled the cold, still air with the sounds of dove-like bubbling and harsh hisses resembling smokers clearing their throats and spitting.

'I make it twenty-six,' Phil said, counting them through a pair of binoculars, at which point he reached into a long bag and pulled out the barrel of . . . a telescope. 'We mustn't get out of the car or we'll disturb them, so use this,' he said, fixing it to my window.

What we were observing was a 'lek' – an established display ground where the males battle it out for supremacy and the chance of impressing reclusive camouflaged females watching nearby. Their territories are little more than the turf they are standing on, and day after day they gather together to square up to one another like bar-room brawlers, strutting about in menacing pose in the hope that over the years they will eventually secure a prestigious place at the centre of the arena. Once there they can enjoy no-strings-attached sex with the majority of the females, who then wind up doing all the chick-rearing.

Their aggressive posing is not all bluff either. Males do go for each other now and again, and as if to illustrate this a mallard that mistakenly dropped in on the lek, standing there for a second or two like a skittle surrounded by black bowling balls, was forced to beat a hasty retreat as the furious grouse turned on it.

'The good news is that counts here are steadily going up, and we're now working on expanding their range,' Phil said. 'But across the UK as a whole they remain in decline so there's still a long way to go nationally.'

To find out exactly how many black grouse live in the North Pennines, Phil uses his pointer dogs to pinpoint females with young in the autumn, while spring time means early starts and an exhausting daily race against the clock to visit all the lek sites at dawn before the males disperse.

The display we were watching was rapidly drawing to a close, and with rankings reaffirmed and an agreement to reconvene 'same time, same place' the following day, the males began heading off to feed. As did we, with Phil dropping me off at my guest house in time for breakfast opposite the silent couple from the evening before. I was bursting with enthusiasm about what I had just seen and desperate to tell someone, but looking at them eating their toast without exchanging a word

I decided to spare them. They were obviously having enough fun.

There can be few more bizarre experiences of bird-watching than a game drive without any guns.

It was a sunny October afternoon in Hertfordshire, and a light breeze played through the narrow band of trees in front of me. To my right and left, spread out in a line, were dozens of people standing still amid the flowering weeds at the edge of a wide ploughed field on a farm near Royston. Many were dressed in tweed jackets and wearing ties, or in suits with wellington boots on. No one said a word, and all eyes were turned upwards towards the top of the canopy. Beyond the screen of trees barking dogs could be heard, whistles and men shouting, and through gaps in the foliage the bare earth of a neighbouring field was visible, as were fleeting glimpses of black labradors running and beaters waving bright flags. A hare trapped between the approaching commotion and the silent line of spectators ran past me trying to find refuge in the scrub, and then I heard the sound we had been waiting for: a whirring of wings and a call much like a window swinging open on a rusty hinge: *crrrrrrreak*, and right over our heads two grey partridges that had been flushed up and over the tree line flew off at speed down the field behind us and into a line of cover. And then more came, high and fast in a small group, called a covey, and more still as the beaters neared. But no shotguns were raised. No birds tumbled to earth with a puff of feathers drifting down behind them. And when the last of the partridges passed overhead, light orange head and chestnut tail visible as it glided close to us on bowed wings, it wasn't met by a volley of gunfire but a ripple of applause.

'I could have bagged a couple of brace at my peg,' a chap in a tweed cap joked as we made our way back to the coaches.

He looked like he could well have done. But, just like the black grouse, there simply aren't enough grey partridges left to spare any more, except on carefully managed farms such as the one we were visiting.

To save driving around England looking at pear trees in the vague hope of spotting a partridge, I had gone 'undercover' and disguised myself as a normal person to attend a special Game and Wildlife Conservation Trust conference on the species, which included the 'fly-past'. Sitting through hours of speeches and debate seems a hefty price to pay to see a grey bird, but this is no ordinary grey bird. Such is its popularity that the conference held in its honour, organized by the trust which has a grey partridge for its logo, was packed, with a diversity of delegates that included everyone from landowners, gamekeepers and research scientists to conservationists and undercover birdwatchers. One common cause united them, apart from the delicious free lunch, and that was a shared love of profiteroles . . . I mean, partridges.

The grey partridge is a plump-bodied ground-dweller – never ever found in pear trees – that has made its home on our arable farms. Unlike introduced red-legged, or 'french', partridges, the more subtly patterned greys are a native species, often referred to with affection as 'Englishmen', and one thing they are good at is laying eggs. Their clutches number in the mid-teens, and in a perfect world a female could expect to raise thirty to forty young during her short life. Supposing half of her chicks were female, then their young would add hundreds more partridges to the population, and if my maths is right we would eventually become completely overrun with partridges and be forced to declare a state of emergency and flee to the mountains to escape them. But something is keeping this from happening, and it's not the army. Instead of adding to their numbers year on year, the population has slipped by a massive 85 per cent since the 1970s. And we now know why.

Of all our birds the grey partridge is reckoned to be the one that has been studied the most, and unravelling the story of its decline has shed light on problems faced by a host of other farmland birds as agriculture has intensified. In short, it needs cover in which to nest and hide, enough weeds to support insects on which chicks feed during the summer, and enough seeds and greenery titbits to eat in the winter. It doesn't sound like a lot to ask. Remove one of those fundamentals through excessive use of sprays or the plough, however, and the population grinds to a halt and starts going into reverse. Which is what happened. And having lots of predators like foxes and crows about hasn't helped matters either.

So couldn't we just plug the gap and get them off the Red List by rearing loads of grey partridges, like we do with pheasants, and releasing them into the wild? Wouldn't that sort it? Well, it seems not. Apparently captive-bred birds are so devoid of survival skills that restocking attempts generally end in fat foxes and failure. Instead habitat is the key – as it is with so many species in trouble – and the heartening news is that farmers are now being paid to provide strips of good ground for wild grey partridges through direct subsidies and environmental grants. It was farming practices that first helped them prosper, and later killed them off, and it is new farming practices that could bring them back.

This much I learnt during my day at the conference, until my false moustache began to slip in the middle of a tea break and I was forced to make my excuses, grab a pocketful of profiteroles and leave. 'Sorry, must dash, my estate can't run itself, you know, what with all the, er, gun-type people and shooty dogs and plough tractors and thingys . . .'

Autumn had become an exhausting rush from one place to another and I was beginning to realize, with twelve Red List species seen so far, just how difficult it was going to be to achieve the goal I had set myself, given that there was no sign of the pace slowing and there was so much else to consider – such as turning up to work now and again, putting out the rubbish, walking the dog every day, and asking my wife and children how they were once a week.

So I decided to give up.

And then, as it was the weekend and I had already walked the dog, sorted the rubbish and asked my family how they were (fine, as it happens), I decided that abandoning my quest having come so far would be madness, and that the rational course of action was to get in my car and drive 330 miles to Leighton Moss in Lancashire. What could be saner than that? After all, I had a date with a peanut feeder, and a bird that I had to catch in the act of sneezing.

In 1897 two German ornithologists were looking through trays of small bird skins at the British Museum when they spotted two that appeared to have been wrongly labelled. The slight plumage differences, subtle enough to have been overlooked before, were enough to distinguish the birds as distinct species: the marsh tit and the scarcer willow tit. Of course it is one thing to tell them apart on a museum workbench, but when they are flitting around in a tree it is quite another matter. They are virtually identical: small and plain brown with light underparts, pale cheeks and black caps. Added to that, confusion over their identities spilled over into confusion over their names, as the marsh tit prefers dry woodlands while the willow tit favours trees and scrub in damp areas. So in essence what you are faced with is twins who have swapped names, and as they are on the Red List I needed to see both – and know which I was looking at.

I had found out that marsh tits were resident in a wooded area near the entrance to Leighton Moss, a large reedbed reserve close to Morecambe Bay, and when I called in advance I was told that they were currently visiting the bird feeders.

'Are you sure they're marsh tits and not something else?' I asked.

'Yes, marsh tits,' the lady on the phone confirmed.

'Definitely?'

'That's right.'

'No doubt about it?'

'No,' she sighed. 'Um, listen I'm sorry but I've got some visitors to attend to . . .'

'So you're sure?'

'Yes, as I said . . .'

'Great. Right, keep the feeders topped up – I'll be there in about six hours . . .'

Ever since the UK's felled forest cover hit a low point at the beginning of the last century, we have been planting more and more trees – and not just commercial blocks of conifers – so you might assume that woodland birds would be doing fine. Yet while some are indeed thriving (like blue tits, great tits and robins), others, such as marsh tits and willow tits, are quietly disappearing and it is not entirely clear why. Woodland is complicated. It supports a huge density and variety of species, and unpicking the myriad inter-relationships to make sense of exactly what is happening behind the green curtain has proven far from easy. Overgrazing of undergrowth by deer may be having an impact on some birds, while the predations of grey squirrels may be affecting others; and then there is competition between species to consider; and a shortage of nest sites; and forestry management practices; and . . . the list goes on. But whatever the causes, the fact is that our woodland bird populations have tumbled by a fifth since 1970, and while the overall decline has now levelled out, numbers of marsh tits and willow tits have kept on falling, which is a shame as, apart from anything, they are cute little birds. In fact, were the government to refine its key targets and indicators regarding wild bird populations and introduce an 'index of cuteness' then these two would surely be on it and getting more of the attention they deserve.

When I arrived at Leighton Moss, screeching to a halt in the car park in a cloud of dust, I was so keen to see a marsh tit that I ran to the visitor centre and arrived breathless at the counter, asking for directions to the bird feeders with the kind of desperation in my voice that could have been interpreted as extreme hunger.

A screen had been put up in front of the feeders so it was possible to observe the live entertainment, and I sat down and waited, watching chaffinches, great tits, pheasants, rabbits and rats gorging themselves on the free food, doubtless thinking to themselves: 'Here we are putting on a great show, and all we get paid is peanuts.' And I waited . . . and waited . . . but still the star act failed to arrive. And then, just when I was considering having a wander and coming back later, a small black-capped tit appeared from the dense foliage of a tree opposite and landed on one of the hangers. It didn't have a short white stripe on the back of its head, so I knew it wasn't a common coal tit – making it a marsh tit. Excellent! Unless, of course it was a willow tit that just happened to have dropped by . . . I was stumped. It did have a glossy cap, clean white cheeks, uniform wing colouring and a neat little black bib under its bill, which all pointed to it being a marsh tit rather than the slightly untidier-looking willow tit, but I didn't feel confident enough to claim it with any certainty. And then it sneezed, or rather gave a call which sounded like *pit-chew!* before grabbing a nut and flying off. And that sound, unique to the marsh tit, is without doubt the best way to tell them apart.

That brief encounter was not all my trip to Leighton Moss had to offer. Following one of the two main footpaths I found myself at the Lower Hide positioned beside a large expanse of water on the far side of the reserve. I lifted the latch and entered to find the dozen or so people inside had turned to face me and were grinning madly. Before I was able to back out and run for it, one of them pointed towards the window in front of them and whispered loudly: 'Look! Just in front of the hide!' And another who could hardly contain their excitement added: 'A bittern! Look!'

And there it was, slowly making its way across a narrow stretch of ground in the sunlight less than 15 feet from the hide: one of Britain's rarest and most elusive birds, and among the trickiest of the Red List species I hoped to see. Oblivious to our presence it stalked slowly across the grass at the water's edge, mottled buff-brown body tapering to the point of its dagger-like bill, and snatched a dragonfly from a plant before making its way into a dense thicket of reeds to our left and disappearing from view.

You could birdwatch for a lifetime and never dream of finding yourself anywhere near as close as we were to this shy and highly camouflaged marshland hunter, and had I arrived five minutes later I would have missed it. More than that, I would have missed out on something I was beginning to appreciate about birdwatching: just how much it can be about sharing the experience. Those in the hide before me were quite obviously delighted that someone, anyone, had arrived in time for them to proudly point out such a special sighting.

Now if you were in charge of marketing birds and looking for a species to champion the conservation cause, you probably wouldn't pick one that determinedly shuns publicity, has a slightly depressed look about it, spends its life hidden away in impenetrable waterside vegetation and is best known for standing completely still amid reed stems with its beak pointing straight upwards to avoid detection. Yet, against the odds, the bittern, a large skulking member of the heron family that doesn't want to be seen – and seldom is – has managed to attract fame and fortune and become something of a wetland icon. It is a disappearing act that we want to see more of.

To lose a species once might be regarded as a misfortune – to lose it twice looks like carelessness. And that is what nearly happened with the bittern. Hunting and the draining of wetlands meant that by the late 1800s the deep foghorn sound of 'booming' territorial males could no longer be heard drifting over our reedbeds. But as luck would have it, twenty-five years later it made an unexpected comeback, recolonizing from Europe and gradually spreading until eighty booming males could be heard – the silent females being almost impossible to detect. Then things took a turn for the worse as reedbeds dried out, starving this fish-eater of food, while pollution, development and cold winters added to its woes. By 1997 only eleven males were counted. The bittern faced its second extinction in Britain.

Once researchers had worked out why and what needed to be done, two major schemes to save the reluctant celebrity followed, costing more than £6 million in total and leading to the creation and improvement of swathes of marsh habitat across England.

That is an awful lot of cash. Can any bird be worth that much?

Sarah Alsbury, project manager of the second tranche of work, told me that in terms of boosting biodiversity it could actually be considered value for money. 'Bittern-friendly reedbeds are attractive to a wide range of other species as well. Water voles, freshwater fish, rare moths and numerous birds have all benefited, as well as human visitors who enjoy the diversity of wildlife the reserves offer, so it has been well worth it.'

While it may be boom time once again for bitterns, with the number of recorded males now topping seventy-five, for many birdwatchers these enigmatic gourds-on-legs remain as abstract as atoms: you're told they're there, but you just can't see them. I knew just how lucky I had been to get such a good view. But not all birds were proving so obliging . . .

They say that the world makes way for people who know where they're going. I'm glad to say the opposite is also the case: people go out of their way to help those who appear lost.

I was back at the far tip of Cornwall and wandering around with no sense of direction. The sign at Land's End showed it was 3147 miles to New York and 874 to

John O'Groats, but there was no arrow pointing the way that read: 'Wryneck: 200 yards'.

There was one in the area . . . still! And after five weeks of searching I hadn't seen one . . . still! But unlike the grey partridge demonstration, no fly-past had been arranged – only a flock of geese which gave me the 'V' sign. So I resorted to asking anyone wearing binoculars if they had any information, and while everyone was more than keen to talk they were short on answers.

'Oh yes, I've seen one along the cycle path.'

'Brilliant! Where exactly?'

'Just by that stone wall over there.'

'Really? What time?'

'Oh, I can't remember. It was a couple of years ago.'

There were plenty of twitchers about chasing rarities, constantly checking their pagers and looking as if they always needed to be somewhere else, and I stopped near a farm where a couple were peering intently through their telescopes at something in the distance. I sauntered over in the hope they had found what I was after. Instead they told me they had spotted a North American bird called a buff-breasted sandpiper. Blown off course on migration, it should have been sunning itself in South America rather than kicking around in a muddy field in Cornwall.

'It's next to the golden plover,' the woman said, letting me use her telescope.

'Wow! A golden plover!' I enthused, taking a look. It was the British species that got me excited. The American rarity was completely wasted on me. Still, anything that was as lost as I felt right then deserved a look, and it was nice to know that unlike so many New World vagrants this strong flying wader at least stood an outside chance of making it home.

'I'm trying to find a wryneck,' I sighed, and they nodded sympathetically, and made a few helpful suggestions.

I got the feeling that unless I was given an exact location, with a search area less than a metre square, I could end up wandering the coasts of Cornwall for the rest of my life in the hope of stumbling across one. I had visions of myself sleeping rough with other itinerant wryneck hunters, foraging for food in the bushes, drinking moonshine, tattooing images of the bird deity on my weather-beaten skin and engaging in ritual human sacrifice. Yes, I needed to see one, and fast.

Fortunately, I finally came across someone who had been keeping tabs on local bird sightings of interest and who was able to give me precise directions to a place just up the road called the Nanjizal Valley.

The valley leads from farmland down to the sea, and on one side overlooking a small cove is a house and garden. The wryneck, I was told, had been seen on the garden wall and also below on the footpath that morning, so was unlikely to have gone far.

I arrived at 1pm and stationed myself slightly up the hill with a view of both spots, and waited, remembering the advice I had been given about taking my time. There were two other birdwatchers in the valley also looking for it, but they soon gave up. I wasn't going anywhere. This, I decided, was my final attempt to see the bird, and I was determined to sit it out until I did.

An hour later, after nothing had stirred, I was driven to go on the pish. Unlikely as it sounds, 'pishing' is a genuine tactic employed by desperate birdwatchers. It involves repeatedly making a 'pish' sound that vaguely resembles some kind of avian alarm call and, so I had read, this can lure little birds out of hiding to see what the commotion is. Not only was this faintly ridiculous tactic probably futile with wryneck, but having never heard anyone actually doing it I'm sure I was getting it wrong. Still, there was no one around, so I made my way down the path hissing 'Pish! pish! pish!' like I had an extreme strain of hayfever. A blackbird hopped out from under a bush in front of me and gave me a look as though I was a complete plonker. Even animals can make you feel embarrassed sometimes, like when you're peeing in a field and cows start watching. So a few pishes later, recognizing that it wasn't working, I gave up trying to talk to the birds and sat back down in a patch of sunshine. I had been up since dawn and promptly dozed off, dreaming that a multitude of wrynecks alighted around me while I slept, snuggling up in the warmth of my crossed arms and the folds of my clothing.

When I woke up it was 3pm. I continued my vigil, looking first at the garden wall and then at the path below, and then at the garden wall again, and then at the path, and then at a line of fencing just to make things interesting, and then back at the garden wall, and then I realized something: I would never see a wryneck. If the species existed at all and I was not the hapless victim of some elaborate ornithological prank, then it did so to teach me how to birdwatch. In the weeks I had spent trying to find one I had learnt so much. It had taken me to places I would never have visited, introduced me to birdwatchers I would never have met, and shown me birds I might never have seen: buff-breasted sandpiper, chough, black-tailed godwit . . . Above all it had taught me how to look, and how to enjoy simply being alone in the countryside. In many ways, I thought, it would be a shame if I ever did see one.

And at that precise moment I did.

It was not a good sighting, but it was enough: a fleeting glimpse on top of the garden wall of a small bird hopping across a flat stone, with pointed head and body held horizontal. My heart leapt. It was exactly the right shape and I grabbed at my binoculars, desperately panning left and right and spinning the focus wheel until I had it in view, a precious split second in which I was able to make out a faint eye stripe, like a bandit mask, before it flew down off the wall and disappeared. It was over all too soon. I was elated, and also strangely disappointed. So, while well aware that the elusive bird was perfectly able to spend the rest of the day feeding out of sight, I walked up the path to get a better view of the wall in the hope it might show itself again. Half an hour passed without anything, and then out of the corner of my eye I spotted a grey-backed sparrow-sized bird flying down from the garden across an expanse of bracken to the path from where I had come. Doubling back I scanned the track and beneath a slight overhang where the soil had crumbled away I saw movement and lifted my binoculars to get a clear sighting. It was the wryneck, feeding on ants without a care in the world. I even had time to set up the telescope I had been lent and got a really decent look at its intricate markings and the dark mark down its back as it went about its business. It was 5.30pm. I never imagined I was capable of spending four and a half hours alone in a valley looking for a bird – or anything come to that – but it had been worth it, and I was filled with relief and a real sense of triumph. This was my wryneck, all mine.

When it flew off and I walked back up to my car I thought: Shall I? And then: Why not! I got out my mobile and phoned the Rare Bird Alert service. A few minutes later my mobile bleeped as a new message arrived, and I had the satisfaction after so much frustration of finally reading a text that I didn't need to chase up – my own. *03:10:2007. 17.47. Cornwall, Wryneck. 1.5mls SE of Land's End, west of Polgigga on S. side of Nanjizal Valley along track to bay, on seaward-facing wall by main house before flying to track below.* There hadn't been enough room to add: *Thanks must go to everyone involved for their help, the man who gave me directions, my friends and family for being so patient, my parents, the workmen who built the A30, all those unsung heroes who have strived so hard behind the scenes and whose names escape me, but most of all you, the dear text reader, for without you none of this would have been possible* . . . etc, etc.

CHAPTER SEVEN

WHEN IT COMES TO BIRDS IT IS IMPOSSIBLE TO KNOW everything and see everything. Not only is there an exhausting variety of species out there for the birdwatcher to spot, but there are endless ways in which they can be seen. You may have been lucky enough to have encountered an osprey, but have you witnessed one snatching a trout from the surface of a lake? Or a cuckoo stealing into another bird's nest to lay an egg? Or a dipper feeding underwater? Or a honey buzzard tearing open a bees' nest? Or swifts mating on the wing? No one has seen it all. And it is beyond anyone to remember more than a tiny fraction of all that is known given that our fact-laden species are subject to such biological, geographical, behavioural, statistical, political, visual, ecological and cultural scrutiny that you could fill libraries with everything that has been written about them. But while no one can know it all, conversely, no one knows nothing about birds. We're all bumping along somewhere in between, looking and learning together, which is a comforting thought.

Well, it would be comforting, but I was reaching the stage where I knew enough to know how little I knew, and had seen enough to recognize just how much there is to see, and I was beginning to feel a little daunted by the amount of looking and learning that lay ahead of me. I had read a few bird books – well, mostly looked at the pictures – and identified a few species in the field without the need for a second opinion. So how else could I improve my birdwatching skills?

Given that my target was forty species, perhaps Tom Gullick wasn't the best person to phone at his home in Spain for advice. Like many birdwatchers he keeps a list of all the birds he has seen. Except that he is a 'world lister', one of a select band with sufficient time and money who have amassed staggering tallies on their travels. More than that, he is the world's number one. He has seen more varieties of birds on earth than anyone else – an astounding total that tops 8,700. But even though this British-born birder is still going strong at seventy-seven, driven by what he describes as 'a natural instinct to hunt and collect', he doesn't expect to see everything. The global total of just under 10,000 is constantly changing as identification techniques become more refined and DNA analysis enables local races of bird to be reclassified as distinct species. Added to that, a number of countries are now too dangerous to visit, some islands are so remote it would take an age to tour them in search of endemic species, and many birds are becoming scarcer.

'If you get to see about 90 per cent of all the birds there are then you really can't hope for much more. But how many I eventually see . . . well that all depends on how long I live,' he said. 'The thrill is in the finding, for yourself or for others, and no new bird is ever boring. Probably the highlight for me was sitting in the rainforest on an island in the Gulf of Guinea staring at a bird that was believed to be extinct – the Sao Tomé grosbeak. That was a special moment.'

So, I wondered, what basic tips could he give me?

'The key is the four Ps,' he said. 'Planning, patience, persistence, and pounds if you're going to be travelling.'

A certain bird beginning with 'w' had taught me all about patience and persistence, and certainly cost me a few pounds, but what about planning?

'When starting out people need to know what they are likely to see when they go somewhere,' he said, 'and prepare by not only looking in books, but also listening to tapes of the birds.'

Bother. Everywhere I turned experts were recommending learning bird sounds as a useful identification tool. It had certainly helped with the marsh tit and I knew they were all probably right, but, to be honest, I dreaded it. I had walked through woods filled with song and it baffled me how anyone could make sense of all the peeping, trilling, chirping and cheeping, which sounded to me like someone had run through an electrical store pressing the 'on' buttons for all the electric toothbrushes, house alarm keypads, computer games and alarm clocks. Not only were there all the elaborate songs to remember, but also the everyday communication calls to consider – and a chaffinch has over a dozen of those for starters.

The root cause of the auditory conundrums is an organ called a syrinx, a double-sided arrangement of membranes and muscles at the bottom of a songbird's windpipe – as opposed to our larynx at the top. This is capable of producing complex layers of sound that can be delivered at speeds too rapid for us to decipher and in patterns too intricate for us to fully describe. As a result, bird-guide authors have been forced to create their own language of sound, tapping out interpretations that look as if someone has lent an elbow against the keyboard: *tchrrrr, djarrrrrr, trk-tk-tk-tk, pseeeeep, rak-aaaaak* . . . While a useful reference, and often surprisingly accurate, there is no way you can learn the sounds from books even if you regularly repeat them out loud, which I did try one evening, 'Tchrrrr! Tchrrrr! Tchrrrr!', until my wife, knowing that I was also trying to get to grips with birds' scientific names, suggested with a smile that I become familiar with another Latin term: *Decree nisi*.

As books were not the answer, there was nothing for it but to buy birdsong CDs and begin by focusing on species one was as likely to hear as see: like owls, and secretive woodland species, and dawn chorus singers you can't be bothered to get out of bed to look at. Fortunately, as winter was drawing near most of the birds had shut up for the year, so I could revise in peace in preparation for the spring ahead. I tend to learn quickly and forget quickly, but incredibly, after days of repetition, I actually began to remember a few of the dozens of extracts, helped by the fact that they were arranged in alphabetical order. Should a peregrine, pied wagtail and puffin all land outside my bedroom window in that order and launch into their vocal renditions I'll be laughing.

My children tested me now and again, and I'd rather been hoping that with the impressive ability of their omega-3-soaked brains to absorb information, they might want to join in. But it was not to be. My eldest daughter had threatened to call Childline if I took her on any more walks that required the wearing of binoculars, while my youngest had developed a heartening interest in all the sciences except ornithology, even declaring one night: 'When I go to university I want to take chemicals!'

'Er, I think you mean chemistry,' my wife had quickly corrected her before I launched into a lecture.

Ah yes, the sweet things children mistakenly say. Like 'runny babbit' for 'bunny rabbit', 'dedicated coconut' instead of 'desiccated coconut', and 'no' when they mean 'of course, Father'.

I tried infectious enthusiasm to win them over to the joys of birdwatching: 'Wow! Look at that song thrush!'

'What, Dad, you mean the meadow pipit? Boring.'

'Er, is it a meadow pipit? Oh, yes, I think you're right.'

And I tried reverse psychology: 'God, aren't birds dull? Let's not go out and see any!'

But no one was falling for that.

Then I tried patronizing them into submission: 'When I was your age I used to spend hours outside in the fresh air on my own exploring the natural world.'

'Why, didn't you have any friends?'

Like most children, they wanted their wildlife to be dangerous and exciting, or cuddly and endearing, and few birds qualify for either category when pitted against such stars as lions and crocodiles and baby pandas. However, my youngest did agree to come with me on a trip one Saturday after I promised her flamingos.

Slimbridge Wetland Centre in Gloucestershire is the headquarters of the Wildfowl and Wetlands Trust. It is part zoo, housing the world's largest collection of swans, geese and ducks, and part nature reserve, and this mix of both the tame and the wild in one place has made it a popular attraction – 'bringing people and wildlife together for the benefit of both' in the words of founder Sir Peter Scott. On top of that it is the only place on earth where you can see all six species of flamingo.

Flamingos are not on our UK Red List – or pink list even – but, like sticks of candy floss, they were enticing enough to buy my youngest daughter's company for the afternoon. I was planning to see a far less colourful bird on our return journey, but in the meantime Slimbridge provided a welcome diversion, as well as the chance to get a flavour of an added extra Britain has to offer birdwatchers in the winter after the passage migrants have tailed off and the summer visitors have departed:

big flocks. From parties of small birds in our woodlands and gatherings of finches and thrushes in our fields to vast congregations of waders and wildfowl at our watersides, winter is a season of coming together, of safety in numbers and a shared need to find food. And on the afternoon in November that we visited the reserve beside the River Severn there was certainly plenty about. Away from the captive bird enclosures and the flamingos, the stretches of open water and wet pasture were crammed with all manner of duckery, from wigeon, pintail and teal to shoveler, shelduck and pochard, and there were notable long-distance travellers out in force including white-fronted geese and much beloved Bewick's swans. The smallest and rarest of our three swans, Bewick's have been faithfully undertaking a 2,600-mile pilgrimage from the tundra of northern Russia to winter at Slimbridge ever since first appearing two years after the reserve opened in 1946. Not only do these elegant visitors escape the clutches of an Arctic winter, but they also get fed, and in full view of the heated Peng Observatory. They are close enough for viewers to be able to tell one from another by their individual yellow and black beak markings, and to read their leg ring numbers: white H61, yellow 407, white BC1 – I think I also spotted one which read H5N1, though that could have been my paranoia about bird flu.

They say that if you provide the right habitat, the birds will come. The same applies to people. Lay on free parking and cars start arriving. Add an accessible, modern visitor centre with a shop and dining hall and queues start forming. Throw in some friendly swans, geese and eye-catching exotic species and . . . well, any organization that can boast over one million visitors a year to its nine wetland centres must be doing something right. On the back of this public support the Wildfowl and Wetlands Trust carries out conservation work at home and abroad and campaigns to conserve the world's wetlands, half of which have been lost over the last century.

It struck me that with the tame ducks you can hand-feed on one side and the hides to view wild birds on the other, Slimbridge illustrates a fundamental dichotomy in our relationship with wildlife: the desire to reach out and touch, and the recognition we need to leave well alone. But why do we want to get close? Why do we have such a strong inclination to befriend? A bird is never going to give us a hug! And yet there is some part of us that wants to make a pet of everything, a yearning for love that unfurls our bread-filled hand in friendship. Conversely there is a wish to see nature at a distance free from our stifling embrace. We also like our wildlife wild. If on safari all the animals in the Serengeti ran up to say hello we would feel cheated. Then again supposing everything ran away out of view we would want our money back. If we have provided for nature we demand to see it, and on our terms.

All of this presents a difficult balancing act for those who act as guardians of our flora and fauna. You can't tantalize TV audiences with breathtaking images of the wonders of the natural world, then tell everyone it's all strictly off-limits. On the one hand you need to keep the enthusiastic crowds back, and on the other people are more likely to support conservation appeals if they have a chance of actually encountering the animals they are paying to help.

Sadly the compromise that results can mean an overly regulated experience, a look-but-don't-touch-keep-to-the-marked-paths-please-wash-your-hands-if-you-have-come-into-contact-with-anything-living approach. And I couldn't help but think as I sat in one of the Slimbridge hides peering at the wildfowl feeding on the open ground, wouldn't it be great to burst out of the hide with my daughter and charge down towards the water's edge with arms spread wide scattering the flocks of birds so that they wheeled and circled above us, before returning flushed and breathless to the hide, opening the door and declaring to the rows of scowling birdwatchers inside: 'Well, that was fun!'

All of which reminded me that if I did indeed want to witness a sky filled with masses of swirling birds we had to leave and get to the Somerset Levels in time for sunset.

After a dash down the M5 we arrived at the Shapwick Heath National Nature Reserve to find the road so filled with cars that we were forced to park a good distance from the entrance and walk as fast as we could. Bear in mind that this was a minor road next to an area of marsh miles from the nearest town, and it was Saturday evening in mid-November. What on earth would bring so many people out?

The light was fading and the clear sky beginning to colour as we finally strode through the entrance gate and onto the straight main path which ran beside a water channel and between stretches of reedbed into the reserve. My daughter took the lead as we picked up the pace. There were people ahead of us – some in groups, some with binoculars – all walking in the same direction, and there were people behind us, funnelling from the road into the reserve. It reminded me of fireworks night, crowds wrapped in coats and scarves gathering at dusk. But while the air was charged with a similar sense of anticipation, there were no vendors selling glow sticks or charity collectors rattling buckets – and not even the faintest whiff of fried food.

We didn't know how far we needed to walk, but people in front of us had stopped and others were slowing and I overheard someone saying: 'Apparently this is where they came in yesterday.'

So we took our place in the line of people scattered along the path.

'Do you think it's this busy every night?' a woman nearby asked the man standing next to her.

'I reckon it's just because it was on TV this week,' he replied. '*Autumnwatch*, somebody said.'

Everyone was looking towards the horizon. It was like some kind of UFO convention field trip. But it wasn't points of light we were looking for, it was moving flecks of black.

'There they are!' my daughter said excitedly. And in the distance a cloud of dots could be seen heading towards us above the distant treetops. Starlings. Thousands upon thousands of them coming in to roost.

As winter flocks go, evening congregations of starlings

are among the most remarkable. Huge numbers, swollen by birds from Europe to reach millions on occasion, assemble from miles around to spend a noisy night together, and Shapwick Heath is one of the best places in Britain to witness the spectacle. What makes it so special is not just the weight of numbers, the flying tonnage of birds, but the aerial displays they put on as they twist and turn in tight formation like swirls of smoke in the evening sky.

The first group of starlings tracked to our left, headed over the path without much in the way of mass acrobatics, and then landed in the reeds out of view. And as a second wave flooded in people moved slightly further along the path to get closer to the roost site, as if wanting to be immersed in the flock as it touched down.

'Wow!' my daughter grinned, as the birds came in low over us.

More and more starlings arrived, some in small groups, others in pulsing ribbons that stretched and contracted like amoebic organisms before settling amid the restless throng in the reedbed. It was impossible to estimate the numbers, but it took at least half an hour for them all to arrive, draining from the sky until there were none left. Well, just one. After the show had drawn to a close and we were walking back to the car I spotted a solo starling flying over us that had obviously lost track of the time.

Given how many there were, you wouldn't imagine starlings were in any kind of trouble. But, much like house sparrows, this widespread and adaptable species has suffered a significant enough decline to get onto our Red List. Lose half of our ospreys and there would be an outcry; shed a few million starlings – we've lost two-thirds of the population since the 1970s – and it hardly warrants a mention. The fact of the matter is that starlings have few friends. Their greedy antics make them unpopular as garden visitors, their appetite for soft fruit crops and cereal grains and anything else going has put them in the bad books of farmers, and they are despised in towns and cities for their noisy and messy communal roosts – incurring the wrath of Parliament back in 1949 after stopping Big Ben by sleeping on the clock hands.

But there is little denying that despite voracious appetites and jerky, pointy, busy natures, they are attractive birds. In the spring their plumage loses its winter peppering of white dots and becomes dark and glossy with an iridescent sheen of purple and green, while their bills turn yellow. On top of that their clicking, wheezing, rattling medley songs, embellished with mimicry, are impressive, and they have complicated sex lives which include plenty of infidelity and such sneaky cuckoo-like tactics as laying eggs in companions' nests. All in all there is lots to understand and admire.

Starlings weren't that common at all a couple of hundred years ago, but gradually spread and became so abundant that they were widely regarded as pests, and exterminated in their thousands. Just as with house sparrows the killing made no difference. Instead it is thought that agricultural changes have succeeded where guns previously failed, particularly the loss or intensive management of pasture where the birds often worked in our interests by gorging on nuisance invertebrates. The adults may be pumping out enough eggs and raising enough young, but the juveniles that leave home simply aren't surviving in sufficient numbers, and the number of big roosts is dwindling. While at one time people were paid to get rid of them, the population slide has been so dramatic that it is now illegal to kill starlings.

Not everyone would want them all back in the same numbers, even if it were possible to engineer. But the decline of starlings does highlight changes in our countryside that may be more significant than the loss of rare and fussy species living on the edge of their range in Britain. As one conservationist told me: 'We ignore the story of common species in decline at our peril.'

The fact that the Americans have plenty of starlings to spare tells another tale. The world is littered with animals and plants that have been introduced to other countries either by accident or intention, disrupting local ecosystems and in many cases pushing native species into extinction. Rabbits and rats, hares and honeybees, toads and trout, ducks and deer . . . the list goes on and on. If you had to put everything back in its rightful place before man started moving species around it would take a lifetime of research just to draw up your removals list. As for the task of getting our starlings back in their box, forget it. They are now firmly established in New Zealand and Australia, and from a batch of a few dozen brought over to North America in the late 1800s and released in Central Park they have spread to pest proportions, now numbering several hundred million.

Should we ever need a few more over here I'm sure the American farmers would be happy to oblige.

The artist Raymond Harris-Ching, whose illustrations in the *Reader's Digest Book of British Birds* helped inspire my original interest in birds as a boy on the Isle of Eigg, lives just a few miles over the border from the Somerset starling roost, and later that month I was lucky enough to get the chance to meet him.

Given the name I half expected a wizened old Chinese man with a drooping grey moustache to answer the door of the impressive historic town house when I called. Instead a robust New Zealander in his late sixties dressed in a white linen suit with a handkerchief in the top pocket and blue braces greeted me and took me through to the front room which overlooked a secluded garden and church beyond.

Despite having no artistic family background – his father was a train driver and his mother in the Salvation Army – Ray Ching, as he is more commonly known, discovered he had a talent for drawing at an early age, which later developed into a passion for painting birds.

'I was motivated in the beginning not by an interest in birds or birdwatching, but I had a desperate desire to own stuffed birds,' he said. 'I asked a local museum if they would lend me them and it was, for a time, as good as owning them. In the act of drawing and painting them I possessed them.'

His abilities were such that after early exhibitions in New Zealand he was invited to England by publishers interested in compiling a book of his own work. But that idea was put on hold when Reader's Digest realized he was just the kind of artist they had been desperately seeking to illustrate a book on British birds.

'They had been unsuccessful in finding someone despite looking at as many as a hundred possible illustrators and, as I understand it, they weren't far off giving up,' he said. 'In the end they were considering getting six or so artists to do the book spread over a couple of years. I agreed to do them all myself, all 240-odd plates, and in ten months.'

Given the detail in every picture it was a monumental achievement.

'At some points they were coming out at the rate of two a day,' he said. 'By the end I was a physical wreck, and I had spent my advance and was flat broke.'

'The starling is one of my favourites,' I said, opening an edition I had brought with me. 'And the great black-backed gull with all the aggression in its expression, and the mistle thrush with its defiant pose, and then there's the focus on the face of the sparrowhawk, and the cirl bunting singing and . . . how did you get their natural qualities so right?'

'Fluke,' he said, straight-faced. 'Not only was I no ornithologist, but when I arrived in Britain and began work on the book I hadn't even seen a blue tit!'

I was stunned. I had somehow imagined he had travelled the country watching birds hour after hour, diligently sketching in the field, noting the alertness in the eye of a heron about to strike, the strained pose of a cuckoo projecting its song . . . Instead he had completed the book without so much as picking up a pair of binoculars.

'I did my absolute best, but in a haze of ignorance that is really quite alarming looking back on it,' he said. 'A couple of times a week boxes of bird skins from museums would arrive at my house in Blackheath. I would unpack them and wonder at the beauty without necessarily knowing what they were. Once I had established the species I would draw them, paint them, parcel them up and mail them back.'

He reached into a drawer and pulled out some papers – among them the original life-sized drawings for a great black-backed gull and a woodpigeon from which he had painted the final plates in gouache. And among the papers were notes from expert ornithologist and artist Robert Gillmor who, along with the many books he read, helped ensure accuracy.

'He gave me feedback from which I could make alterations,' he said. 'But when he told me that I had painted the water rail with two left feet I said: "Jesus, just tell me the important things, we don't have time for details!"'

The artist told me that despite the success of the book he drew a clear line between that one-off detour into illustration and his ongoing life's work. Much as I attempted to stick the two disciplines together – arguing that the book's illustrations were artistic – he determinedly prised them apart.

'I was a painter before the book and I'm a painter now,' he said. 'The Reader's Digest illustrations are a terribly small part of my output.'

So did he enjoy birds outside the artist's studio?

His eyes lit up. 'If I was able to have a second shot at life and come back again and was of independent means I would spend the best part of it travelling the world looking at birds. I think it's the greatest pleasure of all.'

But Australia, not England, is where he does his bird-watching when he can. 'There's something that spotting a bird can deliver that you cannot get in any other way. It's a wonderful thing. People who don't birdwatch at all are missing out on a great joy.'

Now I was under the impression that drinking herbal tea made you a good person, but apparently there's more to it than that. To make a difference you have to actually do something positive – and that doesn't mean going shopping, however much we may be lulled into believing we can buy our way to a better world. Sometimes we have to make sacrifices, we have to set an example, and I was conscious that in reality I had done precious little of either. I liked to believe I was doing my bit, if only by instilling the kinds of values in my children that I had read about on the sides of the shampoos we used, such as 'respect', 'balance', 'kindness' – even though there was the danger that they might grow up joining anti-dandruff marches – but the truth was I could point to little which showed I was willing to turn talk into action. My environmental credentials needed a boost. And so I did what everyone in such circumstances should do: I volunteered for a morning's conservation work.

The winter meant a relative lull in terms of the birds

I planned to see, so I joined a woodland charity called Moor Trees for a muddy few hours on a Dartmoor farm, which was hosting an event organized as part of National Tree Week.

About twenty people had turned up, mostly environmental science students, and we were led to a sloping field, shown how to plant and stake a tree properly, then given a spade each, a bag or two of saplings and told to spread out and avoid planting in neat, regular patterns. So off I went brimming with enthusiasm and got to work. I cut away a section of grass turf about a foot or so across, then dug out the soil to about a foot deep, gently positioned a young oak tree in the centre, back-filled around its roots with earth, pressed it level with a heel, hammered in a wooden stake, fed a protective plastic collar over the tree and fastened it to the stake. I heaped a little more soil around the base and, hey presto, a new tree was added to our countryside for generations of people and wildlife to enjoy. It brought a warm glow of satisfaction on a cold day.

And then I set about the process again for an ash tree, and a birch, and another oak, and . . . I was knackered. I looked about me and everyone was happily digging away, pacing themselves a little more wisely and showing no signs of slowing. So I carried on, planting a hawthorn, a rowan, a crab apple, another oak. Off came the coat, up went the sleeves. Another oak . . . another ash, until I reached a dozen in all. It was back-breaking work, but how much better I felt for having done it. And you never know, in the future one of my trees could provide a home for woodland birds, many of whom have struggled in recent years – in particular our smallest resident woodpecker, the lesser spotted woodpecker.

The lesser spotted woodpecker has more problems on its plate than simply bearing the geeky 'lesser spotted' name tag. Its population has dropped by almost three-quarters since the 1970s – which is not only a problem for the species, but a major headache for birdwatchers as it was hard enough to see even when it was more common. There are only a couple of thousand pairs left, thinly scattered through the broadleaf woodlands of southern England and Wales, and unlike the bolder and bigger great spotted and green woodpeckers, the sparrow-sized lesser spotted woodpecker spends its life creeping about in the uppermost branches of deciduous trees, hidden away in the dense canopy. That means that the best time to see these petite black and white birds is during the winter when the trees are stripped of leaves.

They have dwindled alarmingly in the South West, but some areas still have a few, and on good advice I visited Yarner Wood, part of the East Dartmoor Woods and Heaths National Nature Reserve, arriving in the late afternoon as the hikers and dog walkers were heading home.

A track from the car park leads up through a section of birch trees, across heathland and returns through stands of old oak trees and I walked the route scanning the treetops for any sign of movement, without any luck. The light was beginning to fade, my neck and shoulders were aching from looking through binoculars at the canopy, and I didn't fancy a return journey the next day, so I quickly walked the route again, and just as before everything that could have been a lesser spotted woodpecker wasn't. I didn't want to see blue tits and great tits right then, and yet they kept flitting around in my line of sight trying their best to look woodpeckerish. I'd have time for them another day, only right then they were just confusing matters. If I had had a tannoy handy I could have broadcast an appeal for order: 'Right, can anything that isn't a lesser spotted woodpecker please assemble at one end of the wood! Thank you.'

I was forced to give up, and was heading back to the car when I saw a small bird with rounded wings crossing in undulating flight from the top of one tree to another just beside the car park. It was like a woodpecker, only smaller.

Hang on a minute!

I quickly raised my binoculars and there it was clinging to a spindly branch, a little bird with a pointed bill, black and white markings on its face and white barring across its black back and wings. I had recently heard a birdwatching adage: you'll know it when you see it – and in this case it rang true. It was a rare moment of certainty, and given how often I mistook birds referred to in identification guides as 'unmistakable' it made a refreshing change. It was a lesser spotted woodpecker – a pied-plumaged Red List species that could serve as the answer to the question: what's black and white and red all over?

Obvious as it sounds, you only ever see something for the first time once, and in that instant of recognition comes a sense of confirmation, that what you have been told is true. In the split second I had brought my binoculars into focus I knew the lesser spotted woodpecker, a bird I had long been aware of from pictures in books, was not just a rumour, it does indeed live in Britain. How could I have ever doubted it?

It flew to another branch and inspected the bark for insects, and as I shifted slightly to get a better view I could clearly make out a dull crimson patch on its head which meant it was a male. I was able to watch it for a minute more before it disappeared deeper into the wood.

A lesser spotted woodpecker, in fact a lesser spotted anything, is never going to feature in those lists one reads of 100 things to see before you die, or even 1,000 things to see before you die, or possibly even 10,000. However, it could feature on a list of things you should see before they die. That may sound a little too gloomy, but at their current rate of decline there is little that gives conservationists much cause for optimism. The bird enjoyed a brief high point in the 1970s as Dutch elm disease swept the country. Decaying trunks and boughs where beetle grubs thrive are a favourite with woodpeckers – especially when insects are in short supply in the winter – and the lesser spotted woodpecker reaped the benefits until the dead elms were either cleared away or toppled by gales. Its numbers then fell with the trees, but alarmingly they carried on falling. The gradual loss of other mature deciduous trees, the fragmentation of our woods, nest raiding by grey squirrels and competition from expanding numbers of great spotted woodpeckers are all believed to have resulted in the population of the littlest of the tribe getting smaller.

Unfortunately we are some way off understanding exactly what needs to be done, and the situation is complicated by the fact our woods are in so many public and private hands. On top of that, quick-fix solutions aren't easy when you are dealing with slow-growing trees. The dozen I planted will take years and years to become of much use to anything at all, let alone lesser spotted woodpeckers, and that is supposing they don't all get blown over because I hammered the stakes in wrong.

Much the same kinds of conservation challenges apply to the willow tit, that lookalike relative of the marsh tit I had earlier seen in Lancashire. Something has happened to the damp woodland it likes to live in and it is losing out to commoner species, so that year by year it has become extinct in more and more areas of the country. It may be that the woods of willow, alder and birch that it favours are drying out, or that increasing numbers of deer are munching all the shrubs it likes to feed in, or that other more aggressive species of tit are nicking all the best nest sites. Either way it was next on my list to track down and I was pinning my hopes on the Midlands.

The more you know, the more there is to worry about. A century ago everyone was blissfully ignorant about the existence of our willow tits at all. We now know what they are, how many there are and that over recent decades they have been haemorrhaging numbers. Only as I got into my car and headed north I began to feel wracked by doubt. I couldn't work out whether the journalist in me had been wooed by bad news. After all, the vast majority of our commoner breeding birds are doing fine. Why should I find myself driving up the M5 to see a kind of tit that looked identical to another kind of tit I had already seen, simply because a figure next to its name on a population chart showed a hefty minus sign? Why wasn't I going in search of success stories, binning the Red List, sneering 'Tough luck, losers!' and burning up the miles to see all-conquering woodpigeons, magpies and collared doves instead? The more I thought about things the more my head became filled with questions. Bird numbers are constantly changing and aren't population targets arbitrary anyway? Is more of one thing bad news if it means less of another? How do we decide where perfect mediums lie? Shouldn't we just let nature take its course? And wasn't that motorway turn-off I had just passed the one I was supposed to take . . . ?

Looking at a map of England, Sandwell Valley on the outskirts of Birmingham is one of the last places you would think to go birdwatching, especially on a damp day in December. Encircled by motorways where the blue lines of the M5, M6 and M42 intertwine with a knotted mesh of green and red A and B roads, the tiny RSPB symbol for the reserve on my atlas looked like a trapped avocet that had flown into a multicoloured spider's web. It took me an age to negotiate the tangle of roads until I finally picked up signs in a busy shopping parade to the north of the city, eventually ending up in a parking area surrounded by scrub where I double-checked the car doors were locked before walking to the visitor centre opposite. If it was bad news for a bird to wind up on our Red List, I thought, then surely things couldn't get any more depressing than ending up living here. I half expected to see contact details for the Samaritans stapled to nest boxes. And if I had been filled with uncertainties before, then arriving in the rain at such an uninspiring location did little to ease it. I couldn't help but wonder: what on earth am I doing?

Twenty-five years ago I would have got straight back into my car and driven off at speed. The former colliery site less than five miles from Birmingham city centre was at that time a sea of mud overrun by diggers hacking away at the valley floor to create a flood alleviation lake alongside the oily slick that was the River Tame, once one of the worst polluted rivers in western Europe. There would have been little wildlife about. But the river was cleaned up, and after the work was completed the scarred brown landscape gradually turned green, plants and animals colonized damp and marshy areas, the RSPB took over and a visitor centre was built on an old mining rubbish tip overlooking the newly created stretches of water.

Today it is something of an urban oasis, with 260 bird species recorded in the valley and 30,000 people visiting every year, including thousands of inner-city schoolchildren, many of whom have hardly set foot off tarmac in their lives.

'For children from urban areas seeing the water, the grass and the trees feels like visiting a real wilderness,' site manager Lee Copplestone told me. 'I remember one boy who had obviously never been out of the city in his life looking at the lake and saying: "I can see the sea!"

This reserve is so important in what it can offer them: a taste of the wild.'

The weather was so foul on the day I visited that a group outing had been cancelled and only a handful of people were about. The high-fenced access to the lakeside hide had been locked up for the day to prevent vandalism, so I followed the footpath down beside the shore. Few buildings were visible in the valley, and it began to feel a little more like a sanctuary. I noticed a snipe feeding on the edge of the reedbed and a couple of shoveler ducks with huge broad bills standing in the shallows, and spotted a group of diving ducks with long hook-tipped beaks being buffeted by the wind out on the choppy water. They were goosander. I had never seen goosander before, but in the bird books they always looked an arresting sight – especially the males with their dark green heads and red serrated bills – and here were twenty of them. They were nice birds to see. My mood began to lift. Maybe this place wasn't so bad after all.

As I made my way back up to the visitor centre something caught my eye: a flash of light red in the leafless trees ahead as bright as a rose caught on the wind and blown between the branches. It settled on a dark, wet bough and I was able to find it in my binoculars, framed between the distant electricity pylons: a male bullfinch.

A male bullfinch is an astonishing sight. When visiting the Birdfair a few months before I had found myself in a marquee devoted to overseas tours plastered with posters of gleaming tropical birds and had wondered which of our homegrown offerings could tempt birdwatchers from Costa Rica or the Amazon or Australia to visit Britain. I had decided then that you couldn't do much better than a bullfinch. Its plumage combines a blush of deep pastel pink with a wash of soft grey, shining blacks and gleaming whites, all neatly arranged as if painted by numbers. Few colours go so well with pink as light grey and black, and the bullfinch's simple palette is what makes it so handsome. No spots or streaks. No garish splashes of yellow or blue or over-ornate patterning. No need for an outlandish crest or wattles. No sense that, like the goldfinch, it has been playing with its mother's make-up. It is striking without being showy: a sophisticated pink-shirted, grey-and-black-suited gent. And the female is also a beautiful bird, with the same glossy black cap, thick short bill and clean white rump, but a warm pinkish brown chest instead. They really do look like a proper couple alongside one another, and they act like it as well, forming devoted attachments so that they are typically seen in pairs.

For such a brightly coloured finch so beloved of the Victorians as a cagebird, the bullfinch is anything but brash. It is a shy species with a soft, sad call that tends to keep out of sight, seeking cover in the woodland edges, orchards and farmland hedgerows where it is found, often being heard initially giving a whistled *peu, peu* or seen flying away with a white behind offering a clue to its identity. But even a rear-end view of a bullfinch is becoming a less and less common sight, and a dramatic population slump since the 1970s, believed to be due to agricultural intensification and the loss of hedgerow trees, has resulted in this dapper garden visitor finding its way onto the Red List. Though surprisingly for such an attractive, gentle bird, not everyone is mourning its decline.

In trying to persuade people of the importance of conserving biodiversity you can appeal to their hearts, their heads or their wallets – and some have attempted to reduce nature's benefits to monetary terms, calculating in trillions of dollars what various natural 'goods and services', such as crop pollination, are worth. The problem with evaluating the living world in terms of its economic benefit to us is that some species regarded as pests would end up in the debit column, and the bullfinch might be among them. Its appetite for tree buds when food is scarce, particularly posh varieties of apples, plums, cherries and pears, which it can speedily scissor off at a rate of thirty buds a minute, has cost orchard owners dear.

While the mathematical modelling required to translate biodiversity into dollars might be in its infancy, back in the sixteenth century they had a clear idea of how much a bullfinch was worth: 1d. That was the price on its head. It was among a selection of birds included in the Tudor Vermin Act – a list of unwelcome wildlife compiled following food shortages and famines – and was caught on perches covered in sticky birdlime or in traps and culled relentlessly, especially as more and more orchards were planted in the centuries that followed. The general licence to kill them was only withdrawn as recently as ten years ago because their numbers were plummeting without the aid of traps and guns, but they are still not popular with everybody.

As someone who does not own any commercial fruit orchards that I am aware of, I felt very fortunate to get such a good view, and all the questions I had been wrestling with on my drive to the reserve dissolved in the moment. The male bullfinch shuffling about on the branch, a plump flush of life on a dismal day, seemed to answer them all. How many bullfinches do we need? Answer: some.

Right, I hope that settles that.

And if I was worried about the journalist in me seeking bad news then I had come to the wrong place. The reserve, created from nothing amid urban sprawl, shows just what is possible, and after the lovely sighting of the bullfinch and all the other birds besides, Sandwell Valley gave me a bonus leaving gift: a willow tit that popped up in the hedge just a few yards from the visitor centre window.

The Liver Bird is not on the Red List, or any ornithology list come to that, so I couldn't count the two I saw perched on top of the Royal Liver Building overlooking the River Mersey. Apart from a few gulls they were the only birds I was able to make out through the fog as the ferry reversed away from the docks at Birkenhead. It was too cold to remain on deck, so I headed for the lounge to warm up and get some rest after the long drive up to Liverpool. Everyone was too busy eating chips, at 3pm, to have bagged all the comfy reclining seats and I settled in and pulled out a book. I could hear a baby gurgling a few rows ahead. How sweet. And then it whimpered slightly. Ah, bless . . . And then it began sniffling. Uh oh. And then like a ticking bomb smuggled on board it exploded in wails and despite the desperate efforts of its parents did not stop crying for the entire three and a half hour crossing to the Isle of Man. I should have felt some sympathy, after all I had been in the same position myself (I once cried loudly non-stop throughout a twelve-hour flight from Cape Town), but after two hours of ear-splitting howls I reached the conclusion that all couples boarding ferries, or planes or trains for that matter, ought to be frisked at security checkpoints for babies.

When the ferry came alongside at Douglas the baby finally fell asleep, everyone got up scowling and disembarked, and I drove in the dark to my town centre B&B. The mandatory two-subject small talk with the owner dispensed with (Weather. Journey. Done.), I was led to a room on the third floor. It was an old house that had been subdivided and subdivided again using some sort of complicated process of architectural long division. The bedroom was barely big enough to swing a cat in – though this would have been difficult to put to the test given that the island's manx cats don't have tails. In one corner was a little bathroom, inside the little bathroom was a tiny shower, and inside the tiny shower was one of those miniature guest bars of soap, presumably because they couldn't fit a larger bar in the room. Dimensions aside it was clean and comfy, and to be honest anywhere I can find a towel that isn't covered in our dog's hairs is luxury. I ate all the biscuits provided and caught up with the news wondering why it is that watching familiar TV programmes in a guest house or hotel can make you feel even further from home.

Arriving somewhere new for the first time at night always adds to the sense of discovery the following morning, and I pulled open the curtains to find I was looking out at . . . well, the rear of another B&B where someone else was pulling open their curtains and looking out. After breakfast I drove out of the capital heading north, and as the road reached the top of a ridge I was greeted with a wonderful view of rolling pasture bordered by neat stone walls and moorland, with peaks rising in the distance fringed with conifers and bracken. The road was virtually empty and it felt as if I had the place to myself. I wasn't in any hurry, so I followed where the route led, stopping at vantage points along the way. I had one person I needed to meet after lunch, and time to kill until the light started fading.

Chris Sharpe heads a team that has plotted every bird species living or landing on the Isle of Man to within 100 metres, filling six shelves with box files of data and resulting in the most detailed bird atlas of its kind in the world. Given the pinpoint accuracy of the survey work, I was somewhat surprised on visiting him at his office in Laxey that the published map of the bird I had come to see was distinctly lacking in detail. Instead of precise locations dotted about the island, there were simply large black squares representing areas five kilometres across. The reason is simple: the risk of persecution. So reviled is this Red List bird in certain circles that he can't afford to take any chances. But how could anyone want to harm arguably our most attractive bird of prey?

The hen harrier is a large raptor that has mastered the art of flying in first gear without stalling, gracefully quartering the ground at low level flushing out prey. A speedy peregrine falcon wouldn't want to be stuck behind one in traffic. Hen harrier females are mottled brown with a distinctive white base to the tail, while the males are a pristine light seagull grey, with a white rump and black wingtips. A delight to behold, you would think. But like bullfinches, starlings and house sparrows, hen harriers have earned enemies among those who consider them a threat to their livelihoods, and although the widespread slaughter of the smaller birds made little difference to their overall numbers, it did drive the hen harrier to the brink of extinction in Britain.

It is not poultry farmers that hate hen harriers, despite the name. The problem is that they eat game birds – in particular red grouse. Given that millions of acres of our heather-covered uplands are carefully tailored to keep wild red grouse happy, and consequently the people who like to shoot them happy, estate owners are not inclined to want to share. Once harriers move into an area, seemingly initially attracted by bite-sized prey like voles and meadow pipits in neighbouring grassland, they can decimate grouse numbers. On one Scottish estate where gamekeepers left hen harriers in peace as part of a five-year project to assess their impact, the raptors famously ate so many grouse that shooting had to be abandoned and staff were laid off. The project findings split the gamekeeping and conservation communities and new research is now under way to try to sort out the situation, but in the meantime relentless killing of this ground-nesting, slow-flying target continues despite them being legally protected, making it the police's number-one wildlife crime concern.

To some extent two world wars helped save them from being lost altogether in the UK. We were too busy shooting people to worry about blasting grouse and harriers. Young, fit gamekeepers well able to handle a weapon were sent to the front line and hen harriers that had been eliminated from everywhere but remote outposts in Orkney and the Western Isles gradually recolonized the mainland. Today there are around 750 pairs scattered across Scotland, Northern Ireland, north Wales and . . . well, it would be nice to say England but apart from winter visitors, ongoing persecution is still keeping them from crossing the border in any numbers. It has been estimated that English moors could support over two hundred breeding pairs. Instead there are fifteen.

The Isle of Man, on the other hand, is hen harrier heaven.

'There's no evidence of local persecution – in fact many people here take a real pride in these wonderful birds,' Chris said. 'The island also provides very good habitat for nesting and feeding, there are a few grouse but no commercial grouse shooting, and we don't have ground predators such as weasels, foxes or badgers.'

Not only do fifty pairs breed on the Isle of Man, but in the winter the island boasts western Europe's largest communal hen harrier roost, with dozens regularly gathering in the lowlands to spend the night together in damp thickets of willow and birch. It was a spectacle I had come to see. I didn't just want to see one hen harrier – I was greedy.

Only I didn't realize how early they began coming in to roost. 'I'd get there as soon as possible,' Chris advised, checking his watch. It was 2pm.

It isn't easy to get lost on the Isle of Man, after all it is only 32 miles long and 13 wide, but as soon as I turned off the main coast road north and began heading west into a large wetland area called the Ballaugh Curragh I found every road seemed to lead the opposite way to the one I wanted to go. Unfortunately I have a lousy sense of direction – spin me around twice on our landing and I would wander up and down for hours trying to find the bathroom – so without a detailed map and with time running out before sunset I began to get desperate. I passed gates I had passed before, bashed the exhaust pipe on the verge attempting an eight-point turn in a narrow lane, and at one point got out and climbed up a wall to try to get some idea of where I was – watched hungrily by two crows who were doubtless calculating how long it would be before I ran out of petrol. And then after two lefts, a right and a left I stumbled across a turn-off signposted Close Sartfield – the Manx Wildlife Trust reserve I was looking for. I parked and ran along the boardwalk that wound through boggy ground and willow thickets until I reached a hide, then climbed a ladder attached to the rear up onto the roof, where I caught my breath and scanned the horizon for birds. Normally standing on top of a hide in full view of wildlife for miles around would be a birdwatching crime of the highest order, but on winter evenings at Close Sartfield it is positively encouraged in order to get decent views of hen harriers coming in to land.

I pulled on a woolly hat and gloves, buttoned my coat against the December chill and paced around the square roof trying to keep warm. Even though it was cold enough without any wind I was hoping the breeze would pick up as it is said to bring in more birds, and after half an hour with no sign of anything I was beginning to get a little anxious.

Forget what you were taught in biology lessons about reproduction, some birds are created by the action of sunlight on the sky. Looking west I noticed that where the weak rays of the pale sun passed through cold air above the distant moors, a tiny dot had appeared. It grew like a swirl of dark gases and spread until it took the form of a living organism. Wings appeared and with them the power to fly free, and tearing itself from the bonds of light, ripping its feathers into ragged fingers in the process, it emerged into the world of living creatures. Behold! A hen harrier, heading straight towards me! It was a female, seeking the darkness of tree cover. Fifty metres away she turned and ditched down between the branches to settle out of sight on low vegetation for the night. It was 3.10pm. And a few minutes later another appeared, oblivious to my presence, and plopped down some distance from the other. Then a male, ghostly grey, floating with buoyant wingbeats above the treetops, hesitated before disappearing down into the surrounding thicket of trees. And then another, darker rufous brown than the females before, which could have meant it was a juvenile, appeared overhead and was followed by a male from the east, and two females, and a male and another female. By the time darkness fell I had counted five females, one juvenile and three males. Not bad for a couple of hours' work, and well worth enduring the cold for, even if I had lost all feeling in my fingers and toes.

But the surprise of the evening still lay in store, when I had an unexpectedly surreal encounter with a group of animals which I later discovered were descendants of escapees from captivity. Driving away from the reserve I got lost again – though that is not the surprising bit – and found myself heading in circles along the dark lanes following my headlights in the hope of coming across a signpost that would point the way to the main road. Around a bend overhung by trees I noticed something up ahead, a mammal like a rabbit in the thick grassy verge. Only although it was much the same colour in the light beams, it looked pretty large for a rabbit, in fact much, much bigger. As I neared it lifted its head to face me, raised itself up on two enormous hind legs and crossed the road in a single jump. Strewth! It was a bloody wallaby. Had I taken a wrong turn and ended up in Australia? Two more emerged from the woods to my right and hopped across the road, and a third paused, blinking in the headlights before disappearing into the long grass.

It seemed my wildlife spotting was coming along in, well, leaps and bounds.

CHAPTER EIGHT

IT WAS STILL AND QUIET IN THE FOREST. SNOW COVERED the outstretched boughs of pine trees and the ground beneath. Tracks of deer and black grouse were visible in the drifts. The sun had just risen over neighbouring mountains and the sky was clear, yet at the corner of a block of conifers it appeared as if it was still snowing. Fragments of something resembling large snowflakes were drifting from the top of a tree, papery scales drizzling down and landing softly in the shadows. In the uppermost branches was a bright finch that looked as if it had dusted itself in red powder paint, an improbable colour amid the dark green and brown of the pines. But that was not the only thing striking about the bird. On closer inspection it looked like it had flown into a tree. The end of its thick bill was strangely distorted so that instead of the tips meeting at a neat point, the mandibles were skewed and crossed over. It seemed like a bird one should feel sorry for, a seed-eater destined to starve, an evolutionary dead end with 'product recall' status that you could return and exchange for two fully functioning greenfinches.

But it didn't look underfed. Clutching a pine cone in one claw in a parrot-like fashion, the large finch prised its partly open bill between two scales then turned its head so that the crossed ends levered the sides apart, exposing the seed within which it extracted with its muscular tongue. It worked methodically, turning the cone deftly against the side of a branch and letting kernel coatings fall through the air onto the snow below, finally dropping the emptied husk to the ground where it landed with a muffled thud. It was a male crossbill. One of our weirdest-looking and least understood birds. And its ingenious Swiss Army beak meant it had the pick of the cone crop well before the ripening protective scales widened sufficiently for other birds to be able to help themselves.

Nearby a greenish-grey female was perched, feeding. It was a peaceful scene in a remote corner of the Scottish Highlands far from towns and traffic. Conifers covered the surrounding hillsides in densely planted rows sandwiched between exposed mountain tops and open moorland below. The only sound was that of the birds working the cones, melting ice pattering on the snow beneath and . . .

'CHIP! CHIP! CHIP!'

The pair of crossbills raised their heads in surprise.

'CHIP! CHIP! CHIP!' Once more the hard mechanical chiselling noise reverberated through the forest.

It was a sound they recognized and they took off, flying above the trees until they located the source and landed nearby, clinging to the tops of neighbouring spruces and looking down at a clearing where two men knelt in the snow. One in a thick black coat was holding what looked like a TV satellite dish in one hand. The other, wearing a brown woolly hat and waterproof trousers, was scanning the pines with a pair of binoculars. Beside the men a CD player repeated the noise on a loop: 'CHIP! CHIP! CHIP!'

The crossbills answered the familiar sound, chirping back in a similarly repetitive fashion, and as they did the noise was switched off and the parabolic reflector was held up towards them, catching and focusing their replies on a sensitive microphone at the centre.

After a few seconds the two birds became bored and flew off, quietly calling to one another.

'Amazing!' I whispered loudly, tracking them with my binoculars and lifting my woolly hat off my ears to hear them better as they went.

Ron signalled with one hand for me to remain quiet as he turned the reflector to follow the departing birds, catching every last fragment of sound before they disappeared.

'I never realized they were so bright!' I said. 'Do you think they were Scottish?'

'We'll see,' Ron smiled, packing away his recording equipment. 'Right, on we go to the next location.'

It was mid-January and I had joined senior research biologist Ron Summers, one of the UK's leading authorities on crossbills, who was heading a team carrying out the first comprehensive survey of their range and population. Only not just for any kind of crossbill. We were a 45-minute drive north of Loch Ness searching for the scarce Scottish crossbill. It is Britain's only endemic species. Every other bird in the UK lives somewhere else in the world as well, but the Scottish crossbill is one of a kind, and it is ours, making its home in the conifer forests of north-east Scotland and nowhere else.

So if it is so special, why haven't we heard more about it? Why aren't crowds flocking to see this real national treasure instead of heading in their thousands to gaze at the dark waters of Loch Ness nearby in the vague hope of glimpsing a mythical monster? (Which, incidentally, I saw clearly on a rock eating a dolphin when I drove past and would have photographed if I hadn't been saving my film for birds.) Why isn't our only unique species emblazoned across tourist brochures the world over? Why are there no Scottish crossbill tours, T-shirts, novelty mugs, amusing car stickers?

The simple reason is that they are hard to find and virtually impossible to tell apart from other types of crossbill. The Scottish crossbill is a pedant's delight and a PR disaster.

We have three different species of crossbill, their ranges overlap, they share the same plumage colours, and they all behave and look much the same, except for miniscule variations in the depth of their peculiar beaks. The common crossbill, which has the slimmest bill, is the most widely distributed and can be found in evergreen forests across much of the UK. Then there is the parrot crossbill from Scandinavia and Russia, which is slightly more heavyweight and breeds here in tiny numbers. Finally there is the Scottish crossbill, which is somewhere in between. It has a bill roughly 1.5mm thicker than the common crossbill. Try spotting that 50 metres away through binoculars! No wonder the coach tours haven't got started. 'And on our left a Scottish crossbill, or a common crossbill, or maybe it's a parrot crossbill . . . well, forget it . . . anyway, on our right a huge loch that might have a monster in it!'

We're not the only ones that are confused. The species look so similar that even they get their wires crossed and occasionally mate with each other, leading to cross-bred crossbills. As such it was originally thought that the Scottish variety was just a sub-species of one of the other kinds, but the fact that it hasn't hybridized itself out of existence and has managed to retain its individual characteristics over time supports the argument that it is a species in its own right. On top of that it also has a 'Scottish accent' – a unique call which Ron first identified and which helped seal the case for its formal recognition.

However, given that nothing is simple with crossbills, even their sound is too subtle to distinguish with any confidence by ear. Instead you need to record the calls, then analyse them with a sonogram, which turns noise into an image. And *even then* the sonogram smudges of lines look so similar between species that they take an expert eye to tell apart.

It is reckoned we have a few hundred pairs, but no one is sure. And no one knows exactly where they live as they move around following the cone crops, raising young whenever and wherever there is food about. Little wonder they are on the Red List labelled 'data deficient' – which was what Ron and his survey team were trying to rectify. By visiting 850 forest locations, playing taped 'CHIP! CHIP! CHIP!' crossbill calls to lure in the birds, then recording their replies for sonogram analysis, they aimed to accurately count and plot Scottish crossbill numbers.

I was lucky to be able to tag along for a morning, and had flown up from Exeter at short notice as it was half the price of travelling by train and less exhausting than driving. Obviously I felt a little guilty about flying, but was reassured to discover that the aircraft had an 'A' rating for noise – though had it been worse I'm not sure how one would offset noise pollution. Do voluntary work in a library? As the plane touched down at Edinburgh the stewardess said: 'You're very welcome to Scotland,' which didn't sound like much of an advertisement, and after sorting out a hire car I had travelled north from the capital through the breathtaking snow-covered Cairngorms and wide river valleys to Inverness where I spent a night in a refreshingly figurine-free B&B before meeting up with Ron the following morning.

Half an hour after our first crossbill encounter we had arrived at the next location north of the Cromarty Firth. But it was far from easy to get to the exact spot.

Following the coordinates on a GPS device we had to fight our way through dense hillside conifer forest, wading through the snow until we came to the specified position, a narrow gap between pine trees where Ron set up his playback and recording equipment. There wasn't a bird to be seen. The trees around were silent and seemingly devoid of life.

'CHIP! CHIP! CHIP!' The tape burst into life, hammering its noise into the forest. It was a bit like fishing, waiting excitedly to see whether anything would take the bait.

Nothing showed at first.

'CHIP! CHIP! CHIP!'

Then small curious birds appeared from nowhere: a coal tit, a crested tit, a goldcrest, tiny shapes flitting between the branches.

'CHIP! CHIP! CHIP!'

Finally, as if drawn in by a powerful magnet, a crossbill landed above us. It was a green-coloured female, shining in the sunlight as she perched at the very top of a spruce tree like a Christmas decoration. Was her bill thicker or thinner than the first birds we saw?

Her replies duly recorded we set off for the third site on the list, which was even more inaccessible, but worth it as a flock of at least a dozen intrigued crossbills paid us a visit, including juveniles, whose bills only start crossing over at the ends when they are a month old. Our final GPS point, however, drew a blank.

I was thrilled to have seen any crossbills at all. They are incredible birds. But had I actually seen a Scottish crossbill? I'd have to be patient and wait until the recordings were analysed over the months to come. Fingers crossed.

Every village has one mad resident. Ours was fortunate in that this was either not the case, or I was that villager. As winter turned to spring I could be seen wandering around the lanes peering at trees and hedges or standing alone with my hands cupped behind my ears looking confused. Those who didn't know I was trying to identify birds were probably justified in crossing the road with a nervous smile to avoid me.

Since moving to Devon I had increasingly grown to love living in the countryside. I no longer felt the need to take an occasional drag on the car tailpipe to remind myself of being back in London, and the mead-drinking, hobbity folk that I imagined inhabited the West Country turned out to be really quite normal. Among those I met there wasn't an ankle bell or baler-twine belt to be found. The only local affliction that I could identify was a chronic case of the raffles. Every single event held in the area included a fundraising prize draw, so that you couldn't get through the door without being accosted to buy a raffle ticket. I didn't attend any funerals but I am sure it extended to these as well. ('. . . Let us join in prayer for Mrs Smythe who will be so dearly missed, but before we do does anyone have . . . let me see . . . ticket number 27? Ticket 27 anyone . . . ?')

A welcoming and thriving community meant there was always lots going on. For a start there was the village fete, where one time I thought I had scooped first prize in the men's baking section – only to be later informed the judges put the trophy on my cake because they had mistaken it for a place mat. And there was a local family dog competition, where Oakey got a bit over-excited and came away with a rosette for best hard-on in show. Then there were plays and clubs and nature talks and plenty else besides. But I had to put it all to one side because I had a busy couple of months ahead of me. With time off work arranged, a family worryingly eager for me to disappear for a while and lots of ground to cover, I set off on the first of many long-distance trips planned for that spring. The village was losing its mad novice birdwatcher for a few weeks. It was safe to step outside once again.

My first port of call was the Highlands and I was delighted to be back. It was mid-April and the Cairngorm mountains were capped with snow and swathed in heather with its complex coloured fabric of greens, browns and toasted purples, broken in places by odd-shaped blocks of plantation conifers that resembled giant jigsaw pieces scattered across the hillsides. I had driven north along the A9 before turning east beside the River Spey past Aviemore to eventually reach a village called Boat of Garten about 30 miles south-east of Inverness. The village lies next to one of our few remaining tracts of ancient Caledonian pinewood, Abernethy Forest, and in a clearing among the towering Scot's pines close to the shores of Loch Garten is probably the world's most famous nest, home to an annual wildlife soap opera that has been running for the last fifty years – a year longer than *Coronation Street* – and which has been watched from a hide, and more recently live online, by more than two million people.

In 1959 the RSPB took the bold step of announcing that ospreys were back and breeding in Britain – and that anyone could come and see them. Bold because it was also news to egg collectors, who had contributed to the extinction of this majestic fish-eating raptor in the UK forty years earlier following a century of persecution and hunting for stuffed cabinet displays. Instead of the location being shrouded in secrecy, the battle for their survival was to be played out in the full glare of the media spotlight, with the forces of a nature-loving majority pitted against a villainous few. The conflict between opposing values that ensued captured the public imagination as committed conservationists triumphed over vandals and egg collectors, creating in the process an icon among birds that helped shape attitudes regarding the preservation of other vulnerable species.

The osprey dynasty lives on, their rebuilt treetop nest site now bristling with CCTV cameras and watched by round-the-clock teams of volunteers. Tens of thousands of people visit Fortress Garten every year, pumping an estimated £1.5 million into the local economy. Little wonder the village Boat of Garten, which grew up around a river crossing and railway junction, has embraced its avian benefactors and branded itself 'The Osprey Village'. Likewise plenty of plant and animal species also owe a debt of gratitude to the osprey, for the biodiversity-rich Abernethy land protected in its name houses thousands of species of flora and fauna –

900 types of beetle for example, none of which, let's face it, were ever going to attract maximum-security protection otherwise.

I suppose I shouldn't have been surprised, then, when I was stopped by a couple outside my B&B who had seen me unpacking binoculars and asked: 'Is Henry back yet?'

'Who? Sorry, I don't know the other guests here.'

'And how's EJ doing?'

'EJ?'

They were referring to the ospreys. Had I been following developments on the reserve's website I could have told them that apparently Henry wasn't back, EJ had laid three eggs and her new mate Orange VS was proving a diligent partner.

The successful recolonization by ospreys over the last five decades means that they have dropped off our national Red List, but they do share their Speyside home with an equally impressive flagship for Scottish bird conservation, the capercaillie – the bird I had really come to see. It looks like a glossy black turkey on steroids, has a name which sounds like a highland fling, makes a sound like clopping hooves and popping corks, has one of the most indigestible diets of any of our birds, and is famously elusive. You need to get up at dawn to stand any chance of a decent sighting, and I had been told by the reserve to arrive at 5.30am the following day. I ate early in the local hotel's Capercaillie Restaurant, which I felt sure would bring me good luck, and wandered back to my B&B along the main road, passing a community hall which bore two plaques on the outside wall: 'Young People – Highly Commended, 2002' and 'Older People – Highly Commended, 2002'. Clearly the village's middle-aged residents were the local troublemakers.

It is strange how excited one can become about a large grouse. After laying my clothes out ready for the next morning like a neat spread of sushi, with sock rolls in the centre, I had turned off the light and spent two hours listening to the alarm clock ticking, desperately trying to get to sleep. The capercaillie was one of those birds I never really considered I might one day get the chance to see, and I couldn't wait. They hang out in the treetops over winter stuffing themselves on pin-sharp pine needles – surely only crabs eaten by seabirds could be more uncomfortable to swallow – then in the spring they come back down to the ground to feed in the low shrub layer and mate. I had heard just how impressive the posturing macho males could be. These testosterone-fuelled, battle-tank birds armed with beaks like secateurs compete for dominance at forest clearing 'lek' sites, much like the black grouse I had seen in the North Pennines. They fan their tails and strut before females with heads held high uttering guttural sounds, and are so aggressive, so I had read, that they have been known to attack passing people and cars. You don't mess with male capercaillie in the spring. Even the gangs of middle-aged troublemakers roaming Boat of Garten would give them a wide berth.

When the alarm sounded I opened the curtains and looked outside, relieved it was neither wet nor windy. There was a light frost on the ground and the trees opposite illuminated by street lamps were motionless, as if frozen solid. I ate breakfast, which had been laid out the night before, and defrosted the car windows with half a mug of tea, then drove the mile or so to the lakeside car park at Loch Garten, arriving half an hour early. I had been expecting to meet up with one of the wardens so I was surprised when a car emerged from the darkness a few minutes later and the two people aged in their twenties who got out told me they were visitors rather than staff. At this time of day? Another set of headlights could be seen snaking along the forest road, and a second car pulled in. Birdwatchers too! And another, and I discovered they had also come to see capercaillie. Gradually the car park started filling up. It seemed I wasn't the only one invited.

As it turned out, this was one of the daily dawn 'Caperwatches' run at Loch Garten during the lekking season from April until mid-May, and they regularly attract dozens of people from all over the country. Conveniently some of the local capercaillie have chosen areas underneath the osprey nest in which to display, which means they can be viewed from the osprey hide without being disturbed during their speed-dating sessions. But it still amazed me that so many other people, young and old, were also prepared to get up before first light to see the birds.

A warden arrived as the sky was just beginning to lighten and we were led along a path to the osprey centre, where we took up positions in front of the viewing windows. Looking through them was like gazing back thousands of years on a long-lost landscape:

tall scattered native pine trees rising from a boggy expanse of blaeberry, juniper, cotton grass and heather. You could almost imagine a herd of mammoth passing through in front of us. The osprey nest was visible straight ahead, quite a distance away, and on the TV monitors in the room you could see the feathers on the back of the female huddled over her eggs were silver with frost. There were a couple of roe deer to the left, and a flock of finches flew overhead – Abernethy Forest is a particularly good location for Scottish crossbill – but there was no sign of capercaillie.

'Look out for any movement,' one of the assistants said. 'It may not be much, perhaps the shifting of a branch in the trees or a head above the heather. Don't be afraid to speak up if you see anything.'

They were out there – we were told one had been seen on a CCTV monitor just before we arrived – but as hard as we looked we could see nothing. Thirty pairs of eyes scrutinized the ground cover and treetops. Where were they?

In such situations it is only natural to want to be the person who spots the hidden treasure first and cries out 'There's one!' to the delight of all. Then again no one wants to be the over-excited berk who gets hearts racing over a bird-shaped rock and has to spend the next five minutes apologizing. However, after an hour without even a hint of capercaillie, a false alarm would have at least livened things up a bit.

People began chatting, and I overheard one of those 'you-should-have-been-here-yesterday' conversations I could have done without. Three males had been displaying apparently. Great views. This wasn't information sharing, it was showing off. I began to wonder how much birdwatching boiled down to a simple game of oneupmanship.

A second hour passed, and frustration was beginning to set in. Two hours is a long time to stand in the cold staring at an expanse of empty vegetation. Was that one? No. And that? Still no. I never realized it could be so hard to spot them. Everyone was getting desperate. The gathering needed a keen-eyed hero − and fortunately there was one in our midst. I heard a murmur among a group at the far end of the hide, a bird had been seen. Conversations around the room tailed off. Ears pricked up. Excitement spread through those assembled, and one by one lenses turned to the right as directions were shared. 'See the dead tree? Go left a bit and look through the gap behind it. There.' Could it be? It was! A female capercaillie visible a long way off sitting in a low conifer having a prickly breakfast of pine needles. Unlike a black male her plumage was an incredible mix of camouflage brown and grey barring and mottled chestnut patterning, with an orange breast and lighter underparts. It was very odd seeing a hefty game bird that you would normally associate with life on the ground perched up in a tree.

By sharing telescopes everyone was able to get a decent look at her. We had all been hoping for a male in picture-postcard pose but were relieved to have seen a capercaillie at all, and the man who spotted the bird was thanked with a ripple of applause, muffled by the fact everyone was wearing gloves.

I spent the remainder of the morning exploring forest trails that threaded between the weathered trunks of Abernethy's tall pines. It was light and calm and quiet beneath the canopy. Lichen and moss covered fallen branches and the ground was soft and thick with ferns and herby foliage so that it felt like walking on a spongy seabed with a gentle swell of green waves high above. It was a magical place. But old trees are intimidating. When you enter ancient forest you step into a process thousands of years old, an experiment in time and matter that can make you feel like meaningless carbon fluff beneath the legs of giants. I needed to get away from the aloof pines and find some plants I could look down on, so I drove to an area of moor nearby, and along a single-track lane close to Loch Garten I spotted something by the side of the road crouched down in the shelter of overhanging tree roots. As it stood up I saw it was another female capercaillie and I slammed on the brakes to avoid hitting her as she doubled back and walked off into the wood. Running over a red-listed capercaillie would not have been a good idea. There are only a hundred to a hundred and fifty in the 50-square-mile reserve, and perhaps a couple of thousand in Scotland in total. It is a species facing its second extinction in Britain, so it wouldn't have done much for my conservation credentials to have been seen peeling a precious female off my front bumper.

Wiped out by the late 1700s due to over-hunting and the extensive felling of open native forests, the capercaillie was reintroduced into Scotland a few decades later for sport and multiplied with the spread of newly planted pines to a population numbering tens of thousands. Demand for wood during the war years then knocked back numbers, and the unsuitability of the dense, drained conifer plots that followed, coupled with an increase in foxes and crows as gamekeeping dwindled, added to their troubles. On top of that another unlikely killer lurked in the woods: deer. Not only have expanding numbers munched their way through the rich and varied ground cover that provides berries for capercaillie and insects for their young, but high fences put up to keep deer out of new plantations were claiming scores of lives. It isn't easy for a fast low-flying 12lb capercaillie to stop dead in mid-air, but a mesh fence of thin wire virtually invisible in poor light and a low mist usually does the trick.

'We found one five-kilometre section of deer fencing at Abernethy accounted for the deaths of twenty-five capercaillie in six months, along with a couple of tawny owls, black grouse and woodpigeon,' Loch Garten site manager Richard Thaxton told me. 'When we realized what a problem fences could be we took out 25 miles, and any that had to be kept were extensively marked to make them more noticeable.'

The next morning I rose before dawn once again with that sense of superiority you get when you are up and about early while all the duvet slugs slumber on, and by 5.30am I was back at Loch Garten for another Caperwatch. Thirty new bleary-eyed birdwatchers who had dragged themselves from their hotels and B&Bs were gathered in the half-light.

'Oh you should have been here yesterday,' I told a

party of 'scope-wielding birders who had travelled up from Yorkshire. 'There was a female feeding in a tree. Great views.'

I had returned in the hope of seeing a male, though for the first hour or so it was much the same story as the day before: CCTV views of a female osprey thawing out on the nest and nothing stirring on the frosty ground below. It was so atmospheric I hardly minded. Then news filtered through that a male had indeed been glimpsed flying in and a dozen of us were taken to a forward hide where we might stand a better chance of spotting him. He had disappeared among the dense understorey and once again the search continued. After ten minutes or so I saw a small dark shape a long way off above the heather through my binoculars. It could have been a head, a trick of the light or dirt on the lens. I knew my judgement had become seriously impaired by wishful thinking so I kept quiet. Ever since the morning before I had begun to hallucinate capercaillie everywhere I turned: in the treetops, on the ground, by the village bus stop, queuing at the local shop checkout . . . Except this time the dark form moved, like a periscope above the low foliage, and I could see what looked like a thick pale beak. It was a male capercaillie, there was little doubt, moving steadily and cautiously in front of a boulder at the base of the distant tree line, but he was still well hidden and I had done well to spot him. This was my moment to shine.

'Hey, I think . . .' I began.

'There he is!' someone next to me called out. 'In front of the rock!'

Bother.

The high-powered telescopes swung into action, and the 'finder' was congratulated as the magnificent black male shifted into view, his red eye wattles clearly visible, along with a rough goatee-beard of black feathers under his chin and two white patches like gleaming rivets on his broad shoulders. Even at a distance he was a thunking great bird, and I could have admired him for much longer, only we needed to swap places with others waiting patiently back at the osprey centre.

The sense of relief and satisfaction at having seen such a secretive and special species was mixed with a desire to see a lot more of capercaillie. One day, I promised myself, I would return to this place. In fact I was beginning to realize that far from taking me a step closer to an end, every success in the task I had set myself was leading me back to a new beginning. Bit by bit I was learning what was out there, and how much was worth seeing. I was enjoying myself. I wanted to start out all over again.

There are some things you never want to see in your life, like geriatric naturists playing beach volleyball or your car airbags. Another is a dead eagle. The crime-prevention poster beside the track showed a police officer holding a poisoned white-tailed eagle up like a tattered gown, huge wings half opened, head slumped to one side weighed down by a massive hooked bill. It was a pathetic sight, our largest bird of prey reduced to a crumpled carcass. Not only is it surprising that anyone would want to be rid of one, but perhaps more astonishing is the fact that there are any here to kill.

Like the osprey and the capercaillie, the white-tailed eagle has made a comeback – and it could take some getting used to. They are enormous. When one flew over an Asda store in Dunfermline in 2007, people phoned the authorities to report that a condor had escaped from a zoo. We aren't used to barn-door-sized birds of prey in our skies. And why should we be? Few are alive today who could remember growing up seeing native white-tailed eagles soaring over Britain. The year that the First World War ended marked the final assault in a battle lasting centuries to exterminate this massive raptor when the last one was shot in 1918 over Shetland. They were on the hit list of sheep farmers, fishery owners and gamekeepers, and they made an easy target. Unlike wary golden eagles which hunt for fresh prey in the rugged uplands, white-tailed eagles, also known as sea eagles, are more lowland and coastal opportunists that will readily scavenge free hand-outs, even if the meat on offer is the bait in a deadly trap or laced with toxins. With the right weapons at our disposal we were able to polish off the last of these pinnacle predators. They were history, and as the decades passed our bird books no longer bothered to feature pictures of them. Even my copy of the *Reader's Digest Book of British Birds* only included a tiny reference tucked away near the end.

Eagles don't generally undertake lengthy sea crossings as you don't get the kinds of strong thermal updraughts over open water needed to keep their bulk airborne. On top of that, white-tailed eagles tend to nest near where they were born. There was no way we were going to get them back unless birds from Scandinavia started chartering flights here – which is exactly what happened. In the mid-1970s the Norwegian Air Force kindly began flying in young eagles as part of a long-term reintroduction project. Dozens were released in the Hebrides, followed by a second wave in the 1990s along neighbouring mainland coasts, and today juveniles from eagle-rich Norway are still being flown over every year, this time to repopulate the eastern Scottish seaboard. White-tailed eagles are no longer a novelty, they are here and breeding, and the best place to find them is the Isle of Mull which, with ten pairs, has earned the nickname 'Eagle Island'.

To get to 'Eagle Island' I drove west out of 'Osprey Village', passing through a hamlet along the way where half a dozen people were standing around looking at a squashed red squirrel in the road ('Squirrel Village'?) and on through 'Lame Dog Town' and 'One-eyed Cat County' to the port of Oban to catch the ferry. It was a quick crossing and on arriving I checked in at a characterful B&B near Salen in the centre of the island where the choice of breakfast cereals was simply muesli (I liked that), then got straight back into the car to explore.

The Isle of Mull is the second largest of the Inner Hebrides and time-consuming and perilous to drive around as a visitor because you are either examining the rocky shoreline in the hope of spotting otters, looking at herds of red deer on the vast expanses of moorland or scanning the clouds above to see if there are any eagles about. At one time the island was overrun with toddlers every summer visiting the colourful harbour Tobermory, which featured in the popular kids' TV show *Balamory*, then the eagles began to steal the limelight with *Springwatch* appearances, and birdwatchers flooded onto Mull boosting the local economy to the tune of millions of pounds.

'Whenever our eagles appear on TV, the phones start ringing in our Eagle Watch booking office almost immediately after, sometimes even during the programmes, with people wanting to come,' said Dave Sexton, Mull's RSPB officer.

Despite the grisly crime-prevention poster I came across on the island, persecution here is now a thing of the past. Eagles are worth a lot more alive than dead.

I met up with Dave at a special observation centre beside Loch Frisa which offers views of an active nest every spring and summer, avoiding people tramping all over the place disturbing breeding birds. A quick glance at the visitors' book showed just how much the eagles stir up strong emotions: *Words cannot really describe today. Fantastic. An incredible and moving experience. Thank you. The eagles are the best thing I've ever seen!*

Somehow I can't imagine people saying the same thing of tree sparrows or twites.

'We've had people burst into tears on seeing the eagles flying overhead. They really can have a profound effect on people,' Dave said.

You get an idea of the size of the birds from some of the exhibits at the centre. I was shown one of their regurgitated pellets of undigested food. Come to Mull and handle solid dried bird puke! There's a crowd puller. But it was more interesting than it sounds, and one of the assistants pointed out a large object embedded in the soft palm-sized oval of fur, fish bones and feathers. It was the skull of a fulmar. Anything that can eat a whole one of these gull-sized seabirds is a hefty predator. I was also given one of the eagle's primary feathers to look at. These are the longest on its 8-foot wings – the 'fingers' – and laid along my outstretched arm it reached all the way from the tip of my middle finger to halfway up my bicep. That is a big feather. As for their nests, they can reach the size of a double bed. But where was the Loch Frisa nest? Where were the resident eagles, come to that?

'You see the opposite side of the valley?' Dave said, lending me a telescope.

'Just about,' I replied. It was a damp and murky day.

'If you follow the conifers along the ridge and find the top one, then go left a bit to the next trunk, a quarter of the way down is the nest where the female is sitting on two eggs.'

'Ah. Hmmm. Yes,' I nodded, even though I hadn't found it.

'She's moving slightly,' he said.

I did notice something, only from three-quarters of a mile away it could have been anything: a buzzard, an owl. One really needs to be able to discern at least an identifiable feature or two to claim a proper sighting. At most I could conclude it was a bird of some kind, and 'a bird' is not a species on the Red List.

'Yes, I've got her, I think,' I mumbled, trying to focus

properly on the distant speck, a little disappointed I had come so far to see so little.

'Look!' Dave said abruptly.

'Okay, okay, I've got her,' I repeated.

'No, look!' he cried.

I turned round and he was staring at the sky. (Note to myself: straight up is a good place to look for eagles.) A white-tailed eagle was flying straight towards us. Heavy, dark brown and vulture-like, it beat a path high over the open moorland on broad rectangular wings and I could clearly make out its weaponry: sharp powerful talons and a vicious hooked bill. This was a bird that would fail a health and safety appraisal. Its short wedge tail was not yet white, indicating it was a juvenile, and among the wide feathers overlapping like roof tiles on its upper wings were two yellow tags that identified it as a bird born a couple of years ago. It flew past us and across the loch where a pair of ravens rose from the trees below to mob it, looking tiny by comparison.

'They're inspiring birds,' Dave said.

Of that there can be no doubt.

The ravens then peeled off and headed towards the ridge opposite and Dave pointed out a golden eagle perched high up on a rocky outcrop on the moors further off, and a second white-tailed eagle – an adult that circled the nest momentarily before landing. That was a lot of wingspan for one morning: two white-tailed eagles, one golden eagle and two ravens. 'Eagle Island' had certainly delivered.

I should have written something gushy in the visitors' book before I left, but didn't. Not because the experience of seeing a white-tailed eagle wasn't special, but because I had also found it strangely unsettling. They were stunning birds, magnificent symbols of freedom, might and majesty, a conservation success story and rectification of past mistakes that should have been a cause for celebration. But to me there was also something sad and lost about them, as if they belonged to another time and place. It was a sense of pity that stirred within me as much as pride. We had killed them off and imported replacements. The eagles felt more like symbols of our power and supremacy than their own.

Having said that, while I had been looking up at what were third-generation British-born white-tailed eagles and wrestling with mixed emotions, they had probably been peering down at me thinking: 'Oi, squirt! You're on our turf now!' Our country is now their country once more. And I wasn't going to argue with them.

I still had seventeen Red List birds to track down and only limited time, so I had to leave Mull the next day and head south in search of a species that was far smaller, less media-friendly and with no visitor centre to its name. My destination was Haweswater in the Lake District, and after a night in a B&B near Penrith I left the ironed track of the M6 and followed winding roads west past sheep-clipped landscapes criss-crossed with mile upon mile of dry stone walling – exhausting to look at given how many generations of bad backs it must have taken to build them all.

Once a natural lake, now a reservoir, Haweswater lies within steep valleys strewn with boulders, scree and scattered trees, and Riggindale at the south-western end has the kind of wild, unforgiving landscape beloved of the ring ouzel. If you have never heard of a ring ouzel, then basically it is a mountain version of a blackbird, though a thousand times less common. The word 'ouzel' comes from the old English name for a blackbird, 'osle', and the 'ring' refers to a crescent of white across the chest. Think of a male blackbird that has a white serviette tied around its neck and you pretty much have a ring ouzel. It doesn't sound like much to get excited about. After all, you sometimes get blackbirds with albino patches of plumage and no one is sticking them on the Red List as a special case for conservation. But while appearances may be similar, ring ouzels are very different from their lowland relatives. They don't live here all year round for a start. Instead, they are summer visitors from the Mediterranean basin, and apart from those that drop by on south and east coasts for a breather on migration, they are seldom seen below 1,000 feet. Ring ouzels are real upland birds, tough but wary, embodying the wilderness spirit of the mountainous regions where they live, and happiest as far away from people as they can get.

Ironically, choosing to nest amid the crags, gullies and rocky outcrops of remote rugged areas means that they now have to put up with a steady stream of visitors. High ground is equally attractive to hikers. Get away from it all and you find the world and his dog turn up on your doorstep! So considering ring ouzels just want to be left alone, was it right for me to go looking for them? Perhaps not. Then again I had kept my distance long enough – a lifetime in fact. I just wanted to see one once, and didn't much rate my chances in any case. The information I had on where they might be found in the north and west of Britain was lacking in detail, and I had read that they were extremely shy, hard to approach and most often seen flying away. While they provided the perfect excuse to visit scenic uplands, there was no doubt they could be a challenging species to track down, and I was a bit concerned this might involve me wandering our national parks for weeks on end.

Honesty compels me to confess that ring ouzels had already eluded me once on my travels. I had spent a few hours searching for them around the funicular railway base just below the snow line on Cairngorm Mountain while staying in Boat of Garten. I had even taken the lift up with skiers to try to get a decent view of rocky ground below and seen a couple of other species of interest but not what I was after. I was pinning my hopes on the Lake District where they breed every summer, and was ready to put in the miles.

Parking by Haweswater I pulled on my walking boots and followed the trail to Riggindale. It was bitterly cold for April and there were pockets of snow on the upper slopes between exposed knuckles of bare rock. The harsh terrain was once home to England's only nesting pair of golden eagles, but the female died in 2004 leaving a lonely male who has spent the past few years tending an empty nest in the hope of company. He wasn't about on the morning I visited, and while a few hardy birdwatchers who had braved the freezing winds were scanning high ridges for a sign of him, I was focusing on the boulders further down and listening hard for the mournful piping of a ring ouzel. Fortunately their song is a doddle to remember. Imagine the sound of a novice musician playing a high note on a flute two or three times in a row. Basically that's it, repeated for good measure.

They were not to be heard or seen, so I doubled back and made my way along a high path which ran through areas that should have been ideal for them. There was short turf where they could forage for worms; low bushes that would provide a pre-migration banquet of berries in the autumn; piles of rocks among which they could safely raise young; and a stream running down to the reservoir supplying a source of water. But there were no ring ouzels that I could find.

Across the country ring ouzel numbers have plummeted by 60 per cent since the late 1980s. There are plenty of theories as to why, from dry weather and over-grazing affecting food sources in their wintering grounds to forestry reducing nesting sites and human disturbance preventing breeding, but none have proven conclusive. They have disappeared in their thousands, and no one is exactly sure why. Just as lichens indicate how clean the air is, I like to think ring ouzels signal how wild our wild places really are, so it is a worry that they are rapidly retreating.

After several hours tramping around I decided to give up on Riggindale and move on, this time to Snowdonia. I had no accommodation booked, only a vague sense of where I was heading, and it was dark by the time I reached north Wales, driving south into the national park, through Betws-y-Coed and east along the A5.

Finding a deserted lay-by near a high lake called Llyn Ogwen I pulled in and slept in the car, waking at dawn the next morning to find I was surrounded by mountains. On one side was the Carneddau group of summits, and on the other the Glyderau range, which I was aware was supposed to be a good place for ring ouzels. It certainly looked the perfect habitat. The shattered peaks had sent rocks tumbling down the hillsides, and bracken, heather and tough grasses covered the flatter expanses. This was climbing country, with steep trails winding off in all directions across the sparsely vegetated slopes, though it was too early in the day for any hikers to be up and about.

I brewed a cup of tea on a camping stove by the car to warm up and wake up, shielding the flame from the wind with my road map, before setting off up into the Glyderau. Climbing a track from the road I followed a stream that raced down past me, treading carefully up the steeper sections and stopping every now and again to look around me and listen. Up and up I went, with no reckoning of how high ring ouzels might be, until I reached patches of snow on the upper slopes of one of the mountains and decided I had probably gone too far. I was exhausted. I sat on a boulder and gazed out at the summits before me and the dark lake below which spilled into a wide valley, wondering where on earth the ring ouzels were hiding and whether it was wise for me to be so far up a mountain without proper equipment. There was no one about, no one knew I was there and I didn't have a clue what the name of the peak was that I had climbed. On top of that I could only remember that the lake I had parked beside was called Llyn-something. Should I have fallen and needed to guide mountain rescue teams to my location, I couldn't have narrowed it down beyond 'Snowdonia, in Wales'. So I made sure I didn't fall, and as rain clouds rolled in I followed the track down and returned to my car.

Cairngorm, Riggindale, the Glyderau, and yet still no luck, but I had one more location on my list and on I went, stopping along the way for a microwaved chicken curry in a pub restaurant with the kind of dated furnishings that reminded me of something an Elvis impersonator might wear. Having said that, I wasn't exactly looking my best either after a night in the car. I had also decided for the first time in my life to grow a beard. This was not the result of going into a hairdresser's, pointing at a picture of Bill Oddie on the wall and asking for that look. Rather it was motivated by general laziness when it came to shaving, and at such an early stage my facial set-aside was far from even and very itchy.

I arrived at the village of Llanbedr close to Cardigan Bay on the western edge of Snowdonia in the early afternoon and took a narrow tree-lined lane that wound up a valley called Cwm Bychan into the Rhinogydd range of mountains. Up until then I believed that the early morning I had spent the previous August birdwatching at Thurlestone Marsh in Devon, when I saw black-tailed godwits and a red-backed shrike, could never be bettered. Little did I know it as I pulled up in the drizzle at the top of Cwm Bychan, but the next hour would be at least as memorable, if not more so.

A field situated next to a hillside farmhouse served as a car park, and as I locked up and pulled on waterproof trousers in readiness to hike up Rhinog Fawr mountain, I heard a piping sound. It was one of those don't-tell-me, I-know-this-tune moments . . . A ring ouzel? A doddle to remember, I think I said. Only, when a new song takes you by surprise it takes a while to register, no matter how much you have listened to it on CD before – much like learning foreign language phrases and being momentarily stunned overseas when someone actually uses them. The sound came again and I couldn't help but break into a grin. Of course it was a ring ouzel! Its melancholic notes were drifting down from a rocky sheep field above and I searched with my binoculars but couldn't locate the singer, so I climbed over the wire fence at the bottom of the field and scrambled up the slope. Where was it? Again it called out. Ahead was a stunted tree surrounded by short grass and I was sure the sound was coming from a heap of rocks behind, so I approached as close as I dared and knelt down on the damp ground, wiping the rain off my binocular eye pieces. Again the clear sound. Again nothing obvious among the rocks. And then I saw a shape, a movement and there it was. Not behind the low tree as I had expected, but perched among the upper branches. Its white chest band was clearly visible and once more it opened its yellow bill and sang for me, before flying off across the slope. It was not a short dash to neighbouring cover that you might expect of a blackbird, but a long flight that seemed to go on and on before it landed on bare ground and began to feed among the scree. I had finally seen a ring ouzel. I couldn't wait to tell . . . well, there was no one I knew who would be remotely excited by such news.

The obliging bird had saved me a long walk. However, I decided to explore a bit further rather than return to my car, and took a track which led past the farmhouse and over a winding stream that fed a lake at the head of the valley. In the small stream I saw the brown head of a large, long-beaked bird peeking above the bank. I had last seen goosander bobbing about on Birmingham's Sandwell Valley reservoir and the female ducking out of view behind a tuft of sedge was the last thing I was expecting to see up here, but my bird book verified that they do indeed breed near upland rivers. That is one of the things that keeps birdwatching stimulating: same bird, different place – likewise different bird, same place.

Then a two-tone song filled the air, only I didn't have to think twice to identify it. *Cu-ckoo, cu-ckoo.* Along with 'quack' most people know this one, and it does make things easier when birds sing their names. As my binoculars didn't have rain guards the initial view was of a blurry grey dove-like bird in a nearby tree. A telescope would have been handy, only the bright blue one I had been lent had developed a fault and in trying to fix it I had made things far worse. So I dried my binoculars on a sleeve and simply walked up to the tree the cuckoo was in and got a perfect view of him. More often heard than seen, a male cuckoo is a handsome bird, with a slate-grey head and back, orange-yellow legs, barred underparts and white dots on his dark tail.

Sadly, like many of our long-distance summer migrants they are being heard and seen a lot less these days. It is thought climate changes and habitat loss on their wintering grounds in Africa make it harder for them to find food, and once they get here, happy to stuff themselves with furry caterpillars other birds won't touch, they face the added difficulty that dunnocks and meadow pipits whose nests they frequently parasitize are far less common than they once were. So I was grateful to see one, or rather two, for as he sang, his wings drooping and throat puffed up with the effort, another male swooped by and the pair of them chased each other between the trees.

Further on past a field of dejected rain-sodden lambs the path led through an area of old upland oak woodland. The leaves were just emerging, giving the forest a light wash of vivid green, and beneath the boughs a thick spongy layer of moss coated the ground and anything on it. Doze off here and you could wake up covered in the stuff. It was just the kind of place that I had read in books would be home to such birds as . . . and there was one straight ahead: a pied flycatcher on a branch by a nest box. It had been years since I had seen one of these attractive little black-and-white birds. Then a male redstart in distinctive grey, black and orange breeding colours landed on a stone wall close by, and when the wood gave way to moorland above I rounded a corner and saw perched on a rock a pair of ring ouzels, the female a drab brown next to the male. It was perfect. Everything was where it should be, as if posing for one of those illustrated nature information boards you get at the entrance to reserves that are typically crammed with an unfeasibly impressive range of labelled species.

It was a shame to have to leave such a beautiful valley, made all the more enchanting by the birds that lived in it, though I had bad photos and good memories to treasure. I had seen more species than I had dreamt possible in a morning. But the high was tempered with a low. A little black cloud that had been chasing behind me over the previous few days finally caught up as I sat in a lay-by thinking over my successes. I felt guilty. Guilty about deserting family, friends and work, for taking time out, for enjoying myself alone. I might have left with everyone's blessing, but they were certainly lying to make me feel better. Surely they couldn't cope without me . . .

It was time to return to Devon and throw myself fully into family life once more, convinced that by rattling through household chores I would feel better and earn a bit more time off for good behaviour. So I busied myself trying to buy my way to a clear conscience. I cooked, cleaned, hoovered, mowed the lawn and nearly did some ironing. It was exhausting. And as it was the half-term holidays I even took my daughters to a Plymouth Argyle football match as a 'treat'. ('No you can't bring your violin. And put down that copy of *Pride and Prejudice* and practise the swear words I taught you.') After a few days I reckoned I had earned plenty of brownie points, though surprisingly no one had been totting these up. The guilty feelings subsided, enthusiastic washing up slipped into overnight soaking and my focus drifted back to the Red List birds that lay ahead. I had fifteen species left to see, including some pretty weird and some extremely rare ones, and a little more time off work, plenty of spring left and a glorious British summer to come. Yup, everything was going just fine . . .

According to chaos theorists, a tiny event like the flapping of a butterfly's wings in one country can set in motion a course of events with major consequences elsewhere, such as a tornado in a neighbouring continent. If that is the case, then I know who to blame. It was late April 2008 and some pesky butterfly fuelled up on high-octane nectar in eastern Europe was at that moment flapping away for dear life, stirring up a storm that would send my stress levels through the roof.

CHAPTER NINE

MAY IS A GREAT MONTH FOR GETTING OUT AND SPOTTING birds as our breeding species are generally brighter, bolder and noisier than ever and doing their best to be noticed. They want to identify themselves – which is a great help as I was having trouble doing it for them. It is also a good time to engage in a little naked birdwatching. Nope, not in that way – I didn't want to frighten them all away – rather, stripped of binoculars. On early morning puppy walks through a nearby forest I tried to focus on sound, and was beginning to appreciate how right the experts were to go on about the benefits of learning birdsong. It is not simply about knowing, but about paying attention, and the more I listened, the more I saw. That call in the conifers as pin-thin as pine needles was a goldcrest. And that hard mechanical *chik!* was a great spotted woodpecker. The *peu-peu-peu* of water dripping in an enamel bath? A nuthatch. Familiar birds became new triumphs. And the ticking sound that accelerated into a sweet trill? It was a wood warbler perched on a thin branch and shivering with the effort, a first-ever sighting that would have passed me by had I not recognized its song from the CDs I played in the car on my commute to and from work.

I have the dog walks and birdsong revision to thank for leading me to my next species of high conservation concern – another warbler, but one that is part mouse, part insect.

For anyone not interested in warblers, now is a good time to make a cup of tea. For those prepared to give them the benefit of the doubt, let me begin with a warning: you are about to enter a world of small, non-descript, brownish, skulking birds. There are rewards. I haven't thought of any yet, but I feel sure there must be some.

While many birds are unmistakable, our fourteen breeding species of warblers can be totally mistakable, and none more so than the four varieties I faced on the Red List: the aquatic warbler, the grasshopper warbler, the rare marsh warbler and Savi's warbler. Theirs are the kinds of pictures one flicks past in bird books, little beige lookalikes that appear far too difficult to tell apart. They spend most of their publicity-shy lives hidden in dense cover and even their names are off-putting – it's that 'warbler' word that makes it all too easy to lump them together and file under 'birds for the experts'. The more I read about their scarcity and secretive natures, the more I realized how difficult it would be to hear, let alone see, even one type of Red List warbler. Already the aquatic warbler had eluded me and I was inclined to write the other three species off as a lost cause. They just didn't seem worth the effort.

However, the grasshopper warbler had other ideas. The commonest of the four by far and easily my best bet for success, this summer migrant numbers in the thousands, though they are thinly spread across Britain and spend most of their lives creeping around at the base of thick vegetation like mice. Actually clapping eyes on one is no mean feat as the only time they tend to surface from the scrub in which they feed is to sing – and singing is what warblers do best. The sound of a grasshopper warbler has been likened to the continuous clicking of an angler's reel being wound or a freewheeling bicycle wheel, and it was this bizarre noise that stopped me in my tracks while walking Oakey early one morning during the first week of May less than half a mile from where I live. Rattled off at an astonishing twenty-six double notes per second, the unmusical song is so unvarying and unremitting, lasting minutes without pause, that it is easily confused with a chirping insect, and so high-pitched that dogs hear a lot more grasshopper warblers than people.

'Hey, do you know what that is?' I smiled down at Oakey.

He looked at me, peeved that the walk had come to a standstill, and gave me the kind of look which said: 'Some kind of warbler. Big deal.'

The far-carrying song was emanating from an impenetrable swathe of gorse beside a lane skirting the western fringe of Dartmoor, but was hard to pinpoint. Singing grasshopper warblers tend to turn their heads to project their sound over a wide area which means that it can come in waves and deflect off neighbouring objects. Up and down I walked, and on and on it reeled, until finally I spotted the bird, perched on a sprig of gorse. Of course as soon as I saw it, it saw me and flew off, but not far and a few minutes later I had a perfect view. Its streaky brown plumage wasn't going to win any beauty contests, but the song it belted out from the top of the bush like a clockwork toy that wouldn't unwind, bill open, yellow gape vibrating as it flooded the morning air with hundreds of notes a minute, was mesmerizing. Such vocal stamina in a bird weighing no more than 14 grams that has just arrived after flying here from West Africa deserves appreciation. It forced me to rethink my position on warblers. Short fancy tunes and brightly coloured plumage seemed easy by comparison. It was like discovering the dreary-looking pupil from your schooldays had turned out to have an extraordinary talent.

Over recent decades it has been a boom and bust cycle for grasshopper warblers. They can breed in most kinds of overgrown open places, and took advantage of scruffy young conifer plantations to increase their numbers and range during the 1960s. However, the evergreens eventually matured and swallowed up the land, while rough, rank areas elsewhere became harder to find as agriculture intensified. Added to that, droughts and overgrazing in sub-Saharan Africa made their winter quarters less hospitable. The result was that a colour-coded map of their distribution across Britain dwindled from an almost uniform flush of solid crimson as numbers peaked in the mid-1970s to something resembling a mild case of the measles twenty years later. Despite a recent upturn there are far fewer grasshopper warblers around than there were thirty years ago. Then again, there may be more than there were sixty years ago, so whether theirs is a good news or a bad news story largely depends on your starting point. That said, if the decline of the last three decades were to be repeated then it would be hard to put any positive spin on the situation.

So given that grasshopper warblers are considered worthy of Red List status, is any specific action being taken to help them? Well, not a great deal. As I was beginning to discover, turning conservation concerns into conservation action is not always straightforward.

Dr Andy Brown is principal birds specialist at Natural England and another of our Red List authors. 'Diagnosing the real causes of decline in any species is a tricky business and requires high quality research which may take several years,' he told me when I visited him at his offices in Peterborough.

'Once we know the causes we need to devise appropriate solutions and would usually seek to put them to the test in the real world. Then, when we know our solutions will be effective, we're ready to halt or reverse our target species' decline – though more often than not it requires a bucket-load of highly targeted money to make a difference.'

He suggested that when it came to helping widespread birds, the choice is often between spreading resources evenly but thinly or concentrating them in the best areas. And as for our scarcer 'conservation dependent' birds – a depressing term if ever there was one – levels of funding need to be sustained even when the situation is improving or you run the risk of returning to square one.

'When the birds are sufficiently abundant and widespread to be self-sustaining you can stop,' he said, 'but there may be decades between the start of our interventions and when we can let them go.'

Just a stone's throw away from his upper-storey window is the headquarters of the Joint Nature Conservation Committee, which guides the government on its national and international conservation obligations, and I took the opportunity to meet up with birds and surveillance adviser Dr Helen Baker.

She told me that while small-scale schemes for rare species on the brink had delivered success stories, a major hurdle was the time required to influence wider change.

'The biggest frustration is the years it takes for legislation to get through the various processes to positive action on the ground,' she said.

'But there's a growing recognition that the health of our environment is absolutely crucial, that we can only push it so far before there is no forgiveness left in it and it begins to fail us.'

'We can't turn back the clock two hundred years,' she added. 'Some bird species that are emblematic of the state of the countryside and that were once common we simply will not get back in the same numbers as there have been significant changes in so many ways. In addressing their recoveries we have to decide how many we want and where we want them.'

That final phrase struck me as hugely significant. As things stand *we* decide – and what a responsibility that is. Our wildlife depends on us, and looking after it has, crudely speaking, become something of a numbers game, a cost-per-bird management exercise governed by lists and targets and spending priorities and directives, with an eye to the bottom line. How many bitterns do we want? If you know where to look, you can find out. (A hundred calling males by 2020 is the national target, as it happens.) And how many can we afford? (Well, they are pricey. Reedbed restoration projects since the mid-1990s have so far worked out at roughly £150,000 for every newly recorded breeding male.)

Before leaving Helen to get on with her work, I asked her how I could help make a difference, preferably without having to spend hundreds of thousands of pounds.

'Everyone can,' she said, 'by simply going out and enjoying the countryside, and making it known why.'

Phew! From an environmentalist that sounded refreshingly undemanding.

I had no idea exactly where I was, and I was not likely to be told. The Land Rover was parked in rough grass on a farm somewhere in Wiltshire. It was an RSPB vehicle, but unmarked so as to avoid drawing the attention of any eagle-eyed egg thieves. Such secrecy would not be out of place on military manoeuvres, which was appropriate given that we were near Salisbury Plain MoD land and passed two tanks on the drive to our location. Nick Adams was sitting beside me, and ahead of us was a huge ploughed field which we were surveying for one of the UK's rarest breeding birds using telescopes fixed to the vehicle windows. The dry earth was covered in hundreds of thousands of flint stones. Somewhere among them, we had been told, was a well-camouflaged stone-curlew sitting on a nest, and the challenge was to find it.

No surprise who spotted it first.

'You see the wheel tracks at the far edge of the field?' Nick said after about ten minutes.

'Uh huh,' I answered, peering through the telescope he had lent me.

'Follow them forward until you reach a green plant, then 11 o'clock from that is a lighter patch of soil, and the female is back a few feet from that.'

It was the first really hot and sunny day in May and a heat haze was blurring distant views. 'What, that rock behind?'

'That's her,' he said.

'That's a bird?!'

It was hard to believe, but as Nick was manager of the Wessex Stone-Curlew Project I had to take his word for it.

The stone-curlew is quite an odd-looking bird, if you actually manage to see one. With its goggle-eyed stare and knobbly-kneed legs it would be a prime target for playground taunts. About the size of a crow, it is a wader that doesn't wade, a gangly-legged landlubber that nests on open bare ground and feeds on worms, beetles, spiders and other such delicacies, mostly at night – hence the big round eyes. Its plumage is a warm sandy brown, streaked with thin lines of black, and it has matching accessories: yellow beak, yellow irises and yellow legs. However, what I was looking at was none of these things. It was quite obviously a rock.

I heard a car approaching, and the farmer whose land we were on pulled up alongside, got out and strode over towards us. He wasn't wielding a shotgun or shaking his fist, which was a good sign. In fact he seemed surprisingly pleased to see Nick.

'So you got my call. Spotted them then?' he asked.

Nick nodded and pointed at the distant rock. 'That's the female on the nest. We'll mark it out and then the contractors can drill seed around her.'

'Good.' The farmer smiled. 'I was sure they were nesting somewhere around there.'

Good? But this was a farmer speaking! An obscure bird that had flown in from southern Europe or northern Africa for the summer had chosen his arable field as a nest site, forcing farm workers to sow around it at some inconvenience and depriving him of a swathe of crop . . . and he was happy with the situation?

'I'll leave you to it,' the farmer said. 'And don't forget to look for the other pair I told you about.'

Once he had left I asked Nick whether I had heard correctly.

'Around here the farmers are fantastic. We couldn't do anything without their help,' he told me. 'Having stone-curlew on their land enables them to qualify for higher level environmental stewardship grants, but they go above and beyond what they're paid to do. I've known some prepared to lose money forgoing a section of crop because they said they were honoured to have them as they are such iconic birds of this area.'

Grants for rocks! I laughed to myself.

And then the rock I had been staring at moved, and I saw it had a black-tipped yellow beak.

An accountant for seventeen years, Nick quit to pursue his passion for birds full-time, and the bottom line he now keeps a close eye on is the number of stone-curlews in his Wessex patch – a figure that has shown a healthy profit over recent years, rising steadily from a low of forty pairs in the 1980s to 120 pairs today. The area holds a third of the national population. However, the species is so vulnerable to disturbance and the predations of egg collectors that as yet there is no facility enabling the public to view them, so I was fortunate he allowed me to accompany him for a morning on his farm visits to locate nests – not that I could offer much in the way of help given that I had yet to get to grips with the basic differences between a lump of flint and a sitting bird.

'Look, there's the male coming in,' Nick said. 'Just to the left.'

A flat-headed plover-like bird was cautiously step-ping from the vegetation at the side of the field onto the stony ground 300 metres away and heading towards the female. I could clearly see his warm light brown colouring, cream lines above and below his wide eyes that emphasized a slightly dumbfounded appearance, a light stripe across his folded wing, and his short black-tipped bill. I was aware they were wary birds, but I did not believe just how wary. On spotting a pair of rooks overhead he froze so as not to alert them to the presence of the nest ahead of him, and only when they moved off did he once more creep forward, pace by pace, hunched over and constantly checking around him as if suffering from a combination of severe arthritis and chronic paranoia. After twenty minutes he had covered barely ten feet, eventually reaching the nest and hunkering down on the ground while his mate tiptoed away to feed, melting into the vegetation nearby.

They are highly distinctive, weird even, and the sort of bird you might expect to see on some documentary about flat arid regions in Africa – which makes it all the more interesting that a few stone-curlews turn up here every summer, favouring plains cropped short by sheep or rabbits, and well-drained chalk fields and downland. Their presence is yet another example of the diversity of habitats on offer in Britain, even if we can't promise much in the way of space. Apart from Wessex, the only other UK stronghold for these migrants is the dry sandy Breckland of East Anglia, where it is possible to see them from hides in Norfolk.

As I was discovering, our Red List birds face a diverse range of difficulties. Spray the fields, slay the partridges. Marshes dry out, bitterns die out. Deer fences go up, capercaillie numbers go down. But few birds in England would reckon on being bombed. Yet stone-curlews do find themselves in the line of heavy artillery fire on a scale that would explain a startled look and paranoid disposition. The reason is that rabbit-cropped grassland and airfields on military bases, such as Salisbury Plain and Porton Down, are tempting places to settle for the summer, and quite a few stone-curlews opt to nest among the ruts of tank caterpillar tracks and on firing ranges. No risk from egg collectors to be sure, and if they keep their heads down it can be a safe bet, especially as Defence Estates now makes a point of protecting them – even, apparently, keeping troops away from nests with 'mine field' signs.

Because they nest in the open, farmers' fields are their most favoured nesting sites. But there are two main problems, both of which contributed to an almost vertical drop in stone-curlew numbers as agriculture intensified and sowing regimes changed. Ploughs and harrows destroy the eggs and chicks, and any light green fuzz breaking through the soil when they take up residence rapidly grows into uniform, dense crops. The stems only need to be a few centimetres high for stone-curlews to desert a nest, because sitting birds like to be able to look around them so they can see predators coming. The answer has been to pay farmers to create special, bare stone-curlew plots. But not everything always goes to plan.

'Now you have to help me remember where the nest is,' Nick said, starting the engine and driving down a strip of weedy game cover beside the field. 'The plot that was created for them is over there.' He pointed to a square a couple of hundred metres wide in a neighbouring field. 'And as you can see they are . . . well, not on it. Unfortunately they don't always do what you want them to do.'

As we neared, the pair flew a little way off on long black and white marked wings, and watched us from a safe distance. All our birds are subject to basic legal safeguards making it an offence to kill, injure or take them from the wild, destroy their nests or collect their eggs. However, a select number have an even higher level of protection which means that it is against the law to even disturb them at the nest. The stone-curlew is among them, so if I hadn't been with Nick, then the two birds eyeing me suspiciously from a neighbouring field could have turned me in. Having said that, without Nick I would never have managed to find a stone-curlew in the first place – and there is no crime that I know of involving the reckless disturbing of rocks.

Once we had parked, Nick got out and began making his way carefully along the furrows looking ahead of him. Finding a sitting stone-curlew in a stony field on a hot and hazy day is one thing; finding its nest once it has flown is quite another, because it isn't a nest at all, more a shallow scrape in the earth decorated with a few little stones or rabbit droppings, and the eggs, roughly the size of hen's eggs but more pointed, are a speckled muddy brown and easy to overlook.

The last thing I wanted to do was trample on the precious clutch and end up discovering stone-curlew egg yoke in the tread of my shoes at the end of the day, so I kept well back, following behind at a distance. It proved extremely hard to pinpoint exactly where the birds had been, but eventually Nick found their scrape amid the scattered flints with a single egg resting in the centre. He measured and weighed it carefully and we pushed sticks into the ground to signal to the farm workers which area to avoid before returning to the Land Rover.

Eggs change in weight as an embryo develops and the figures Nick recorded meant that he could calculate when the one we found was laid, how many of its twenty-seven days of incubation remained and the exact date when the chick would hatch, enabling him to circle the date in his diary, accurately advise the farmer and return to ring the youngster before it took off foraging. Like other conservationists working with the birds, he also regularly has to stand guard when farmers are working the fields and lift chicks out of the path of oncoming ploughs until danger has passed, and he engages in a bit of gardening – weeding areas around nests so they don't become too overgrown. No conservation work for any of our Red List birds is as hands-on as that for stone-curlews.

'It's a full-time job throughout the summer, but all the work is paying off,' Nick told me. 'And there's nothing more satisfying than an individual bird returning the following year that you had ringed and put in long hours trying to protect.'

Skylarks don't sing requests, but if they did they would probably draw the line at the French children's song: *Alouette, gentille alouette, alouette je te plumerai*. Translated it is all about plucking skylarks for the pot, which was once commonplace here as they were widely eaten, with Mrs Beeton among many serving them up as a delicacy stuffed and baked. Those netted by the Victorians that were spared the pot frequently ended their days as caged songbirds, some with their eyes barbarically put out in the misplaced belief they sang better blind. Worse still, others were plagued in the wild by the attentions of sensitive poets and musicians. In bygone days it didn't pay to be noticed. Far safer then for birds to keep a low profile, look awful, sing badly and taste foul.

The skylark is certainly not much to look at, but it is a lot to listen to as it launches into uplifting song, rising and hovering over open countryside for minutes on end pouring out an unbroken stream of rapid trills and high-pitched warbles like an overwound music box. Being a tree-fearing bird of grasslands, heaths and wide cultivated fields without song posts, it chooses to sing from the sky, and the overlapping airborne arias of several birds dotted high above their territories can create the effect of surround sound for anyone walking beneath them. But from the 1970s onwards skies over our arable lands began to be emptied of song as cultivated fields that once provided perfect habitat were turned into super-efficient agricultural factory floors, more than halving skylark numbers in the process. There was less cause for celebratory poetry and music as the lark ascending became a case of the lark descending. As the population of one of our best-loved birds plummeted, pushing it onto our Red List, its public profile soared. The skylark became an ambassador for wildlife in decline.

We no longer eat skylarks, and while they are still pretty common and widespread the current population of 1.7 million pairs wouldn't go that far towards feeding the nation in any case, even if we got inventive with leftovers. Farmers are rightly focused on producing crops rather than little birds. But that doesn't mean we have to shove skylarks out of the picture altogether, as I found out when I visited a commercial farm in East Anglia which, perhaps surprisingly, is run by the RSPB.

Located in Cambridgeshire, Hope Farm is 180 hectares in size and grows a mix of mainly wheat and oilseed rape. But it is no woolly eco-project run by bearded, yurt-dwelling, mung-bean munchers. In fact, when I arrived I was the only one around with a beard, and no one demanded I take my shoes off and play the acoustic guitar. Hope Farm is a serious business-like operation, and also a massive experiment.

'We had been lobbying to try to improve the plight of farmland birds, but we'd never put our money where our mouth was,' farm project manager Chris Bailey told me. 'To that end we bought this site in 1999 following a huge appeal for member contributions. It's one of the most adventurous and far-reaching things the charity has ever done, a unique project run for profit with the aim of improving biodiversity.'

The farm looks like any other in the area: neat, tree-less large flat fields of green, yellow and brown, weedy margins and a stretch or two of hedgerow. Walking around I came across no bird hides or nature trails. The only thing that caught my eye as out of the ordinary was a scattering of bare squares in the fields of wheat, as if whoever was responsible for sowing the crops had run into problems with the equipment jamming.

The reason, Chris told me, was skylarks.

The main problem for skylarks has been that most of our wheat is now sown in the late autumn rather than spring. It sprouts early, remains dormant through the winter frosts and then puts on a growth spurt when the weather warms up. This has a double-whammy effect on ground nesters. After the summer harvest all the stubble is ploughed up ready for the next planting, leaving no winter pickings for farmland birds, while in the late spring fields that would once have been newly tilled are instead like lush lawns. Skylarks can get one brood in before the growing wheat crowds them out, but really need two or three during summer to keep their numbers up. They are also forced to nest in crop tramlines where predators can find the eggs and young more easily.

Despite all of the problems associated with winter wheat, Hope Farm still grows it, and not even organically. 'We are regularly visited by farmers and farming organizations and have to show them what can be achieved on a typical modern farm,' Chris said.

All the team has done is put in the kinds of stand-ard environmental measures covered by farming grants. Nothing fancy. And the result has been that crop yields have remained competitive and farmland birds have thrived.

For skylarks, the solution has been the creation of the unseeded plots a few metres across within the crops. The patches of bare earth and weeds, similar to those for stone-curlews only much smaller, provide useful foraging areas at negligible cost. They have proven so successful at Hope Farm, trebling skylark numbers since they were introduced, that they are among a list of measures all farmers can now adopt to receive special grants.

So where were the skylarks?

'You should see one soon enough,' Chris said as we turned and headed back towards the farmhouse. And at that moment, right on cue, one rose over the wheat field in front of us and hung on the breeze singing.

It's what skies were made for.

Some birds you want to hear as much as see. If you were to read bird books looking for recommendations, however, then you would probably neither want to hear nor see a fellow Red List farmland companion of the skylark called the corn bunting. A selection of terms I came across to describe its appearance included: 'nondescript', 'dull', 'inconspicuous', 'undistinguished', 'plain', 'scruffy', 'drab' and 'dingy'. And its song? 'Repetitive', 'unmusical', 'monotonous', 'incessant'.

The corn bunting looks a bit like a chubby skylark, but without the short crest or white outer tail feathers. In fact if you subtracted all the interesting distinguishing features from all the birds in the world you would end up with a corn bunting. That may be a little unfair, but physically there isn't much about it that sets it apart, which ironically is one of the best ways to identify it. The corn bunting is streaky brown, lighter on the underside, and is not only easily overlooked out in the countryside but also in books on British birds because the standard way species are ordered means it is typically on the last page. About the most noticeable characteristic is that compared with other small finches and buntings it is tubby looking, sporting a rotund belly that has earned it such nicknames as 'corn dumpling' and 'fat bird of the barley'.

The corn bunting has had to put up with a lot more than insults over recent years. Its population has dropped by more than 85 per cent since 1970, making it one of the biggest fallers on the Red List. The decline has been for much the same reasons as our other farmland birds in trouble, and there are now only 10,000 pairs left patchily scattered across mainly eastern areas of England and Scotland.

Does anyone care? Perhaps surprisingly the answer is yes. Its song, which Simon King had described when I met him at the Birdfair as being like 'rattling keys', is much cherished as one of the evocative sounds of our arable lands in summer. The corn bunting even made the top ten in a poll of the nation's favourite farmland birds, which shows what a forgiving lot we are. (And, yes, as it happens there are more than ten species of farmland bird. If you believe the government's birdwatching bureaucrats – the ones with binoculars who don't work for MI5 – then the 'official' figure is nineteen.)

Despite all the negative descriptions, I wanted to hear and see a corn bunting, and my tactic on leaving Hope Farm was to drive along B roads through Cambridgeshire with my windows down stopping every few hundred yards beside arable fields and listening hard for its jangling song. The queues of tractors backed up behind me were obviously delighted, and I could see in my rear-view mirror that farmers at the wheel were even waving at me vigorously, which was so friendly. Some even raised a finger or two as they passed, presumably pointing out birds of interest up in the sky above.

I had no luck, and as the light began to fade I decided it was time to find a quiet lay-by where I could sleep in the car. It isn't easy finding a private spot in flat fenland where you are visible for a hundred miles around, but eventually I came across a farm track leading off the road, and pulled in beside the base of a giant electricity pylon, where I switched off the engine and got out to stretch. I couldn't have picked a better place to park. Almost immediately I heard a corn bunting and saw a dark speck perched fifty metres away in the centre of a flowering field of yellow oilseed rape like a midge floating in a bowl of custard.

As my binoculars were packed away in the car boot I got out a tiny spare pair stashed in the glove compartment that were about as powerful as opera glasses – appropriate given that I was watching a fat bird singing – and brought the dot into focus. I could barely make it out, but just then another male started up right behind me and I spun round and saw he was perched on one of the pylon struts, chest puffed out and head thrown back, notched bill wide open chucking out his song. It was the kind of perfect sighting that made me want to say thanks. So I did. I stood beneath the pylon in a field of oilseed rape somewhere in Cambridgeshire looking up at this podgy passerine singing and I said: 'Thanks!'

And then I got into my car and fell asleep with the sun setting in a blaze of crimson and the sound of corn buntings jangling in my ears.

Supposing our turtle doves wrote postcards they might read as follows: 'Terrible journey. Left Africa hungry. Flight a nightmare – most of my friends gunned down over Malta and France. What a welcome to Europe! English food lousy: portions way too small.'

Life for this summer visitor is fraught at every turn. There is too little to eat in drought-hit over-grazed areas of Africa where they spend the winter, too few farmland weed seeds here to raise enough young, and to get from one empty larder to the other they pass through regions of southern Europe where migrant birds are illegally hunted in vast numbers. Little wonder we have lost eight out of every ten turtle doves in the UK, and two-thirds of the European population.

Back in the 1970s when Lee Evans went birdwatching as a schoolboy at Cley on the north Norfolk coast, he used to regularly watch hundreds of turtle doves flying over.

'Now you can sit there and not see any. It's an abysmal situation,' he told me.

Lee is one of Britain's top birders. When he isn't acting as a bird tour guide he is chasing around the country trying to see as many species as he can every year with the kind of single-mindedness that has made him among the most renowned characters in twitching circles. Such obsessive devotion has brought its rewards, but also comes at a personal cost: he has been married four times and lost an eye in a serious road accident.

As twitchers generally like their birds rare, I was interested to know how he regarded declines in some of our common species, given that he has seen at first hand changes in bird populations over the years.

'The fact so many birds are becoming scarcer is a real worry,' he said when I called him up. 'At one time grey partridges, spotted flycatchers, tree sparrows, corn buntings and willow tits were simply bread-and-butter birds. Now you have to be prepared to travel to see them.' Obviously, I could back him up there.

The Red List species that gave him most cause for concern, however, was the turtle dove. 'You see them less and less, year after year,' he said. 'It could go the same way as the passenger pigeon if we're not careful.'

The turtle dove is the smallest of our five species of dove and pigeon, and the only one that migrates. Those that dodge hunters' guns on entering the EU return here in April and May and nest in trees near open spaces where they can find seeds, raising their young on milk – well, the next best thing, a nutritious regurgitated milky substance produced in their crops. They are among our most attractive birds, with pale pink chests, blue-grey heads, a short ladder of black and white on their necks, white-edged wedged tails and chequered dark feathers fringed with orange on their backs like tortoiseshell, though this is not the reason for the 'turtle' name, which derives instead from their soft purring *turrr turrr* song; a sound reminiscent of long, hot, lazy summer days.

Despite their precipitous decline you would think they

would still be relatively easy to see given that the last population estimate was 44,000 pairs. However, during the course of two days I struggled to find a single turtle dove, which led me to one of two possible conclusions: the absolutely outlandish notion that I might be a rubbish birdwatcher, or the far more probable deduction that the figure is a gross over-estimate.

I was looking in the South East where they are supposed to be most common, and in May, and even remembering to hold my binoculars the right way round, but they were simply not to be seen. After success with skylarks and corn buntings, my East Anglian farmland bird odyssey was grinding to a halt, and I was getting more than a little anxious. In fact I was ready to call the British Trust for Ornithology to tell them that their statisticians really did need to check their facts as, far from there being 44,000 pairs, the turtle dove had now disappeared from Britain. One day we may find a few thousand tucked down the back of a giant sofa in Norfolk along with a load of loose change and biro tops, but I wouldn't count on it.

I visited Lakenheath Fen in Suffolk, and found none, and Fowlmere in Cambridgeshire, which was also supposed to be a good site, but drew a blank. I also drove up and down country lanes between the two scanning fields and copses without any luck. Finally I decided to try Paxton Pits Nature Reserve beside the River Great Ouse south of Huntingdon, where I had heard they are regular breeders.

One of the best things about looking for specific species is that you can't help but encounter others of interest along the way. Paxton Pits reserve is a series of flooded gravel quarries surrounded by a wealth of wildlife-rich habitats, and attracts over 100,000 visitors a year, many coming to hear singing nightingales, which are virtually guaranteed every spring in the scrub and thickets a short walk from the car park.

It was mid-afternoon when I pulled up by the visitors' centre in bright sunshine and I started off along the main trail that loops around Heronry Lake, soon reaching an area of grassland surrounded by dense hawthorn bushes.

That must be a thrush warbling away, I thought as I strode along the gravel path. A weird-sounding one though. And there's another . . .

I had seen the signs for guided evening nightingale walks, and was a bit disappointed there were none planned for the day I was there as I had never heard a nightingale before.

Little did I know, I just had.

Nightingales not only sing after dark, but also quite happily in the day, and because I hadn't expected to hear one I mistook the songs emanating from the dense bushes by the path to be those of song thrushes, or blackbirds, or something else I hadn't yet learnt on my birdsong CDs. I didn't put two and two together.

Then a low-energy lightbulb switched on in my head and I realized what I was hearing, and wondered that I could ever have doubted it. The more I listened the more amazed I became. The nightingale's song is an incredibly powerful and varied mix of phrases, some as mellow as rich red wine, others squeezed into thin trills or hammered out with mechanical urgency. And when one of the shy robin-sized brown birds finally emerged from a thicket and perched in full view I couldn't resist pulling my mobile out of my pocket and phoning home.

Dispensing with small talk, I said with some urgency: 'Hi, it's me, quick, get the girls on the line!'

'Why? What's the matter?'

'I've got a bird they need to hear.'

My wife sighed. 'They're watching *Lord of the Rings*.'

'*Lord of the Rings*? Forget that.'

After a brief pause my youngest daughter came to the phone.

'Hi, Dad. What is it?'

'I'm going to hold up my mobile so you can hear this bird. It's a nightingale and it has the most beautiful song of any of our birds. Now listen hard,' I said, then like the celebrity-watchers I had seen in Leicester Square I reached out my phone towards the singing nightingale as it poured out its intricate repertoire a short distance from where I stood.

'Did you hear it?' I asked a minute later, pressing the receiver to my ear once more.

'What? Oh, yeah,' my daughter replied. 'Can I go now? It's a good bit in the film.'

'Sure, okay,' I said.

I was so full of enthusiasm about the nightingales and so proud that I knew what they were that I wanted to tell everyone who passed by.

A young man with binoculars around his neck was

heading quickly up the path towards me, and when he paused I said: 'Are you looking for nightingales?'

'Great, aren't they,' he said, smiling. 'No, actually I'm on my way to see something else.'

'Oh, what's that?' I asked, a little put out.

'It's a kind of woodpecker that's quite rare.'

'Oh yes?'

'It's called a wryneck.'

My mouth fell open.

'It's just around the corner apparently,' he added, dashing off.

I felt as if I had been slapped around the face. After all the effort I had put in trying to track one down in Cornwall it hardly seemed fair to be told one was 'just around the corner'. I cursed under my breath, knowing that I had to go and look, and followed him to a spot opposite boat moorings on the Great Ouse where a half dozen other birdwatchers were gathered. Of course the wryneck was nowhere to be seen, and I began telling the young man, a student called Ed, in a patronizing and knowing way how hard they were to find when he interrupted and said: 'Look!' And there behind us was the little grey woodpecker in full view on the path beneath a tree. As easy as that.

The first time I had seen one it had been something of a relief. This time I could enjoy it more. But there was something special about the sighting that had nothing to do with the bird, and everything to do with the people around me excitedly savouring the moment. As texts were fired off new people arrived, some straight from work in shirts and shiny shoes, and as they joined the small gathering those there first immediately offered them the use of their lined-up telescopes to ensure they saw the bird before wasting time setting up their own equipment. This act of thoughtfulness and the pleasure all seemed to be taking in the shared experience made a lasting impression.

'I've been waiting years for this,' one man beamed as he absorbed the bird hungrily through his binoculars. 'The early nineties was the last time one was spotted here.'

It made the weeks I spent trying to see one seem trifling by comparison, and I got the feeling he could have stood there patiently watching it until the sun went down, and that I would still find him in the same spot the next morning, with one of those 'Police Aware' signs stuck on his back.

However, I had to leave him and the others to it because I was sure I had heard a turtle dove calling from a line of trees a little way ahead. Only there was a problem. Hanging around on the path between me and the bird I hoped to find was the wryneck. To get to see the dove would mean frightening away the wryneck. To frighten away the wryneck meant being thrown in the river by a group of angry birdwatchers.

I had no option but to turn and walk the entire two-mile length of the circular path around the reserve in order to end up where I wanted to be just a couple of dozen yards ahead. And of course by the time I got there the turtle dove was gone.

Jinxed by a wryneck yet again.

I gave up on turtle doves. Instead, after a night in a

B&B on the outskirts of Cambridge I drove to Thetford Forest Park to meet up with BTO research ecologist Greg Conway, an expert on a red-listed bird with a scientific name that cries out to be part of some ornithological Gregorian chant: *Lullula arborea*.

Thetford Forest is Britain's largest lowland pine forest. Straddling south Norfolk and north Suffolk it was planted after the First World War by the newly established Forestry Commission at a time when our wood stocks were perilously low and fast-growing conifers provided the answer. What had once been heath and grassland became impenetrable blocks of green-topped pit props, and eighty years on it is still a vast commercial plantation – only much more besides as the area has increasingly been managed with recreation and conservation in mind.

Having said that, it was hard to imagine the spot we had driven to was managed for anything much at all, least of all wildlife. It was a mess. A swathe of conifers had been cut down, the trunks taken away and the remaining roots grubbed up by diggers and dumped in rows. It might not have looked pretty but this woodland clearing, Greg assured me, provided ideal habitat for the bird he was studying and that I had come to see: the woodlark.

The woodlark looks pretty much like a skylark, only it is slightly smaller and paler with a short white-cornered tail, a dark patch at the corner of its wing and a long, thin, light stripe above its eye. It is also far less common than a skylark and has experienced something of a population rollercoaster ride over the last century – knocked back by severe winters and the loss of sparsely wooded heaths, then regaining ground where dense forests have been felled and young conifers planted. Its numbers were up in the 1950s, down in the 1960s, up in the 1970s, down in the 1980s and up in the 1990s. Supposing you could buy shares in birds then the fluctuating fortunes of woodlarks might well ward off a wary speculator. However, of all the Red List birds they would probably have been the soundest investment twenty years ago when they hit a low of 250 pairs. Since then their numbers have steadily climbed to over 3,000 pairs and they are spreading outwards from strongholds in the South and East. The woodlark's sweet, descending song may be one of the saddest around, but these days it has plenty to sing about, and the fact it can be heard more and more is good reason to feel cheerful.

'What they need are areas of grass cover and bare ground for foraging in, and the felled areas are perfect for several years until the new trees grow too tall,' Greg said, parking near a heap of sun-blanched roots at one edge of a huge rectangle of cleared land bordered by conifers.

While the habitat may be good, ground-nesting woodlarks are vulnerable to predators like foxes, crows and adders, and potentially sensitive to disturbance by visitors using the trails, such as dog walkers. Exactly how much of an impact this has on their numbers was being studied by Greg, and he had even rigged up more than a dozen motion-sensitive cameras beside nests to identify which animals are woodlarks' worst enemies. Dog-owners beware: your beloved pooch's grainy mugshot could be pinned up as part of a rogues' gallery on a wall in Greg's office.

One moment I had never seen a woodlark in my life, then Greg pointed at a bird perching on an upturned tree root poking through a tangle of gorse and grass a short distance away, said, 'There's the male,' and I had seen one. In that split second I crossed from one camp to another. It would be too much to suggest the nation is divided into those who have seen a woodlark and those who haven't, given that the vast majority neither know nor care, but the amoebic sprawl of my life experiences nudged forward a fraction taking in the new sight, and a new sound as it uttered a few liquid notes from where it perched.

We watched it for a while until it flew off to another part of its territory out of view. Unfortunately I couldn't stay longer as I planned to get to Hampshire before dark to visit the home of the man credited with getting us all birdwatching in the first place.

After returning to my car I had only driven a little way past Cambridge and was taking a route along minor roads when I found myself skirting a village somewhere near Royston. Where the road passed a farm and a line of trees I pulled over in the shade and got out. Opposite was a wide weedy field where a number of pigeons were pecking around in the earth, and the fact that there were so many had prompted me to stop. I had scrutinized a lot of arable acres over the previous few days, but had a good feeling about this patch of what looked like set-aside. Through my binoculars I counted more than fifty woodpigeons, and there were at least a dozen stock doves and numerous collared doves. It was like some kind of Dove World visitor attraction. Then I saw what I had been hoping to stumble across: side by side amid the grey throng were a pair of turtle doves. They appeared so small and dainty alongside the heavyweight woodpigeons. Fragile even. And I was surprised at just how colourful and beautiful they were. I hadn't expected to be bowled over by a dove, but with their red legs, soft pink chests and backs patterned like cracked caramel glaze they were irresistible. After all my searching I was amazed to find they existed at all. So to anyone who hasn't seen a turtle dove, it is well worth it. But hurry, while flocks last . . .

After the vast skies and exposed spaces of Cambridgeshire and Norfolk, driving through Hampshire into the village of Selborne was like plunging into a cool pool of green, with its lush meadows and woods of oak and beech. It oozed picturesque rural England – buttercups, bumble bees and church bells. If arable East Anglia is considered the nation's bread basket then this would be the place to have the picnic.

Until fairly recently one could have spread a rug beneath one of the oldest trees in Britain, a 1,400-year-old yew standing in the grounds of St Mary's Church in the centre of the village. Toppled in the gales of 1990 the tree has now been reduced to a smooth-sided stump, a decaying monument amid the churchyard memorials, and after arriving in Selborne in the late afternoon I found myself standing by it pressing my hand against its side. But I had not come to pay my respects to a dead tree, incredible though it was. Instead I followed a path mown in the grass around the side of the church to a tiny headstone hemmed in between others and bearing the simple inscription: G.W. 26th June 1793.

Gilbert White is credited with being one of the first ecologists. At a time when the study of nature was confined to laboratories, and theories postulated from piles of bones and the dissection of plucked and pickled specimens, this Oxford-educated curate was wandering around his parish in the eighteenth century simply watching wildlife in the wild. His was the science of observing the living world in its surroundings, and his compiled letters and meticulous notes became the best-selling book *The Natural History and Antiquities of Selborne*, which has never been out of print since it was first published in 1789. Gilbert White's fieldwork led to a few new discoveries, such as the identification of three mind-bogglingly similar species of warbler on the basis of song, but more importantly he broadened our understanding of the inter-connectedness of life, from the vital role of the humble earthworm upwards, and paved the way for a new approach to the study of the natural world. His book has inspired generations of backyard naturalists and birdwatchers and spawned a kind of citizen science in which we can all participate without the need for microscopes, lab coats and petri dishes. When we record the first swallow of spring or add the name of a new butterfly in our garden to a tally on the kitchen pinboard we follow in his footsteps – and our seemingly trivial everyday lists of sightings are considered useful even today by those tracking the spread of species and the effects of climate change.

Gilbert White's house, The Wakes, stands opposite St Mary's Church, and I was relieved to find a room was available above a pub just across the street. My accommodation over the previous few nights had been divided between B&Bs and lay-bys, and I didn't fancy sleeping in my car yet again.

After dumping my bags there was time for a walk along paths made famous in *The Natural History and Antiquities of Selborne*, through a landscape now protected by the National Trust. I climbed the steep Zig-Zag track carved out by Gilbert White to reach the plateau at the top of Selborne Hill, then retraced my steps down into the valley and strolled beneath the Hanger where tall beech trees cling to the chalk hillside. From there I could look back across a wide expanse of parkland to the rear of his house, now restored as a museum. There was no one else about to ruin the setting, just me, which was fine of course, sharing views that he would have enjoyed over two hundred years before. I spotted a roe deer beneath an oak tree, and a fox further on, two robins and a wren, great tits, blackbirds and chaffinches – a fittingly English selection which I duly noted down, feeling that in some way I owed it to the celebrated recorder of flora and fauna. It was an idyllic place, seemingly unchanged over the centuries, and I could almost imagine bumping into the reverend rounding a corner and being put to shame by his list of sightings.

Being there made me wonder just how much our appreciation of nature is bound up with a sentimental element of nostalgia. When I saw the roe deer browsing among the trees it felt more like a glimpse of the past than an experience in the present, a fleeting link with some intangible age of natural harmony and abundance. Perhaps at the heart of it our love of nature is motivated by such a spiritual yearning, a search for an imaginary paradise where the rivers are always filled with salmon, the woods with birdsong, the meadows with wild flowers, the skies with soaring eagles and secluded corners lie beyond the reach of man. And where better to start looking for that lost Garden of Eden on a calm, warm evening in May than among the beech trees and badger tracks of Selborne.

The following morning I was suffering from a severe case of heavy duvet syndrome and missed breakfast, but eventually managed to haul myself out of bed to visit Gilbert White's house. I snooped around in his rooms, read displayed pages of his original handwritten manuscript and toured the landscaped gardens, making the mistake of taking a shortcut behind by the vegetable plots and falling off a walled ha-ha, which wasn't the least bit funny. I had been hoping the reverend might bless me with a Red List bird or two in his parish, but it was not to be. However, as luck would have it another writer who lived in a neighbouring village a few years after his death came to my aid instead: Jane Austen. Taking a detour to pass by her Chawton home before rejoining the A31 I spotted a small finch in a hedge on the outskirts of the village. It was a linnet, a widespread lowland relative of the twite, only far more eye-catching. Surprisingly untroubled by a car pulling up right in front of it, the obliging bird remained perched in full view on a thorny twig, patiently waiting while I found my binoculars on the back seat, wound down the window and finally got it in focus.

Not only is a male linnet a handsome sight, with a chestnut back, grey head and crimson patches on its chest and forehead, but it also has a charming twittering song which made it a favourite cagebird during the Victorian era. As if to prove that point the bird I was watching deigned to give me a few notes, though only a few before flying off. I'm guessing it spotted the beginner's guides to birdsong CDs on the front seat beside me and decided its music was lost on a gawping first-grader.

As with many of our farmland birds, things started going wrong for linnets in the mid-1970s. Like twites they are dedicated seed-eaters, so the increasing use of bug-killing crop sprays posed little problem. Instead it was herbicides that did the damage. No weeds, no seeds, no food, no broods. And the ploughing up of unproductive overgrown field edges, winter stubbles and the kinds of scruffy, scrubby places where they like to nest made life even harder. Within a decade our linnet population had been slashed by more than half, and with no sign of a recovery they joined the twite on the Red List.

However, their slide has stalled, and it is believed the main reason is that they developed a taste for oilseed rape – of which there is no shortage, as anyone who has recently taken a trip through our yellow and pleasant land will testify.

*　　*　　*

On returning home I had a welcome surprise – a message from research biologist Ron Summers saying that he had analysed the crossbill sounds from the day we spent in the forests north of Inverness. While birds at the second and third sites had been common crossbills, the first pair we saw were indeed scarce Scottish crossbills.

I couldn't stop grinning all day. It was like getting an official exam result with a big fat pass mark on it.

All of which meant that I had nine species left on the list to track down. They included some of the rarest breeding birds in Britain – and I could well imagine that at that precise moment they were busy deciding on their hiding places in anticipation of my arrival.

CHAPTER TEN

I HAVE HEARD IT SAID THAT IF YOU DON'T WASH YOUR hair, eventually it will naturally clean itself. That may or may not be the case, but I can confirm that this principle does not apply to a house. It was late May, the half-term holidays, my wife was having to work extra hours and I was supposed to be in charge. As far as domestic chores were concerned I was letting nature take its course, so by the third day I was surprised to find the washing-up still hadn't done itself, the vacuum cleaner had shown no initiative when it came to tackling the carpets, and the bathroom hadn't even bothered to wipe a cloth over its grimy features, even though I had left a new pack by the sink. It was very disappointing.

My daughters had run out of clean clothes and were

not best pleased that the only washed items I could find for them were firemen's outfits from the fancy dress box, and we were short on food. On top of all that a knee injury meant Oakey was sporting one of those embarrassing plastic head funnels to prevent him chewing his stitches, so that he resembled a table lamp with four legs and bad steering and kept crashing into everything. His insurance policy specifically stated that it did not cover 'civil commotion', though since that just about summed up everything where he was concerned we were unlikely to ever be able to make a claim.

Things were unravelling fast. Yet all I could think about was the birds I wanted to see, the vast distances I had to cover and the precious little time left before I was due back at work. I needed to get a grip. At the very least I had to do some shopping. So I drew up a list. And what did I write underlined at the top above bread, milk, cheese, dog tranquillizer and disposable plates? *Bottle of rosé wine*. I had a sighting from a few days earlier to celebrate and it was the required drink for such an occasion.

There was a time when RSPB warden Paul Morrison and his team toasted every new pair of roseate terns that nested on Coquet Island with rosé wine, but as he told me, 'Eventually numbers began increasing so steadily that we would have been staggering around unable to get any work done.'

The recovery of this summer visitor from the brink of extinction in the UK over the last few years has certainly been worth raising a glass to. Not only is the roseate tern one of Britain's rarest breeding seabirds, it is also one of the most elegant. It looks a bit like an arctic or common tern, only with a lighter back, an almost entirely black bill, a flush of pink on its breast from which it gets its name, and it has much longer tail streamers that were prized in the nineteenth century as decorative plumes for women's hats.

For one reason or another we lost 95 per cent of our 1,000 or so pairs of 'rosies' between the mid-1960s and mid-1990s. Since then conservation work has helped the small population that remained increase by the same proportion of 95 per cent. Unfortunately, that doesn't bring them back up to the original total. Far from it. Instead you end up with just under a hundred pairs. But it isn't maths that has been killing them off. One of the problems is that roseate terns spend the winter months along the coast of West Africa, in particular Ghana, where scores are trapped, killed and their leg rings used to make jewellery. Probably more significant, though, is the fact that the seas around our coast are not as plentiful as they once were. Sandeels and small fish are in short supply, and many of the UK's major seabird colonies are in a state of collapse following a string of disastrous breeding seasons.

Of the perilously small number of roseate terns that return to British waters every summer, virtually all of them nest on Coquet Island, a scrap of land a mile off the coast of Northumberland, so I had to pay the North East a visit to stand a reasonable chance of seeing them.

After a day on the road and a night in motorway accommodation entirely occupied by flocks of plump, pink hen parties I arrived at the port of Amble where, from the estuary boardwalk, I could clearly see the low landmass of Coquet Island with its lighthouse at one end. Birds were circling above the surrounding sea, only from such a distance there was no way I was going to be able to tell a roseate tern from any other kind of tern – and four species nest on the island, just to confuse matters.

Amble Tourist Information Office behind the harbour has an RSPB remotely operated live camera link with the offshore reserve and I was able to pan around the windswept oval of rocks and grass, zooming in on nesting seabirds that covered the turf. But despite crystal clear close-ups, this digital transmission was not the view I had driven for several hours to experience. I needed to share lightwaves directly with the birds, eyeball to eyeball. I had to get to the island.

I met Paul Morrison at the nearby Amble Marina and he handed me a lifejacket, warning: 'It could be a bumpy ride, so you'll have to hold on tight,' before leading me to a rigid inflatable boat where I took up a position at the front. While sea wildlife cruises do visit Coquet Island they are forbidden from landing, so I was lucky to be able to hitch a ride. Paul needed to pick up one of his assistant wardens, who was desperate to return to the mainland for a hot shower.

Stationed in the lighthouse buildings throughout the summer, researchers monitor and protect not only the few dozen visiting roseate terns, but a staggering 30,000 other seabirds that nest on the five-hectare sanctuary. In conservation terms it is probably the most noisy, hectic and hazardous job you can sign up for. Terns are extremely aggressive defenders of their nests, dive-bombing and crapping with precision accuracy and attacking intruders with their pointed beaks. For the volunteers it is like sharing summer with thousands of flying scissors, and Paul showed me his blue cloth hat peppered with holes and scuff marks from attacks over the years.

'I was pecked on the nose last year and someone was hit on the mouth, so those working on the island are now issued with padded safety helmets fitted with visors,' he said.

Once out of the sheltered estuary and in open water he hit the throttle and we crashed through the heavy sea swell, passing rafts of puffins riding the waves and the bobbing heads of curious seals. Then, as we neared the island, a cloud of terns rose from their nests on scalpel-sharp wings and swirled above us in the sunlight, filling the air with grating calls and eyeing the target of my exposed head. A bucket of sandeels as a peace offering might have been an idea, but Paul reassured me that as they were sitting on eggs rather than tending to young they were not at their most belligerent.

The main dilemma I faced was trying to make sense of the confusion of birds and identify roseates among the similar-looking common, artic and sandwich terns, especially as I was having to operate my binoculars one-handed while the other gripped onto the boat as it rose and fell beside the jetty. But Paul came to my aid, pointing out rows of small numbered wooden boxes positioned on three shingle-covered tiers below the lighthouse. Roseate terns tend to nest where there is natural cover to protect their chicks from aerial predators and wet weather, and along with reduced human disturbance these nest boxes are one of the keys to their conservation on Coquet.

And sure enough there they were, sunning themselves outside their prime waterfront residences, some with their long tails cocked upwards, while others circled overhead among flocks of common terns, a favoured companion as they are such aggressive defenders of colony airspace. You would have to travel to the Azores archipelago off Portugal or Rockabill lighthouse in the Irish Sea to see as many roseate terns in one location in Europe, so this really was a special place to find myself. The colours were so pure and clean: bright white feathers, glossy black caps, vivid red legs, all set against a clear blue sky. It was if I had stumbled onto the set for a washing detergent advert . . . *Just how do seabirds keep their whites looking so white?*

All of which should have reminded me a few days later back at home as I opened the rosé wine that I needed to wash some of my daughters' clothes if they weren't to spend the entire half-term week dressed as firemen.

Standing on the top of a hill in Dorset at dusk waving a white handkerchief might have resembled a rather overly dramatic admission of defeat, but that was not the case. Nor was it a signal that I was in some kind of serious trouble – either mental or physical. I was trying to attract a mysterious wide-mouthed long-winged insect-eating night-flying bird. Obviously. And it wasn't working.

Some birds are weirder than others. (Actually some birdwatchers are weirder than others, but given the handkerchief-waving antics I'm in no position to poke fun.) Natural selection has given us such diversity on our doorstep that if you lined all the species up in a police-style identity parade you would be faced with an incredibly varied-looking bunch. At one end there would be the massive mute swan, at the other the tiny goldcrest, and as you made your way along past the geese, gulls, guillemots, divers, ducks, woodpeckers, warblers and shifty-looking skuas and crows trying not to catch your eye, you would come across a number of surprises guaranteed to stop anyone in their tracks. There's the curlew for a start with its preposterously long beak, then there's the puffin painted up like a clown, and the spoonbill . . . evolutionary experiments no self-respecting prehistoric ancestral *archaeopteryx* would have agreed to take part in if they had known the outcome. They are just the sort of characters that make the natural world such a source of wonder. And then, when you thought you had seen it all, one more curiosity would bring you to a halt mouthing, 'What the . . . ?' Huddled on the ground completely still next to the kestrel and the cuckoo, a similar-sized mottled grey and brown bird resembling some kind of giant moth, with camouflage plumage the colour of dead bracken and bark, a flattish head, large dark eyes, a tiny bill surrounded by bristles and a yawn that opened both vertically and horizontally in a unfeasibly capacious gape like that of a basking shark.

It's name? The nightjar. One of the strangest of our

birds. A summer migrant whose unusual appearance, astonishing purring sound and nocturnal habits have made it the subject of superstition through the ages and earned it an assortment of bizarre monikers: goatsucker, fern owl, gnat hawk, wheelbird, razor grinder, puck bird, gabble ratchet and flying toad.

Perhaps what is most surprising about the nightjar is that there aren't more of these kinds of birds around. It is ornithology's answer to the bat, and given the huge smorgasbord of insects that take to the air after dark, its existence makes perfect sense.

By day nightjars sit motionless on the ground or roost lengthways along branches making them virtually impossible to spot, and in the depths of the night they go about their business in silence, twisting and turning above pastures and woodlands snapping up moths and flying beetles in their gaping mouths. Invisible by day, undetectable at night – a tricky proposition for any birdwatcher. However, there is a brief window of opportunity at dawn and dusk to see and hear them when the territorial males make themselves known.

I met ecologist Durwyn Liley one evening near Wareham in Dorset and we drove north to an area of heather-covered heath, muddy moss-lined pools and felled conifers called Morden Bog where he was confident we could find a nightjar or two. Durwyn had studied nightjars off and on for the best part of twenty years, yet he seemed as keen as I was to find one.

'There's something about being out at this time of day as the light is fading and hearing the noise of a nightjar in the gloaming. It's quite magical,' he said as we followed a track that led from the road. 'There is so much that is not known about them, and that sense of mystery adds to their appeal.'

Nightjars nest on the ground in heathland and open woodland – sometimes even synchronizing their laying on the night of a full moon – and we do know that like woodlarks, which share these habitats, they have experienced population ups and downs. Our lowland heaths may be well protected nowadays, but they are a fraction of what they once were. They have been ploughed up, built on or covered in conifers, and the fragments that remain are typically surrounded on all sides by urban development and overrun with dog walkers. As heaths shrank during the post-war years, so did nightjar numbers. They simply ran out of suitable places to live. And then, just when it seemed nothing was going their way, a sound emerged from our forests to gladden their hearts: the buzzing of chainsaws. Maturing pine forests planted between the wars were felled, clearing areas that were ideal for nesting, and yet more trees were toppled in the gales of 1989 and 1990. It was boom time for both nightjars and woodlarks, helped also by more careful management of our heaths, and nightjar numbers more than doubled to over 4,500 pairs by 2004. The reason they, and the woodlark for that matter, have remained on the Red List is because they have failed to regain enough of their former range across Britain.

As the track wound between rhododendron bushes we came across a sluggish slow worm living up to its name as it inched across the path, and further on sika deer hiding in the gorse. There were a couple of hobbies cruising the skies above for dragonflies, and higher up sickle-shaped silhouettes trawling for aerial plankton: swifts. The swift is no land animal that flies, but a flying animal that occasionally lands, spending the first couple of years of its life airborne – eating, sleeping and mating on the wing – before first touching down to raise young, and like the nightjar it has a wide whiskery mouth suited to scooping up insects – of which there was no shortage that evening. The mosquitoes were out in force. It was best to keep moving.

Durwyn led the way past a lake to a wide clearing dotted with a few trees which had been thoughtfully left standing by the Forestry Commission to provide nightjar song posts. From there we climbed up onto a ridge and at the top he produced a white handkerchief from his pocket. 'On territorial flights males display the patches of white on their wings and tails, and seeing this can bring them in for a look,' he said, and flapped it a few times in the air.

I waited for a magician's 'hey presto!' and a nightjar to emerge from the gathering gloom. But no luck. So I gave it a go, with a similar result. Durwyn then clapped softly once or twice, imitating a wing-slapping sound made by the males. A couple of bats were whirring around the tree line below and I could hear restless small birds settling down for the night, but once again no nightjars appeared.

As we returned to the clearing Durwyn stopped abruptly. 'Can you hear that?' he said.

A continuous stream of notes a bit like the sound of

a tropical frog was coming from a dead tree up ahead, changing pitch down then back up again every so often.

Durwyn cupped his hands behind his ears and I followed his lead, amazed at just how much it helped amplify the sound.

'Listen for a *qu-ick* – that's when it will fly,' he said.

On and on the song motored until, just as Durwyn had described, a couple of notes rounded off the performance, silence descended and I saw the bird, gliding down from the tree and flying towards us like a dark hawk. For its size it was amazingly light and buoyant and quiet in flight, and as it passed I could make out the white markings on its tail and long tapered wings.

The nightjar skirted the conifers and we knelt down to see it better against the sky as it patrolled the edge of its territory, gliding with its wings held above it in a steep 'V' before landing in another tree where its vibrating *churring*, as it is known, began again. Another started up further across the heath, and walking back to the car as darkness fell we heard several more filling the air with their extraordinary song.

If the pleasure birds bring us can be considered valid grounds for their conservation – self-interested though it may be – then some sounds must be as worth preserving as sights. Certain species more often heard than seen have become as much a part of our culture as many of their eye-candy counterparts. Their songs may not always amount to much musically, like those of the nightjar, corncrake, cuckoo or tawny owl, but they can still speak volumes. The first cuckoo I ever heard on a family trip out of London didn't just say: 'I am a cuckoo'; it said: 'Welcome to summer in the English countryside,' before going on about cut-price rail fares and Tourist Information Office opening times. Imagine never hearing a cuckoo again, or having the chance to hear one . . .

. . . and then imagine a species that shares our interest in birdsong, but takes it to another level. A hoarder of sound and a master mimic – introducing . . . all the way from south-east Africa, the versatile virtuoso, the superlative songster, the cutting-edge continental cover-artist that is . . . the marsh warbler!

Drum roll, cymbal crash . . . silence.

Well, I would introduce a marsh warbler if only I could find one first. The truth is that while touring schedules do include a few brief UK appearances every year – and back in the 1970s they were well known on the Worcestershire circuit – these days even established venues can't confirm this extraordinary act.

In terms of stage presence the grey-brown marsh warbler is one of the dullest-looking of our warblers, which is certainly saying something, but as performances go its recitals are considered among the most colourful of all our songbirds, even if they do breach copyright laws. Sneaked in among sweet liquid notes and harsh nasal noises are dozens of riffs it has collected on its travels – pinched from other birds heard on its long and time-consuming migration between Europe and its African wintering grounds. Ornithologically speaking you could say the marsh warbler was into world music, only without feeling the need to decorate its home territory with batiks, incense holders, sandalwood picture frames and bamboo place mats. More than two hundred species provide its material, and the average male includes snippets of the songs and calls of forty-five African and thirty European bird species, all memorized and blended with note-perfect precision into its medley compositions.

Given that the UK lies at the north-western extremity of its European range, marsh warblers have never been common here. But for reasons not fully understood they have become rarer and rarer, so that today barely half a dozen pairs breed in Britain – mostly in dank dense nettlebeds in the South East – and only a few pass through on migration. No wonder I had put a question mark next to its name on the Red List and pretty much ruled it out as a potential sighting.

However, I hadn't counted on chaos theory.

The hyperactive eastern European butterfly mentioned earlier had managed to deflect a storm over the Ukraine with all its flapping, sending strong winds west towards Britain. There may have been factors other than butterfly-power at work, such as surface temperatures, air pressure and the like, but perhaps it's best not to let scientific facts confuse matters. Either way, by late May a strong wind acting like a giant pinball machine paddle was batting migrating birds west, driving them across the North Sea and dumping them in the drizzle on our shores. For several days it rained rarities: bluethroats, bee-eaters, rosefinches, orioles, obscure buntings, pipits and wagtails – and among the mix of migrants were marsh warblers.

What was supposed to be a relaxing final few days of the half-term holiday looking after my daughters was suddenly thrown into turmoil. Our computer email inbox started filling up with messages from the 'BirdGuides' alert service I had recently subscribed to, and my mobile was in meltdown with incoming texts. Marsh warbler spotted here . . . marsh warbler spotted there . . . If ever there was a chance to see a marsh warbler it was at that precise moment. Except that I was at least a couple of hundred miles from the nearest sighting, I had two children and a lame dog to look after, my wife wasn't prepared to fake an illness to take time off work on my account, our diary was packed with activities and I had a 'to do' list as long as my arm: *wash clothes, paint cupboard, mend backdoor lock, ring car insurers, ring parents, ring ouzel* . . . (well, at least I had ticked off the last one). I felt like I needed to buy a timeshare in my own life. All I needed was 24 hours.

My hopes were raised when one lone marsh warbler did turn up briefly as far west as Durlston Country Park in Dorset, but by the time I got there in the evening after a quick handover at the front door with my wife, followed by a hair-raising drive, the bird had reset its compass and gone. There was nothing for it, I had to sit tight and wait three days until the weekend when I had a full day to myself. Three long, tense days, during which time there was no guarantee the visiting warblers would stick around. In fact there was every likelihood they wouldn't.

I tried to take my mind off the subject, but it was hopeless. All I could think about was where I needed to be – and right then it wasn't where I was. After 24 hours the initial flood of information had started to dry up, and by day two only scattered possibilities remained. The clock was ticking, the marsh warblers were disappearing, and with them my hopes of seeing one. I don't know what the average life expectancy of a twitcher is, but high blood pressure must take its toll. And as my 72-hour ordeal neared its end I had a decision to make: where would I drive? I could only spare one day. I had to get it right. As I scoured the texts and emails and weighed up the options a single detail among the various short reports kept catching my eye – repeated references to an 'orange bucket'.

Spurn Head on Yorkshire's east coast near Hull is one of the country's prime locations for migrating birds. The sand and shingle spit extends for over three miles across the mouth of the Humber estuary and provides an ideal vantage point from which to view passing flocks funnelled along the thin promontory or dumped by strong winds among the thickets of buckthorn, elder and hawthorn. It is considered such an important location that it has its own permanent bird observatory, one of almost twenty dotted around Britain and Ireland that carry out long-term monitoring of bird populations and movements. Just a short distance from the observatory, sheltered behind the curved neck of the Spurn peninsula and nudging out into a wide expanse of tidal mudflats, is a small headland called Sammy's Point. A path runs to the point along a raised sea wall which separates the sea from paddocks and arable fields behind, and at the time of the migrant bird invasion in late May a standard-sized orange bucket could be found near the far end beside the track. Don't ask me why. No one was elaborating on the origins of the bucket. The fact is that it was there, and it provided a useful marker because exactly opposite, beneath the bank, was an area of nettles, and among them a solitary marsh warbler had taken up temporary residence.

I needed to find that bucket.

Saturday finally arrived and I set off before lunch to cover the 360 miles that lay between my house and Sammy's Point. Only I hadn't reckoned on roadworks and traffic jams along the way. By the time I reached Hull it was early evening, the sun was dropping like a stone in my rear-view mirror, I was stuck behind a police car driving at a snail's pace and a seemingly endless stretch of road still lay ahead. It appeared that geological forces had moved all the villages further apart since my road map was printed, and a quirk in the earth's electro-magnetic field south-east of Hedon meant the clock in my car was speeding up while the milometer was slowing down. I was beginning to run out of day. And then, when eventually I reached the village of Kilnsea at Spurn Head, prised my clenched fists from the steering wheel and got out to ask directions to Sammy's Point, I found that while it was only a couple of fields away, reaching it meant negotiating a time-consuming route leading right then left then right like one of those zig-zag cordons in airport passport control that entail a mile-long trek in order to move a few yards forward. And where the lane ended and I finally pulled up overlooking the sea, I still had half a mile of path to cover. Birdwatching doesn't often require the need to break into a run, but run I did. With binoculars bouncing on my chest I sprinted up the track until I saw it: the orange bucket, glowing up ahead like a beacon of hope in the evening light.

Remembering that I had come to find a bird, not a bucket, I climbed down off the path and found a place to sit among the grass and thistles where I could get a good view of the patch of nettles opposite. I raised my binoculars and observed a couple of little brown birds flitting about the foliage in silence. It was at that moment a terrifying realization dawned on me: that after a three-day wait and seven hours on the road I had reached my destination with a pitifully poor knowledge of how to identify a marsh warbler by sight. Unless these warblers warble they are regarded as one of the toughest bird identification challenges, and everything in front of me seemed to have been struck dumb. I was seriously out of my depth.

The sun was beginning to set and in desperation I collared a passing birdwatcher to try to glean information on what I should be looking for. It turned out experienced birder Graham Shortt was the right person to ask as he had seen it the day before. He also brought with him the luck I needed, for as we chatted a loud, clear sound erupted from the nettles in front of us, and he gave me a nod. It was the marsh warbler, and for a few minutes it delivered one of the most incredible bird songs I have ever heard, with Graham acting as translator as it reeled off its astounding repertoire of imitations.

'That's a quail,' he said. 'A blue tit. Jackdaw – can

you hear the *jack*? That's a linnet flight call, a pied wagtail . . .'

The bird even gave us the odd fleeting glimpse before disappearing down into the cover of the nettles and
rushes and falling silent.

It wasn't a long performance, but it almost called for
a round of applause. And while I can't say my nerves
could stand any more birdwatching against the clock
chasing texts across the country, I will long remember
the little bird that for a brief moment turned a nettle
patch by a discarded orange bucket next to a muddy
estuary into a concert venue.

The ice sheet had retreated, and although the winters
could still be hard it was rain that fell over the barren
land during the long days, not snow. Downpours
collected in gullies between rounded hills and spilled
into rivers, dragging scattered boulders across the wide
flat valleys, and water lay in sheets on the bare ground
or stagnated in pools in the impermeable bedrock. Here
and there vegetation had got a toehold: clumps of vivid
green moss filled crevices, and grasses sprouted where
thin windblown soils had collected in sheltered corners.
Life was stirring once more in this sodden corner of
north-east Scotland newly exposed to sunlight as the
glacial snows had withdrawn. It was 8,000 years ago, in
an area now known as Caithness and Sutherland, and
the mild and moist conditions were perfect for a process
that would create one of the world's biggest bogs.

While hazel and birch did endure for a while, this

was no place for trees. This was moss country. And as the spongy plants that colonized the poorly drained landscape died, their remains failed to decompose in the acidic water that had sustained them. Smothered by fresh growth from above, the fibrous waterlogged matter accumulated and was compressed into a thick mat – peat. Only when temperatures rose 4,000 years ago and Scot's pines invaded the landscape was the formation of this dark carpet briefly interrupted. But then the cold rains returned, the pines perished and once more water-loving plants that were adapted to tolerate such a nutrient-poor environment covered the ground: sphagnum mosses, cotton grass, cranberry and sedges, as well as carnivorous species like sundew able to suck the goodness from invertebrates trapped on their sticky hairs. At the rate of a millimetre a year the peat layer grew, metre by metre over the millennia, and insect and bird life flourished in the vast wilderness.

Incredibly that is the way things stayed. While all but the tops of Britain's mountains and rocky shores were in time exploited and altered by man, this ancient impenetrable blanket bog remained intact, nibbled away only in places by grazing livestock and by the cutting of peat for fuel and distilling whisky. Scotland's 1,500 square mile 'Flow Country', one of our few truly natural habitats, survived.

And then in the second half of the twentieth century the diggers moved in. Drains were cut, helicopters powdered the drying peat with fertilizers and non-native conifers were planted. Trees were on the march once more, and great chunks of the rare and fragile peatlands were destroyed. However, there was opposition, and birdwatchers were among those who rallied to try to save the threatened habitat, funding the purchase by the RSPB of 18,000 hectares, now known as Forsinard Flows National Nature Reserve, where work immediately got under way to cut down plantation trees and block up the drains.

But who on earth would want to come to such a remote reserve? Wasn't opening a visitor centre and laying a flagstone trail across a squelchy patch of peat in this far-flung corner of Scotland just a complete waste of time?

It seems not. Incredibly, more than 50,000 people have visited since the reserve first opened in 1995. That's a big queue for the bog. And of all the places on my itinerary, Forsinard was the one I had most been looking forward to.

After a long drive north, a scotch egg at Scotch Corner, a night in a B&B and a meal in a restaurant with a selection of sayings stuck to the wall including, worryingly, *What doesn't kill you, can only make you stronger*, I made it to Helmsdale in Sutherland. From there a single-lane road with passing places and snow poles on either side led up into the heart of Flow Country, tracking the Helmsdale and Halladale rivers between hills covered in heather and yellow flowering broom. There were red deer on the slopes, and curlew, lapwing and snipe feeding in the rough grass. Then as I neared Forsinard the valley widened and the landscape opened out. Ahead lay an immense panorama thousands of years old, a rolling fabric of greens and browns, broken in places by black peaty pools. All that was missing was a sign that read: *Welcome to the middle of nowhere.* This was what I had wanted to see: large wet undulating space with nothing much in it.

I hadn't just come to experience nothing, invigorating though that may be. Surprising as it sounds, I had travelled all that way to see . . . well, a duck. Only not the type of duck you can find by chucking a handful of bread onto the nearest loch. For a start this particular variety mostly eats shellfish. And they don't much like people, so you won't spot them waddling around a village pond or hanging about canalside pubs looking for leftovers. The duck I was after spends most of its life at sea, diving down for mussels, clams, crabs and lugworms. Its name? The common scoter. 'Common' because thousands can be seen congregating offshore through the autumn and winter, particularly around the coast of east Scotland and Wales. However, a truly British common scoter is anything but common. Virtually all of those found bobbing about our seas are visitors from the Arctic and northern Europe. Only fifty pairs breed here, exclusively in Scotland, and the seemingly unstoppable and largely unexplained decline of this native population has placed them firmly on our Red List.

To ensure I saw one of our common scoters meant not only journeying north of the border, but also inland as they nest beside freshwater lakes, particularly in the Flow Country. So far, so good. Only . . . which lake? There are dozens and dozens to choose from, and not many scoters to spread around. Somewhere in the mossy swamp that stretched for miles in every direction from Forsinard were a few pairs of these small ducks. I had two options: recklessly set off into the marsh never to be seen again, with the outside possibility of being dug up by archaeologists in several hundred years' time and stuck in a freezer drawer labelled 'Forsinard bog man', or, more sensibly, ask for advice.

Being a man, I pulled on my walking boots and set off into the marsh. But within minutes I was forced to beat a retreat, chased back into the car by clouds of voracious midges that plastered every bit of exposed skin and delivered a remarkable bite for an animal the size of a full stop. It was like being attacked by rogue punctuation. Even those that followed me into the car carried on their attack, and I had to stuff bits of tissue in my ears to keep them out.

To save me from getting lost and devoured by carnivorous plants and insects, reserve manager Norrie Russell agreed to take me out searching for scoter. We met beside a river near Forsinard and headed off, hiking up between blocks of plantation conifers onto open ground. There were mountain hares among the thickets of gorse and we passed ditches where the roots of pines that had died four millennia ago were visible, preserved in the peat. The track petered out at the edge of a high plain of wet heather and soft hummocks of moss, and Norrie led the way to the top of a ridge, skirting small shallow lochans where water-dwelling bogbean had been nibbled by deer in a margin around the edges. The view was fabulous: not a house or telegraph pole to be seen, just an unbroken expanse of low vegetation.

This was probably the furthest away I had ever been in Britain from a Spar shop.

Given that we stuck out like sore thumbs on the flat peatland, I didn't much rate our chances of seeing anything, let alone a common scoter. Up ahead was a slightly larger exposed area of water the colour of smoked glass, though it looked empty. A light breeze rippled the surface, keeping the midges at bay, and I was finally able to take the tissue out of my ears and hear what Norrie was saying.

'I said there should be a pair here,' he repeated, scanning the water with his binoculars.

At first I couldn't see anything, but he was right. Two birds that had been hiding under overhanging sedge at the far bank emerged and swam across the lake, little more than duck-shaped silhouettes at such a distance. They were common scoter – though only just.

The word 'scoter' may originate in the fact that these fast fliers tend to 'scoot' about all over the place, and that is precisely what happened. They spotted us approaching and took off, flying low with pointed tails visible, then landed in a neighbouring stretch of water. We moved in closer and Norrie was able to set up his telescope, focus on the male and stand aside to let me have a look.

What I am about to say may come as a surprise to many, given that I am talking about a duck – and was just as much a surprise to me – but as I put my eye to the viewfinder I saw in the magnified circle, caught in the sun on the glinting surface of the small loch, the most handsome bird I had come across on my travels. The male I was looking at was neat, compact and motoring along in an endearing clockwork fashion as ducks do, but his glossy plumage was pure black. Apart from a dapper little wedge of yellow on top of a slightly incongruous bulbous bill, his flawless ebony feathers were incredibly striking, especially as wildfowl can so often look like fashion victims. He dived for a short while and when he reappeared close to the browner female, popping back up to the surface as if filled with air, droplets of water ran off his oiled plumage like liquid silver. He was, quite simply, immaculate.

Of the thousands of people who contributed to the appeal to buy the Forsinard reserve, the vast majority will never visit this remote and precious place, let alone see a common scoter. I can't speak on behalf of the ducks I saw, but for my own part I guess I would like to say thanks.

The scoters do owe a debt of gratitude though. Their situation is increasingly precarious, with habitat changes, pollution and predation taking their toll, so they need all the protection they can get. And while losing the few that remain in the UK, a toehold at the southerly edge of their range, might not be devastating in terms of European numbers, it would certainly be embarrassing.

'We can't expect people in other countries to look after their threatened species and not do it ourselves,' Norrie said. 'They are now extinct as breeders in Northern Ireland and if they disappear from Scotland we're not likely to get them back.'

However, work to safeguard common scoters may all

be in vain in the face of a more profound threat to their long-term survival, and that of other northern species: global warming. Upping the thermostat a couple of degrees would undoubtedly suit many of our sun-loving birds that favour hot summers and mild winters, such as red-listed cirl buntings and woodlarks. It is also expected to result in new arrivals, perhaps night herons and hoopoes, and might even bring back old favourites like red-backed shrikes. But higher temperatures will also shift those species adapted to cold and upland conditions further uphill and further north. Ring ouzels could be squeezed off the tops of mountains, chased upwards by an ascending tree line and lowland competitors, while experts predict capercaillie, Scottish crossbills and common scoter, among others, are likely to be wiped off the UK map altogether by the end of the century if average temperatures rise by 3°C. In search of suitable climate and habitat, European birds faced with such a temperature change would need to move on average over 300 miles, generally in a north-easterly direction. That would place these Highland specialists somewhere in the North Sea. At least scoters can swim, but capercaillie and Scottish crossbill would be left treading water wondering where things had gone wrong.

If you were setting up a museum of agriculture in England, your exhibits of bygone memorabilia should probably include a scythe, an old threshing machine, a horse-drawn plough . . . oh, and a stuffed corncrake.

This streaky brown relative of the moorhen was once familiar across rural England. The repetitive rasping voice of calling males, sounding something like a stick drawn across a comb, rose from hay meadows throughout the summer. But as agriculture modernized, corncrakes died out along with the traditional farming techniques that had sustained them. They now fly right over England on migration from Africa in the spring, bypassing the country altogether in order to reach less intensively farmed areas further north to breed, and you have to travel to the crofting lands of the western isles of Scotland to stand a reasonable chance of seeing one.

Leaving the smart black common scoter admiring his own reflection in the upland loch near Forsinard I drove west across vast saturated expanses of moorland to the coast. I reached the Isle of Skye by early evening, crossing the bridge that links it with the mainland, and on the eastern side of the island I pulled up in a lay-by overlooking a loch, lowered the seat back, wrapped myself up in a duvet and settled down for a night in the car. While I had welcomed the remoteness in Caithness during my drive, I was less keen on it now I was parked all alone by an empty stretch of road as darkness fell. Try as I might to convince myself that crime rates tend to be pretty low in areas devoid of people, I still felt anxious. Wasn't a lone vehicle parked on a moor far from the nearest house bound to attract thieves and murderers from miles around? I could picture bedraggled bands of psychopaths homing in, rattling manacles around their wrists and ankles, tramping over the hills towards me. It also began to rain, heavy drops drumming on the roof of the car like impatient fingers, which didn't help my nerves as it drowned out the possibility of hearing any approaching hordes and caused the windows to steam up. I could neither see nor hear anyone coming. I was certainly doomed.

Somehow I managed to put my fears aside and get to sleep. But not for long. I was woken at 3.30am by two headlights drawing up directly in front of me. Christ! All the murderers had chipped in to hire a car! The bright beams were switched off, and I tentatively rubbed a square of condensation from the inside of my windscreen and peered through. I could just make out in the pre-dawn light a large man getting out and lifting open the boot of the car. He pulled out a long barrel and fixed it to a thicker barrel which had what looked like a telescopic sight on top. I had to act fast! I threw my duvet to one side, grabbed my keys, turning them quickly in the ignition, and without time to put on my shoes I pressed my bare feet on the pedals and revved the engine, pulling away with a screech and flicking on the headlights. As I swung past the car aiming for the road my lights tracked across it, and I saw in the full beams the man standing by his open boot looking startled and holding a fishing rod in one hand.

Oh well, at least I was up in good time to catch the afternoon ferry to North Uist.

The Flow Country might be soggy, but North Uist has practically given up with land altogether. Half of the surface of this largely flat, 17-mile long island in the Outer Hebrides is covered by water. Between the peaty-brown pools and heather-covered moors, livestock graze in wire-fenced fields, while across areas of light soil made fertile by windblown shell sand, known as 'machair', wild flowers thrive and ploughed strips are farmed by crofters. These fields may not amount to much in terms of acreage, but they are home to well over a tenth of our 1,000 or so pairs of corncrakes.

Corncrakes are famously elusive. Their way of life is the total opposite of the plains-dwelling stone-curlews I saw in Wiltshire. A corncrake would have a heart attack if it found itself in the middle of a ploughed field. Instead they nest and raise their young in tall, dense invertebrate-rich vegetation, such as hay meadows, where they can keep out of sight. And a skulking nature has largely been their undoing. When mowers became mechanized these secretive ground-dwellers reluctant to take to the wing were presented with the choice of either breaking cover and running like hell to avoid being harvested, or hiding out and hoping the danger would pass. Being card-carrying agoraphobes they invariably opted for the latter – a major tactical error. Families simply remain within a diminishing crop, herded into the middle by the circling mower until they are killed as the final square is cut. We have literally mown them down in their tens of thousands over the decades, both in Britain and across Europe, and the widespread loss of hay meadows, early and repeated cutting of grass for silage and general agricultural intensification have also contributed to their well-documented decline and led to them being classified as globally threatened.

In North Uist and neighbouring corncrake-friendly isles, crofters are encouraged to cut their grass late in the summer; mow hay fields from the inside out, driving the birds into the margins rather than the centre; and provide overgrown corners and corridors of nettles and irises in which corncrakes can nest in the spring until the meadows have grown sufficiently high to conceal them. These small changes have made a big difference, helping to turn around plummeting numbers, and the hope now is that eventually they will start to expand their range.

I was pretty excited that I might finally get to see one of these conservation causes célèbres. Even hearing one would do, and I had given myself two full days on North Uist to track this Red List species down – and two full nights to be on the safe side, as the males tend to call from dusk through until dawn. If success meant forgoing sleep then so be it. If it meant hiking up and down the island for hours on end then so be it. Whatever it took. I was fully primed for the tough assignment that lay ahead, and as I drove off the ferry at Lochmaddy and made my way to the accommodation I had booked in a village near the north-west coast I decided on my plan of action. I would unpack, grab a quick evening meal, get to bed early, then target the RSPB's Balranald Reserve the following day where there was supposed to be a healthy population.

It was raining when I finally arrived at my B&B in Knockintorran. I parked in front of the house, turned off the engine and wondered why it sounded as if it was still running. On getting out I listened by the bonnet. Nothing. And then the grating sound came again, except that it wasn't from the car but a patch of nettles on the other side of the driveway: *krrek-krrek, krrek-krrek*. I couldn't believe it. It was a corncrake. Then another started up from a scrubby area by a field, and one more from cover near the edge of the road. I had been steeling myself for the possibility of failing to even hear one during my visit, and here I was surrounded by three calling corncrakes and I had only just arrived. It was faintly ridiculous.

I pulled on a coat, grabbed my binoculars and set about trying to clap eyes on the hidden vocalists. Easier said than done. The loudest of the calls was coming from a section of thick grass and irises just off the road, which I scanned and scanned again without any luck. How could the noise be so close and clear yet without a singer to be seen? I was aware they were supposed to be masters of ventriloquism, bouncing their notes off walls and buildings and changing volume by turning their heads, making it extremely hard to place them, but this was beyond a joke. It was as if the corncrake had left its song behind and run off somewhere else. There were hardly enough nettles to hide a sparrow, let alone something several times that size. Only one logical explanation could account for it: someone had discarded a comb in the undergrowth and the wind happened to be rhythmically brushing a stick up and down the teeth. I felt stupid for thinking it could be anything else.

Then I spotted the bird. He wasn't even in the nettles at all, but standing on a small rock between them just 15 yards in front of me looking like a damp young chicken pullet in the rain. His rusty red wings were folded against the sides of his yellow-brown body, and his grey neck strained upwards as he called away, *krrek-krrek, krrek-krrek*. With every utterance it appeared as if the lower half of his pale bill remained fixed while the upper half and head tilted back, like one of those plastic flip-top Pez sweet dispensers. He was so intent on delivering the high decibel territorial sound and wooing passing females with his one and only chat-up line that he appeared oblivious to my presence, enabling me to watch for a while until the rain began soaking through my coat and I decided to leave him to it. He had a long night ahead of him and a few thousand more *krreks* before sunrise.

'Lots of people come to North Uist just to hear corn-crakes, even if they can't be sure of actually seeing them,' Balranald Reserve manager Jamie Boyle told me when I met up with him the next day. 'They're a symbol of a way of life that has been lost, and some visitors even re-member hearing them as a child and long to hear them again. Fortunately, at least here, they still can.'

It had become abundantly clear to me on my travels just how much people do care about our birdlife. However, in my quest to see the UK's species of highest conservation concern I had also been looking for answers to the question of whether we *should* care. Do we really need corncrakes, for example? Would it be so bad if we lost them?

Financially speaking they would be missed. From ospreys to white-tailed eagles I had witnessed first hand the economic benefits of creating reserves and protecting species, and corncrakes certainly have a value in terms of local tourism revenue. On an emotional level I had experienced how life-enriching wildlife encounters could be, even watching a wet corncrake in the rain. The potential for life on earth to surprise and captivate would be the poorer for the loss of such a unique species. From a practical point of view I had heard compelling arguments as to why we need to safeguard the complex web of biodiversity that sustains us – that the natural world is not simply a luxury to be enjoyed on days out, but a life-support system upon which we depend. Pest-eating, seed-dispersing corncrakes may only play a small part, but have a role nonetheless. And I was also beginning to understand just how much birds are embedded in our culture and sense of place. They are a part of what defines a country, like landmark listed buildings. Our existence would not be placed in jeopardy should Nelson's Column or Big Ben be knocked down – unless you happened to be standing under them at the time – but our nation would feel emptier for their absence.

However, there is another argument for conserving species regardless of whether they benefit us or not. It is that we have a moral responsibility to do so. One doesn't need to believe in the existence of a divine designer to marvel at the miraculous set of circumstances that brought every one of our birds into being. Against outlandishly long odds life stirred in our planet's primeval soup three and a half billion years ago, and from the slime multi-cellular organisms evolved, grew scales and crawled onto land whereupon many took up work as estate agents. During the Jurassic Period some of the reptiles developed feathers and launched themselves skyward as birds, and while their dinosaur ancestors bit the dust these warm-blooded high flyers spread across the globe exploiting land and sea. The evolutionary process that followed over the next 150 million years gave us, among several thousand other surviving varieties of bird, the corncrake. The chances of corncrakes, or any other creature for that matter, ever having occurred are incalculably slim. So when people talk about conserving species for their own sake, I can see where they are coming from – though I now draw the line at midges.

Having spotted a corncrake within twenty minutes of arriving on North Uist I had plenty of free time to kill, and the following afternoon during a break in the rain I walked from my B&B across an area of orchid-filled sandy machair to the sea. It was like a stroll through a field guide to wild and unspoilt places. Lapwings swooped low overhead uttering noises like kazoos, calling redshanks and oystercatchers joined in, and ringed plovers scuttled away across the ground ahead of me. I heard corn buntings singing, saw a peregrine hunting and was mobbed by a colony of nesting terns – little terns and arctic terns. It was every bit as good as those memorable occasions at Thurlestone Marsh in Devon and Cwm Bychan in Snowdonia when it seemed new birds were queuing up to be identified. And as an unexpected bonus I was woken the next morning by two male corncrakes hard at work calling outside my bedroom window, and I managed to see one after coming down for breakfast. Believe me, there aren't many B&Bs in the UK that can offer guests corncrakes with their cornflakes.

CHAPTER ELEVEN

I WAS RUNNING OUT OF TIME, MONEY AND CLEAN SOCKS, I had to be back at work in a few days, I was due to catch a flight from Edinburgh to the Shetland islands in 48 hours, and I was driving 500 miles out of my way on the off-chance of seeing a bird that I have to confess I have eaten on several occasions.

The reason for my detour was a note I had spotted a week earlier in a reserve logbook. After seeing the singing marsh warbler in Yorkshire I had spent a night in hostel-style accommodation provided at the Spurn Point bird observatory – half a night, in fact, as the friendly birdwatcher I shared a room with snored so badly I bailed out at 3am, muttering something about going owl watching. As a result I had time to briefly visit the Lower Derwent Valley National Nature Reserve nearby before heading north for Forsinard, and thumbing through a book of recent sightings in one of the hides I came across an entry that set my heart racing. Quail. Two of them had been heard a few days earlier. They weren't making themselves known at the precise moment I stopped by, but in the hope they were still around I had returned, leaving North Uist and driving south to Yorkshire rather than east to Edinburgh Airport.

Quail are quite easy to find in the cold food sections of supermarkets, but in the wild in Britain these tiny, streaky brown partridge-shaped summer visitors are not at all common, and because of huge declines over the last 150 years are on the Red List. Those found in the shops are a domesticated Japanese variety reared for eggs and meat, while our native birds are specially protected, though frequently find themselves on the menu in Mediterranean countries where they are shot on migration to and from their wintering grounds in sub-Saharan Africa. Drought to the south of their range and agricultural intensification in the north have added to their problems. However, just like the red wines chosen to accompany those that end their days nestled between buttered potatoes and steamed broccoli, quail do have their good and bad years. When the conditions are right they multiply at an astonishing rate, laying up to a dozen eggs, then moving on to breed again, accompanied by their young who are fertile within a few weeks of hatching. Wave upon wave can spread north, boosting the couple of hundred typically heard in cereal fields and grassland in Britain every summer by up to ten times, and vintage quail years include 1947, 1953, 1970, 1983 and 1989. Oh for a robust, full-bodied 1989 quail! (Actually, even a sniff of a clapped-out 2008 version would have done.)

I arrived at dusk in the Lower Derwent Valley and parked beside North Duffield Carrs. It was a beautiful still evening, the sky was beginning to flush pink and I settled in at the furthest of the two hides overlooking a section of river and pasture, and waited. What I was listening for was a short, liquid, rhythmic song: *whit, whit-whit*. I heard a quacking, a plopping, squealing, cheeping, tweeting and warbling coming from the marsh, and a yawning and sighing coming from the hide – which was me – but no quail.

I had shut my eyes and was beginning to doze off after my day-long drive when a faint sound jolted me awake. A single quail song drifting over the flat fields to my right. Then silence. I left the hide and walked along a path in the direction the sound had come from, and paused. A roe deer passed by, and a barn owl floated low over the reeds. The sound came again: *whit, whit-whit . . . whit, whit-whit . . .* It was quite a long way off, so I climbed over a fence and crossed a field, wading through long grass already wet with dew, drawing closer. At least I thought I was. Just like corncrakes these shy birds that seldom venture out into the open are known for being able to throw their voice, and I had to double-back and clamber over a dank muddy ditch that was suffering from a severe case of halitosis, cut through a field of nettles and fight my way through a clump of trees until eventually I found myself beside the River Derwent – a cloud of mosquitoes circling my head, twigs in my hair, trousers soaked and covered in slug slime and shoes plastered with reeking mud. I could have qualified as a Site of Special Scientific Interest. The bird called again, and it was then that I realized it was on the other side of the river. And there was no way across. I was stuck on one bank as the light began to fade while somewhere over the water hidden among the tussocks of grass and shadows was the quail singing at me: *twit, twit-twit . . . twit, twit-twit . . .*

The gathering darkness had rendered my binoculars useless. However, unless I was confusing it with a large singing rat, I did briefly glimpse a quail-shaped silhouette moving through the low vegetation opposite, and I decided to beat a retreat, recognizing that I probably shouldn't have been in the farmer's field, and that standing on my own staring across a river in the twilight on a Saturday evening looking a complete state could take some explaining.

It was time to make my way north once more, back to Scotland and Edinburgh Airport, where I treated myself to another night wrapped in a duvet on the reclined driver's seat, trying hard to imagine I was in the first-class section on a long-haul flight. An airport car park is neither the most private nor peaceful place to sleep, surrounded by CCTV cameras and with jets revving on the tarmac nearby, but it had to suffice. I needed to save on B&B expenses before flying out the following morning. A costly cup of tea in the terminal before departure, however, made a mockery of my budgeting.

I'm still paying it off in instalments. On the positive side the café was offering interest-free finance on a glass of orange juice and I got a croissant for breakfast with one of those 'buy now, nothing to pay until 2015' deals.

Tired and still hungry I began a long and complicated journey to reach one of the northernmost Shetland isles. The flight from Edinburgh landed at Sumburgh Airport on the main island where I picked up a hire car. I then drove north to Toft, and from there took a short-hop car ferry to Ulsta on the small island of Yell, headed across rolling Yell moorland to Gutcher, caught a second ferry to the smaller island of Fetlar and finally drove to my lodgings in the hamlet of Houbie, where I staggered up the steps, slumped on the bed exhausted and hoped that when it came to it I could remember the way back.

Shetland is no place for tree spotters – you'd do well to find one. Low vegetation covers the lumps of land like a thin coat of brown and green paint. But if it is sky, sea and open space you are after, then these bleak and lonely isles have plenty to spare. And wind and rain. The day I arrived the BBC's radio weatherman had chirpily reported Britain was enjoying its warmest day of the year so far. He failed to mention Shetland. It was cold, wet, a gale was pounding the exposed archipelago, and despite the fact it was June I had needed the car heating on full blast. This, I decided, must be a tough place to live.

But for wildlife, summer here is sheer luxury. Long days and nutrient-rich waters mean lots of plankton, lots of plankton means lots of fish, and lots of fish means lots of seals, whales, dolphins, otters, and especially seabirds – over a million come every year to raise their young along the rugged coastline and on the windswept moors. Half the world's great skuas nest on the isles, as well as significant numbers of gannets, puffins, kittiwakes, guillemots and fulmars, whose crowded colonies on precipitous sea-cliffs make for one of Britain's great wildlife spectacles.

I was in search of an extremely scarce species with a lifestyle as unusual as its name. Called the red-necked phalarope, it is a type of wader that behaves a lot like a duck. Smaller than a starling, this delicate, thin-necked, thin-legged, thin-billed bird is happier bobbing about out at sea or swimming around lakes than hanging about with gangly muddy-footed worm-eating cousins along the shore. And its breeding arrangements are equally bizarre. Come the spring these long-distance travellers leave the equatorial oceans and head for midge-rich freshwater lakes and marshes at latitudes upwards of 60 degrees north, encircling the globe in a band that takes in Alaska, Scandinavia, Siberia, Greenland and Iceland. Having undergone a plumage change from winter whites and greys to a mix of dark slate streaked with gold on the back and chestnut around the neck, they turn established sexual roles on their head. Instead of settling down to domestic duties, the bigger, brighter females compete for males, then leave them to incubate the eggs and raise the young while they go off looking for another mate. It is a strategy that obviously works, as there are 3.5 million red-necked phalaropes in the world.

In Britain, however, they are anything but common,

and over the last century as collectors plundered nests and increased drainage and unchecked plant growth destroyed favoured shallow pools, they became rarer and rarer, so that today Shetland and the Outer Hebrides manage to attract a couple of dozen at most – the majority nesting beside carefully tended bog pools and flooded peat-cuttings on Shetland's isle of Fetlar. Conservation work has helped them back from the brink, and the Loch of Funzie and neighbouring mires at the fertile eastern end of the island are the UK's number-one site for our precarious population.

After a brief rest, I ventured back out to my hire car and drove the couple of miles to the reserve to see if there were any about. Few places could have looked more inhospitable. The rain was horizontal, waves were breaking on the small dark loch and the grass in the surrounding fields was bent double. The wind was so strong that any phalaropes that might have been there were hiding away in the sedge and rushes rather than braving the elements on the pools and channels. It was hopeless. The only bird I saw was a handsome male red-backed shrike seeking shelter near the RSPB hide before continuing on his migration, which was a welcome surprise – and a far better sighting of this red-listed species than the scruffy juvenile I had encountered nine months earlier in Devon.

The next morning the weather was as bad, and my prospects of seeing a phalarope at the Loch of Funzie just as slim. I spent the day visiting a seabird colony on a neighbouring island and looking for otters, hoping the winds would eventually ease, but if anything they got worse. This was not something I had reckoned on. Wildlife watching was meant to be unpredictable, I told myself, though as I clocked up my second evening at Funzie staring across empty stretches of cold water it was hard to remain upbeat. I had only one day remaining before I had to leave.

The weatherman on the TV that night swept his hand indifferently over the Northern Isles. 'Blowy,' he said, not wanting to waste words. 60,925,000 people across the UK – that is everyone who doesn't live in Orkney and Shetland – won't have cared less. But I was doing enough worrying for them all. This was not a place I could pop back to and I couldn't postpone my return flight. All I needed was a momentary lull in the gale, the briefest window of opportunity.

The forecast proved irritatingly accurate. While the rain stopped, I woke to more strong winds, and returned to the loch where I sat in the car and stared out forlornly. Hope was ebbing away hour by hour.

I had arranged to meet reserve warden Malcolm Smith that afternoon for a chat about conservation work on the island, and I'm sure he could see from the look in my eye that I was desperate.

'Seen one yet?' he asked, leaning back in the chair in his office.

I shook my head miserably, hoping he might take pity.

'Unfortunately the wind means it is far from ideal,' he said, glancing out of the window.

'Ah well,' I shrugged with a pathetic sigh, 'maybe it was never meant to be.'

He checked his watch, thought for a moment, then asked in a serious tone: 'If I took you to a place where I am hoping to find some, do you promise you would keep its location strictly to yourself?'

'To be perfectly honest,' I said, my face brightening, 'I have absolutely no sense of direction and a lousy memory. Your secret couldn't be safer.'

He mulled things over for a few seconds, then got up decisively and pulled on his coat. 'Right, follow me.'

I jumped in my car and tailed him along the main road to a parking place where he stopped, and we headed up onto the moor. I was dressed in trousers, waterproof over-trousers, thick socks, a T-shirt, shirt, jumper, coat and woolly hat, and wished I had put on more layers. The wind racing in off the sea seemed to pass straight through my clothing, and by the time we reached the top of the hill my face and fingers were numb. Where the land flattened out I spotted a couple of fluffy grey balls waddling off into the heather – great black-backed gull chicks – and above us great skuas, powerful-looking piratical birds, flew low overhead. There were nests all around, so we had to watch our step.

A short way ahead was a shallow, muddy upland lochan, the surface roughened by the wind and broken in places by rocks and the stems of sedges. What in its right mind would leave behind the Arabian Sea to come to this desolate spot to breed? I thought.

Nothing, by the look of things. The water was devoid of bird life. My last chance appeared to have ended in failure.

Malcolm paused and scanned the lochan with his binoculars. 'Pretty, aren't they?' he smiled.

Uh? Where? I couldn't see anything.

I looked, and looked again.

Only I hadn't reckoned on them being quite so small. Yes! There they were, riding the waves at one end, half hidden between the rocks, two dainty waders picking insects from the surface: a male and female red-necked phalarope. The boldly patterned female was foraging among the submerged stones while the male, who had a more washed-out appearance, was busy spinning around in the water using his slightly webbed feet to stir up food from the bottom. This was one of the rarest sights in British wildlife. But instead of keeping our distance, Malcolm led me right up to them – and incredibly they completely ignored us.

'They're such approachable birds,' he said. 'I've had them run through my legs, and you see people with huge telephoto lenses struggling to take photos of them because they are just a few feet away.'

We watched and waited in the hope of identifying any possible nest site so that Malcolm could return to record and ring young at a future date, but after a while the two birds flew off to another pool and we headed back to the road. Despite the cold I was glowing inside. This was the final destination on my itinerary. I was going home, and with another memory to savour – just in the nick of time.

As a parting gift Shetland offered me one more special moment that would rival spotting corncrakes from my North Uist B&B. Before leaving, my guest-house owner – who also doubled as island shopkeeper, campsite administrator, part-time postman, coastguard and fireman – told me it might be worth having a quick look through my bedroom window. This turned out to be something of an understatement. Outside in the bay a pod of killer whales were hunting seals, chasing them up against the rocks, the towering dorsal fin on the male cutting through the surf like a black sail as they moved in for the kill.

Now that's something you don't see every day. More to the point, where was a wildlife film crew when I needed one?

My year was as good as over and I had seen thirty-eight of my forty target species. I was two warblers short of a Red List. There was the aquatic warbler, that globally threatened visitor from eastern Europe that only passes through in tiny numbers once a year, which I had tried and failed to see. And there was the Savi's warbler – one of our rarest breeding birds that I had practically no hope of tracking down.

These pesky warblers aside, I had seen far, far more species than I had ever dreamt possible. It was time to stop racing around the country, and enjoy getting to know more about what lived outside my own back door in Devon. And it was lovely to be home – even if there was no full English breakfast on offer and the cereal wasn't in tupperware.

'Have you finished birdwatching now?' my eldest daughter asked during supper on my return from Shetland.

'Actually, in a way I think I've just begun,' I said with a laugh. 'Anyway, it's not really something you just stop doing. Even if you stop looking, you can't stop seeing. It's about interpreting experience and . . .' But by the time I eventually finished my sentence everyone had cleared away their plates and moved to another room.

Yes, it was time to put family first and take things easy.

At least I thought it was.

In July I got a phone call.

'The Savi's has begun to sing again,' the man said.

It was like one of those cryptic spy thriller messages.

'He won't stay singing for much longer. I'd get here as soon as possible to stand any chance of seeing him,' he added, giving me directions before hanging up.

It was an expert I had contacted a few weeks earlier. I had never expected him to call. Less than half a dozen pairs of Savi's warblers spend the summer here, and the risk from egg collectors and disturbance from over-keen birdwatchers means their whereabouts are shrouded in secrecy. When I had first made contact, he told me my ornithological credentials needed checking before we could talk further. I said I didn't have any ornithological credentials, though gave a few details of people he could contact to verify I could be trusted – and had heard nothing more. His call came out of the blue, and I had to act fast.

I immediately rang a work colleague and told him I needed the next day off at short notice as I was owed time in lieu.

'Why do you need a whole day to go to the loo?' my

youngest daughter asked when I got off the phone.

There was no time to explain. It was 9pm and I had a 300-mile drive through the night ahead of me. Grabbing my wallet, binoculars and a coat I rushed out of the door and jumped in the car.

Five hours later I turned off the motorway and followed winding roads to my destination, pulling up in a car park at 3am and setting my alarm for 4am.

Named after the Italian professor who first identified them, Savi's warblers were driven to extinction in the UK in 1860 following the draining of wetlands. A century later they made a comeback, colonizing reed-beds in the South East as part of a general expansion in their European range. However, despite there being plenty of suitable habitat, numbers of this plain little rufous-brown migrant have begun plummeting back towards zero and there doesn't seem to be much that can be done to halt the decline. Within a few years they could be gone from Britain.

It wasn't easy getting up after so little sleep, but I managed to stagger bleary-eyed to the reserve opposite and walked along a deserted public footpath that cut through a dense reedbed shrouded in morning mist. I had only gone a few hundred yards when I heard a distant sound. It was a bit like a grasshopper warbler, except that the fast, repeated notes blurred into a continuous dull buzzing. This was the noise I had come for. Though how could I be sure I was right? The singer was out of sight deep among reeds, so I ran back to my car humming the tone and found the right track on my birdsong CD. It was identical.

Returning to the path I bumped into my covert savvy Savi's contact. He wasn't sitting on a bench in a suit and dark glasses. Nor did he pass me information in a black briefcase. However, he did confirm the song was as I had thought, and even pointed out a bird he felt sure was it, before it disappeared from view.

Aside from overhearing a farmer complain about getting too much money in grant subsidies, the song of a Savi's warbler is arguably one of the rarest sounds in the British countryside. I was one of very few people that summer fortunate enough to have heard it.

And there was another surprise in store. The final bird on the list – the most endangered of them all – decided to put in a late appearance.

To be honest, I had given up all hope of seeing an aquatic warbler. Only five had been recorded so far during the year that I was aware of – as far apart as Shetland, the Thames estuary and Weston-super-Mare. Repeated visits to Marazion Marsh in Cornwall had drawn a blank, my twelve months were up, and I had been forced to shrug it off with a laugh. After all, having seen such a variety of incredible British birds, why should I worry about some obscure little visitor from Belarus? And yet it still intrigued me. This was a species staring down the barrel at global extinction. So when, in late September, I heard a single bird had turned up in the South West, and at a coastal wetland reserve in south Devon within striking distance, I knew I had to jettison my self-imposed August deadline and try one last time.

My alarm woke me at 5am, I woke the dog, he woke

everyone else in the house and I quickly tiptoed out of the front door leaving the commotion behind, jumped in the car and drove in the dark to Slapton Ley, a large freshwater lake near Dartmouth. The aquatic warbler had apparently been seen in an area of rank vegetation bordering reedbeds at the northern end of the lake. I knew my chances of spotting this little Africa-bound migrant in the short time I could spare before work were slim, especially given that a run of clear nights had provided perfect conditions for any bird thinking of undertaking a Channel crossing. However, when I arrived I saw something in the dawn light that instantly lifted my spirits: a lone birdwatcher by the edge of the marsh glued to his telescope.

Parking on the narrow shingle ridge which separates Slapton Ley from Start Bay, I walked over to him as fast as I could.

'Sorry to disturb you . . .' I began, catching my breath.

'He's just in there,' he whispered, glancing at the binoculars strung around my neck and anticipating my question.

'I was just wondering whether . . . What? Really? An . . . aquat . . . ?'

'Aquatic warbler. Yes, there on the ground where the thistle stems are moving.'

I followed his gaze and could just make out something burrowing through the grass in a most un-birdlike fashion, but by the time I raised my binoculars it had disappeared into the reedbeds.

It seemed I had arrived a split-second too late.

The wail of anguish I wanted to let out would have been loud enough to wake my family back at home once again. I silently cursed the fact I had stopped for petrol on the way. I cursed the second slice of toast I had had for breakfast. I cursed the traffic lights, the double-parked delivery lorry, the speed cameras, the local council . . .

And then, just as I was about to start in on the government, the little bird re-emerged from the reeds and, unbelievably, flew back and landed beneath a clump of gorse just twenty paces from where I stood, before edging its way up a thick grass stem into a ray of morning sunlight. There it settled in full view, one of the world's rarest songbirds and arguably the most handsome of our warblers, its yellow-brown upperparts streaked with black and a warm stripe of gold running through its dark crown. This precious little traveller had a lengthy journey ahead of it. Mine was now at an end. And what a way to end my year!

I had managed to see all of our Red List birds, exceeding my wildest expectations. And what amazing birds they were . . . from the Scottish crossbill, with a beak that looked like it had been in a rear-end shunt, to nightjar and wryneck, both masters of camouflage; battling black grouse and macho capercaillie; the secretive bittern and corncrake; supreme singers such as the skylark and marsh warbler; eye-catching bullfinches, yellowhammers and turtle doves, endearing twites and corn buntings . . . And they had taken me to some incredible places, from the mountains of the Cairngorms and Snowdonia to the windswept wilds of the Hebrides and Shetland; from vast Flow Country peatlands and the huge arable fields of East Anglia, to the scenic Isles of Scilly, the coasts of Cornwall and lush Hampshire valleys. Not forgetting all the friendly and knowledgeable people I had met along the way. Preachy holier-than-thou conservationists? Nope. I didn't meet one among them. Nerdy birders? Well, who am I to judge? Bizarre B&B owners? Just the one – a wild-eyed woman in Scotland with dangly earrings the size of wind chimes who asked whether I wanted a roll in the meadow. Only later did I realize she had been offering to make me a packed lunch.

Although it would be easy to consider the Red List grounds for despair, I had discovered plenty to feel upbeat about. Every bird tells a story about the environment, and it seems enough people are now listening. And while I had started out all excited about the rarities on the list, I had learnt to appreciate how we can't take our common birds for granted. I'll never look at a house sparrow in the same way again – in case they're wondering why I keep staring at them strangely.

After my successes I was planning on at least a few months of self-congratulation.

But it was not to be.

A couple of weeks after my final sighting in September, disaster struck. I discovered a new Red List for UK birds was in the process of being drawn up – and with quite a number of additional species set to push up the total.

I took a deep breath and tried to remain calm.

I reminded myself that a longer Red List was far worse news for the birds than for me.

While I had bumped into plenty of likely contenders for inclusion on my travels, there were bound to be others out there that I hadn't seen. But could I really desert everyone once details were finalized, put my job on hold and go traipsing off again?

No. It wouldn't be fair.

Having said that, a quick trip now and again couldn't hurt. I could even persuade my family to join me. I was sure they wouldn't mind a weekend in Wales if the need arose.

Or a few days in the Highlands.

Perhaps even the Isle of Eigg.

Now there's a nice place to start . . .

Appendix

The UK 'Red List'

(As at 2008)

Twite
Tree Sparrow
Yellowhammer
Cirl Bunting
Black-tailed Godwit
Red-backed Shrike
Spotted Flycatcher
Song Thrush
House Sparrow
Reed Bunting
Black Grouse
Grey Partridge
Marsh Tit
Bittern
Wryneck
Starling
Lesser Spotted Woodpecker
Bullfinch

Willow Tit
Hen Harrier
Scottish Crossbill
Capercaillie
White-tailed Eagle
Ring Ouzel
Grasshopper Warbler
Stone-curlew
Skylark
Corn Bunting
Woodlark
Turtle Dove
Linnet
Roseate Tern
Nightjar
Marsh Warbler
Common Scoter
Corncrake
Quail
Red-necked Phalarope
Savi's Warbler
Aquatic Warbler

The Population Status of Birds in the UK 2002–2007:
Birds of Conservation Concern
Royal Society for the Protection of Birds (RSPB), British Trust
for Ornithology (BTO), Joint Nature Conservation Committee
(JNCC), Birdlife International, The Wildfowl and Wetlands
Trust (WWT), English Nature, Countryside Council for Wales,
Scottish Natural Heritage, Environment and Heritage Service
(Northern Ireland), The Hawk and Owl Trust, The National
Trust, The Wildlife Trusts, British Ornithologists' Union,
The Game Conservancy Trust

Epilogue

In June 2009 the UK 'Red List' was revised for the third time, increasing from 40 species at the last review in 2002 to a new total of 52. More than one in five of all British birds are now considered of high conservation concern.

Six species managed to make sufficient gains and dropped off the Red List. The stone-curlew and woodlark have both benefitted from conservation work, while a survey of Scottish crossbills found their population is higher than previously thought. Modest recoveries in numbers of bull-finch, quail and reed bunting also mean they no longer qualify for inclusion.

However, 18 new species in serious decline were added to the tally, among them the cuckoo, herring gull and lapwing. The full list of new inclusions is as follows:

Arctic Skua

Balearic Shearwater

Dunlin

Fieldfare

Golden Oriole

Cuckoo

Hawfinch

Herring Gull

Lapwing

Lesser Redpoll

Redwing

Ruff

Scaup

Temminck's Stint

Tree Pipit

Whimbrel

Wood Warbler

Yellow Wagtail

The Population Status of Birds in the UK, Channel Islands and Isle of Man: Birds of Conservation Concern 3

ACKNOWLEDGEMENTS

I owe a huge debt of gratitude to all those who so generously offered their time, assistance, expertise and enthusiasm to make this book possible. They include, in no particular order: John Chester, Scottish Wildlife Trust warden, Isle of Eigg; Simon King, www.simonkingwildlife.com; Guy Anderson, RSPB; Stuart Piner, Rare Bird Alert; John Swann; Kester Wilson, BTO; Dave Flumm, RSPB; Julian Hughes, RSPB head of species conservation; Dr David Noble, head of census, BTO; Will Wagstaff, Isles of Scilly Bird Group; Craig Hilton-Taylor, manager IUCN Red List; Paul Forecast, London RSPB manager; Phil Warren, Game and Wildlife Conservation Trust; Sarah Alsbury, RSPB; Tom Gullick; Raymond Harris-Ching; Lee Copplestone, manager Sandwell Valley RSPB reserve; Chris Sharpe, Isle of Man Bird Atlas; Ron Summers, senior research biologist; Richard Thaxton, Loch Garten site manager; Dave Sexton, Mull RSPB officer; Dr Helen Baker, birds and surveillance adviser, JNCC; Nick Adams, Wessex Stone-Curlew Project; Chris Bailey, RSPB project manager, Hope Farm; Lee Evans; Ed Taylor; Greg Conway, research ecologist, BTO; Paul

Morrison, RSPB, Coquet Island; Durwyn Liley, ecologist, Footprint Ecology; Graham Shortt; Norrie Russell, Forsinard Reserve manager; Jamie Boyle, RSPB, North Uist; Malcolm Smith, RSPB warden, Shetland North Isles; Martha Devine, RSPB, Shetland North Isles; Andrew Raine; Chris Orsman, RSPB; Barry Yates, Rye Harbour Reserve manager; Chris Morton, Forestry Commission; Adam Griffin, Moor Trees; Duncan Bridges, Manx Wildlife Trust; Liz Grundy, Defra; Joe Dimbleby, CPRE; Alan Goodall and Caperwatch team, RSPB Wales office; David Rogers, senior reserves manager, Kent, Natural England; Radipole Lake reserve staff; Steve Whitehouse; Adrian Thomas, RSPB; Hamish Murray, Dorset County Council head ranger; Warren Claydon; Andy Roadhouse, Spurn Point Observatory; Ian Harding, reserve warden, Stodmarsh; David Feast, reserve warden, Stodmarsh; Steve M.R. Young; Brian Lowe, North Uist RSPB corncrake officer; Mike Tyler, Devon Birdwatching and Preservation Society. Particular thanks to Grahame Madge, RSPB press officer, and Dr Andy Brown, principal birds specialist, Natural England, for their expert input, and to copy editor Mari Roberts. Also to Bill Martin, editor, *The Herald*, Plymouth; all my colleagues on *The Herald*, especially Mike Longhurst and Pete Hale; Nick Lester for accompanying me on my sparrow quest; and most of all my parents Dr Andrew and Penny Elder, and Pat Millner. Also Jay and Tess, Charlotte and Ben, Tam and Mark, Paul and Lindsay, Stuart MacRostie, Steve Boucher and other patient listeners, family and friends. Special thanks to Susan Smith, MBA Literary Agents, and Doug Young, Transworld.

INDEX